HAWAII'S FISHES

A GUIDE FOR SNORKELERS DIVERS AND AQUARISTS

Milletseed Butterflyfish (Chaetondon miliaris) feeding on the eggs of a Hawaiian Sergeant.

HAWAII'S FISHES

A GUIDE FOR SNORKELERS DIVERS AND AQUARISTS

TEXT AND PHOTOGRAPHS BY JOHN P. HOOVER

ADDITIONAL PHOTOGRAPHS
BY
DAVID R. SCHRICHTE
MARJORIE L. AWAI
MIKE SEVERNS
BOB OWENS
AND OTHER MEMBERS OF THE
UNDERWATER PHOTOGRAPHIC SOCIETY OF HAWAI'I.

MUTUAL PUBLISHING

LCC 92-081784

DESIGN
MICHAEL HORTON DESIGN

SECOND PRINTING (REVISED) AUGUST 1994
THIRD PRINTING (REVISED) JANUARY 1996
FOURTH PRINTING MAY 1998
FIFTH PRINTING MARCH 1999
SIXTH PRINTING (REVISED) AUGUST 2000
SEVENTH PRINTING JANUARY 2001
EIGHTH PRINTING JUNE 2002
NINTH PRINTING (REVISED) MAY 2003
TENTH PRINTING MAY 2004

ISBN 1-56647-001-3

MUTUAL PUBLISHING
1215 CENTER STREET, SUITE 210
HONOLULU, HAWAII 96816
TELEPHONE (808) 732-1709
FAX (808) 734-4094
EMAIL MUTUAL@MUTUALPUBLISHING.COM
WWW.MUTUALPUBLISHING.COM

PRINTED IN KOREA

COVER: the Flame Wrasse *(Cirrhilabrus jordani),* one of Hawaii's most spectacular endemic fishes, photographed at Molokini Island, Maui. 80 ft.

CONTENTS

Introduction _____ vi

Acknowledgments _____ vi

Coral Reefs and Aquariums / Author's Note _vii

Diving and Snorkeling in Hawai'i _____ viii

Where to Dive and Snorkel _____ 1

The Environment _____ 8

Classification and Names _____ 10

Fish Anatomy _____ 12

ANGELFISHES _____ 13

BARRACUDAS _____ 17

BIGEYES _____ 19

BLENNIES _____ 20

BOARFISHES_____ 23

BOXFISHES _____ 24

BUTTERFLYFISHES_____ 26

CARDINALFISHES _____ 37

CHUBS and STRIPEYS _____ 39

DAMSELFISHES _____ 41

EELS_____ 48

FILEFISHES _____ 57

FLAGTAILS _____ 60

FLATFISHES _____ 61

FROGFISHES_____ 63

GOATFISHES _____ 65

GOBIES and DARTFISHES _____ 70

GROUPERS and ANTHIAS _____ 74

HAWKFISHES and MORWONGS _____ 78

JACKS _____ 82

LADYFISHES, BONEFISHES and MILKFISHES _87

LIZARDFISHES _____ 88

MULLETS and THREADFINS _____ 90

NEEDLEFISHES _____ 91

PARROTFISHES _____ 92

PIPEFISHES and SEAHORSES _____ 97

PUFFERFISHES and PORCUPINEFISHES ___ 99

RAYS _____ 104

SANDPERCHES _____ 106

SCORPIONFISHES and GURNARDS _____ 107

SHARKS _____ 112

SNAPPERS and EMPERORS _____ 116

SQUIRRELFISHES and SOLDIERFISHES ___ 119

SURGEONFISHES and MOORISH IDOLS __ 124

TILEFISHES _____ 134

TRIGGERFISHES _____ 135

TRUMPETFISHES and CORNETFISHES ____ 140

WRASSES _____ 142

Catching Your Own Aquarium Fishes _____ 161

Photographing Fishes _____ 162

Source Materials _____ 163

Further Reading_____ 164

Table of Invalid or Incorrect Scientific Names 169

Index of Common Names _____ 171

Index of Hawaiian Names _____ 174

Index of Scientific Names _____ 175

Appendix _____ 179

INTRODUCTION

To enter the water is to enter a natural realm not greatly altered by human activity. Except perhaps for the tops of the highest mountains, no environment in Hawai'i remains so unchanged, the abundance and diversity of its wildlife so intact.

Wildlife, of course, is the main attraction of this undersea kingdom. Nowhere else can such a bounty of fascinating, colorful animals be seen at such close range. Most are fishes. Coming in all sizes and shapes, they are everywhere—on the bottom, at the surface, under the sand, in caves, even inside other animals. Their vibrant colors are astounding, their shapes sometimes strange beyond belief. Some have developed elaborate mechanisms of defense—balloons, poisons, hypodermic syringes, electric shocks. Others mimic stones, coral, sponges, plants, crabs, each other—anything to survive and multiply. There are fishes that can fly and fishes that can't swim. Some are as big as a city bus, others the size of a pin. The variety is endless.

Hawaii's Fishes presents underwater photographs and informative descriptions of over 250 species—almost all of the fishes encountered by divers and snorkelers in the islands. Their evolution, classification and suitability for aquariums are also discussed and recommendations given on where to best see them.

Whether snorkeler or diver, whether visitor or **kama'aina**, you will enjoy exploring the undersea world of Hawai'i.

INTRODUCTION TO THE REVISED EDITION

Hawaii's Fishes is now ten years old. Since its original publication scientific names have changed, new species have been described, geographic ranges have been extended, and new photos have been taken. The anniversary seems a good opportunity to make needed changes. I have also revised some common names to better agree with those in current use. A big **mahalo** to my readers for making this book a success and to Mutual Publishing for great support over the years. For the very latest updates, and information about my other books, please visit my website www.hawaiisfishes.com.

ACKNOWLEDGMENTS

This book could not have been written without the scholarship and research of the authors whose works are listed on page 163, especially John E. Randall, Robert F. Myers, Spencer W. Tinker, Margaret Titcomb, and Mary Kawena Pukui. I am indebted to them for most of the scientific and cultural information presented here.

Few photographers working alone could find all the animals and take all the pictures needed for a book such as this. I am particularly grateful to the members of the Underwater Photographic Society of Hawai'i and others who contributed pictures that I lacked.

In addition I would like to thank Jeff Preble, Marj Awai, Bruce Mundy, Therese Hayes, Bruce Carlson, Richard Pyle and John Earle for information, corrections and comments; Linda and Ken Bail of Bubbles Below Scuba Charters for showing me some of Kauai's rare fishes; Mike and Pauline Severns and Dave and Jennifer Fleetham for taking me to see flame wrasses; Hal Ing for some good boat dives; Gert de Couet for reviewing portions of the manuscript; and my editor Stu Lillicoe, whose passing soon after this book was first published left a gap in the lives of many of us who love the sea.

Final thanks go to my enthusiastic and sharp-eyed dive buddies Fenner Shupe and Dan Dickey who spotted many of the fishes in these pages, and to Marcia Stone.

Like many others, I have gained pleasure and knowledge over the years by keeping marine fishes. Few hobbies are so fascinating. I am compelled, however, to wonder what effect the removal of perhaps half a million reef fishes a year has on Hawaii's underwater environment. Many, myself included, feel that Hawaii's reefs are being thoughtlessly overcollected. Even fishes unable to survive in captivity are regularly taken and sold. What can be done?

Careful regulation is one step. The market, for example, may demand Hawaiian Cleaner Wrasses, although in home aquariums these beauties invariably starve to death. If even one exporter supplies them, others are under pressure to follow. To protect our reefs, the taking of these and similar species could be prohibited. No one, then, would have to sell them to stay competitive. Other attractive and easy-to-catch endemics, such as Hawaiian Lionfishes and Bandit Angelfishes, might also benefit from increased protection. Few constitute a large or important part of the tropical fish trade. It's best to leave them on the reef.

A second, more important move would be to strengthen Hawaii's system of marine parks, allowing more equitable sharing of reef habitats between dive-tour operators who want to show colorful fishes to their customers, and collectors who want to catch and sell them. By providing reef fishes a sanctuary in which to live and reproduce, marine parks might even increase the numbers of commercially valuable juvenile fishes outside the conservation zones. Marine parks also make good economic sense as visitor attractions, and could perhaps help pay for themselves through user fees. The enormous popularity of Hanauma Bay on O'ahu and Molokini Island off Maui attest to this.

A third approach, perhaps the most critical, is education. Diving, snorkeling and aquarium keeping open the underwater world to numbers of enthusiasts who share their concern and knowledge with those around them. As a group, marine aquarists probably know more about fishes and corals than do most divers and snorkelers. Instead of condemning home aquariums, therefore, why not use the hobby to stimulate appreciation for the underwater environment? Many threats to coral reefs are more dangerous than fish collecting. Among them are pollution, runoff, dredging, filling, and dynamiting. Governments can help to control these, but will show concern for reefs and their inhabitants only when there is popular demand to do so. Aquariums help create that demand.

I hope that all who use this book will contribute in their own way to conservation of the underwater world, helping to keep diving, snorkeling and aquarium keeping fun for us and for our children.

Hawaiian Lionfish or Turkeyfish *(Pterois sphex)*
This spectacular endemic fish is uncommon and often over-collected. Pūpūkea, O'ahu. 30ft.

The best locations for diving or snorkeling in Hawai'i change with the seasons and, to a lesser extent, with the weather. Here is a summary of information important for planning excursions in the Islands.

May - September diving is best along northern and western shores. During these seasons the surf is predominantly from the south.

October - April diving is best along southern and southeastern shores; at these times surf is from the north or northwest.

Wind is an important factor affecting water conditions in Hawai'i. Trade-winds restrict diving and snorkeling along northeastern and eastern shores about 80% of the year. These shores are diveable only during periods of light, variable or southerly winds, which occur most often in winter. Trade-winds are strongest and steadiest during the summer. Winds at any time of year tend to die down at night and pick up during the day. Diving and snorkeling, therefore, are often best in the early morning.

Water Temperatures range from an average in the low 70s Fahrenheit (low 20s Celsius) during January and February to an average in the low 80s (high 20s C.) during September and October. Most local divers wear a light wetsuit for comfort.

Currents running parallel to shore at some locations can sweep divers away from planned exit points. Areas susceptible to currents are best explored at slack tide. Always swim upcurrent at the beginning of a dive. At the sites listed in the next section currents are not troublesome unless specifically mentioned.

Tides in Hawai'i vary less than two feet and are not an important factor except at snorkeling and diving spots affected by strong currents. Tide calendars are available.

Forecasts and information: For wind, tide and surf conditions at selected O'ahu beaches call **973-4383** (National Weather Service) or **596-7873 / 596-SURF** (the Surf News Network). The Surf News Network gives frequently updated reports based on actual beach observations but uses LOCAL-STYLE WAVE HEIGHT. The National Weather Service reports TRUE WAVE HEIGHT—see below.

TRUE WAVE HEIGHT vs LOCAL-STYLE WAVE HEIGHT: The National Wather Service and most websites report "true wave height." This is the actual height of the breaking wave-face as seen from the beach. The Surf News Network on O'ahu, however, (which gives detailed reports updated at 7 am, noon, 3 pm and 7 pm) reports "local-style wave height"—the wave height seen by surfers in the water *behind* the breaking wave. Does it matter? YES! **"Local-style wave height" is about half the height of the face of the breaking wave!** Local surfers and longtime residents are used to "local style wave height" and know what to expect. All others should mentally double any wave height reports they get from the Surf News Network phone line or website.

Surf reports and forecasts are also available on the Web at:

http://www.surf-news.com/ (reports "LOCAL STYLE WAVE HEIGHTS")
http://www.prh.noaa.gov/hnl/pages/marine.html (features a long range forecast)
http://www.hawaii.edu/news/localweather/surf
http://hawaiiweathertoday.com

For general marine forecasts and coastal wind observations dial the National Weather Service at the following numbers: O'ahu: 836-3921; Kaua'i: 245-3564; Maui: 877-3477; Big Island: 935-9883.

Most photographs in this book were taken at the popular snorkeling and diving sites listed below. After you have explored these there are many more places to try. A number of helpful diving guidebooks are listed under Further Reading at the back of the book.

Unless otherwise mentioned, all these locations have rest-rooms and showers. Visibility at most snorkeling sites is best in the early morning before the wind, waves and people stir up the bottom.

ISLAND OF O'AHU

The main diving and snorkeling areas on O'ahu are on the west shore (the leeward or Wai'anae coast), the south and southeastern shores (from Honolulu to Hanauma Bay) and the north shore. The northeast (windward) shore is rarely dived because of rough seas and wind.

HANAUMA BAY NATURE PARK

Everybody's favorite snorkeling beach on O'ahu is spectacular Hanauma Bay Nature Park on the southeastern shore, ten miles east of Waīkīkī via the Kalaniana'ole Highway (Route 72). Hanauma Bay is a flooded volcanic crater open to the sea on one side. A marine preserve, its sheltered waters are home to a wonderful variety of colorful and very tame sea life. Most of the fishes in this book may be seen there. Hanauma Bay offers undersea adventure to everyone, from novice snorkeler to advanced diver.

Between the reef and the beach are several shallow lagoons (maximum depth about ten feet) that are ideal for beginners. The water is protected and fishes abound, although visibility is often poor and there is little living coral. The reef close to shore is a fossil reef—the remains of coral that grew thousands of years ago when the sea level was higher. Live coral can be found further out in the bay in deeper water. If conditions are calm, snorkelers can see it at the Witch's Brew area around to the right—please don't touch. Fish feeding, once popular in the Bay, has recently been banned. It alters fish behavior and may affect the natural species composition of the reef.

Beyond the reef intermediate and advanced snorkelers will find clearer water and a greater variety of fish life. Several shallow channels lead through it, usually marked by flags; at high tide you can often

1

swim right over it. If you are not confident in the water, however, do not attempt to go beyond the reef. Depending on the tide, a current may be running either in or out through the channels. Walking across the reef is discouraged.

Further out in the bay visibility improves and live coral becomes more abundant. Starting from the channel through the reef just to the right of the concession stand, divers can follow an old undersea telephone cable to a reef of finger coral in the center of the bay at a depth of 30 to 40 feet. When the sea is calm an area called the "Witch's Brew" off the rocky point to the right of the beach is a good intermediate-level dive. You can either swim out or walk around, making your entry off the rocks. Several advanced dives at the entrance to the bay offer an even greater variety of marine life. If you have not been there before, go with a guide; a strong current, the "Molokai Express," sometimes sweeps across the mouth of the bay. The southeast side side of O'ahu is calmest from September to May. Although the bay is almost always diveable, visibility can be poor when surf is breaking across the reef.

For a free walking tour of the bay, visit the information stand sponsored by the Hanauma Bay Educational Programs and the University of Hawai'i Sea Grant Extension Service. The guides are friendly and knowledgeable. Fins and masks (sometimes of poor quality) are available for rent from the concession stand. To ensure a good fit, bring your own.

Directions: From Honolulu take the H-1 Highway east. It soon becomes the Kalaniana'ole Highway (Route 72), which continues along the coast through several residential areas. Just beyond the Koko Marina shopping center the road climbs a hill to the Hanauma Bay turnoff. You can't miss it. To be sure of parking, arrive well before 10 A.M., especially on weekends. The lot is closed when full. Public transportation is available; for detailed directions from your location call TheBus at 848-5555.

KAHE POINT BEACH PARK

If the surf is up at Hanauma Bay you might try Kahe Point Beach Park on the west shore, about 20 miles in the opposite direction from Honolulu. Here you can snorkel or dive along an artificial reef composed of rocks and boulders piled over two enormous underwater conduits. These pipes discharge hot seawater used to cool the Hawaiian Electric power plant across the road. The fishes love it and so will you. If caught in the strong current from the vents, either enjoy the ride or swim to one side to escape. Visibility here is often excellent. Reef fishes of all kinds frequent the outfall, including occasional barracudas and eagle rays. Divers can go on to explore reef areas to the right and left. Kahe Point lies on a fairly sheltered side of the island and the conditions can be good throughout the year. Maximum depths are about 30 feet. Enter the water at a small sandy cove beyond the rest-rooms to the right of the parking lot. You might have to snorkel through some small breakers on your way out. If you see large waves breaking in the cove and many small boys surfing, the visibility might be poor.

Directions: From Honolulu take the H-1 west about 20 miles toward Wai'anae. Approximately 3.3 miles beyond Campbell Industrial Park (exit 1A) is a Hawaiian Electric power station. Just before the power plant turn left into Kahe Point Beach Park. Do not leave valuables in your parked car.

PŪPŪKEA BEACH PARK

From May to September, Pūpūkea Beach Park on O'ahu's north shore offers two popular snorkeling/diving areas: "Three Tables" and "Sharks' Cove." Each has a shallow, protected inlet for beginners with deeper water beyond for the more experienced. Outside the lagoons, expect interesting topography and depths of 30 to 50 feet. There are underwater caves at Sharks' Cove; avoid them if there is any surge or wave action. The deeper caves should be explored only with a guide. Fish life at Pūpūkea is not as abundant as at Hanauma Bay or Kahe Point. The protected waters inside the reef are designated a marine conservation area but, as fishing, netting and spearfishing by snorkelers is allowed, this is largely meaningless.

Directions: Pūpūkea Beach Park is 33 miles from Honolulu International Airport. Take the H-1 west from Honolulu past Pearl City to the H-2 (exit 8A), then north toward Wahiawa. Follow the main highway toward Schofield Barracks (bypassing Wahiawa town), turn right on Route 99 through the pineapple fields and continue down to the coastal town of Haleiwa. Continue through Haleiwa along the coast about five miles to Waimea Bay Beach Park. Less than a mile beyond Waimea you will see a Foodland supermarket on the right and the tiny Sunset Beach fire station on the left. Three Tables is .2 mile before the fire station, Sharks' Cove is beyond it. There are no facilities at Three Tables but it is an easy walk over to Sharks' Cove.

MAGIC ISLAND

Magic Island, at the Diamond Head end of Honolulu's Ala Moana Beach Park (across from Ala Moana Shopping Center), offers a convenient shore dive right in town. Enter the water at a small sandy beach on the Ala Wai boat channel to the left of the lagoon. To reach the best diving areas you must swim out through the channel and beyond the breakwater; keep to the right to avoid traffic from the marina. It is a good idea to use a surface float with a dive flag here. (Unless you are with an experienced guide do not attempt to enter the ocean by swimming through gaps in the lagoon breakwater.) Visibility is fair to poor at Magic Island, but there is a surprising amount of marine life. Expect depths of 20 to 30 feet. Snorkeling is not advised because of boats and poor visibility.

THE *MAHI*

O'ahu's most popular boat dive is the wreck of the *Mahi*, a decommissioned minesweeper sunk as an artificial reef in about 90 feet of water off Ma'ile on the west shore. Most dive charter operators will be glad to take you there. On the *Mahi* you can feed large eels while being swarmed by schools of Bluestripe Snappers and Milletseed Butterflyfishes, watch the resident school of Spotted Eagle Rays and, if you are lucky, find a Whitetip Reef Shark resting in the ship's hold. For a pleasant second dive, the charters often visit nearby "Makaha Caves," a shallow site where you can swim through short caverns and see a large variety of reef fishes. Visibility is usually excellent.

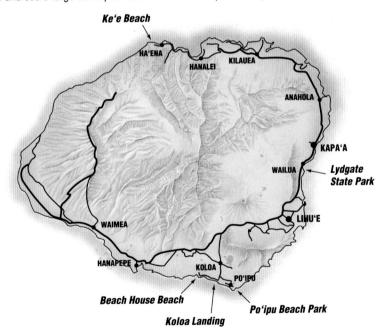

ISLAND OF KAUA'I

Most snorkeling and diving on Kaua'i takes place off the north and south shores. The east shore is usually rough and windy. In any event, a boat is needed to get to the best dive locations. A number of good dive charter operations exist, some of which will take you off-shore to Ni'ihau and Lehua Islands for especially exciting diving.

KOLOA LANDING

The best all-around shore diving and snorkeling on Kaua'i is off Koloa Landing, near the south shore resort area of Po'ipū. This protected inlet is easily accessible by road and, because there are no facilities and no beach, there are no crowds either. Visibility is fair to good and it is usually calm. Coral formations extend along both sides of the inlet; the fishes, which have been fed for many years, are extraordinarily tame.

Directions: From Līhu'e drive westward on Route 50 about seven miles to Route 520. Turn left 3.3 miles to Koloa Town. About 1.6 miles beyond Koloa, bear right at the Y intersection toward the Spouting Horn, then left on Ho'onani Road. Almost immediately a bumpy turnoff on the right leads down to Koloa Landing.

PO'IPU BEACH PARK

If you want to combine beachgoing with novice snorkeling try Po'ipū County Beach Park, several miles further down the coast, next to the Stouffer Wai'ōhai Beach Resort. This small park has a shallow protected area excellent for beginners. The modest variety of marine life here includes schools of needlefishes. There are also a few tidepools to explore.

Directions: From Koloa Town drive about 3 miles down Po'ipū Road. Immediately beyond Poipu Shopping Village and the Wai'ōahi Beach Resort turn right a short distance to the shore on Ho'owili Road.

BEACH HOUSE BEACH

On the road to the Spouting Horn next to the former Beach House Restaurant (destroyed in 1992 by Hurricane Iniki) is a narrow roadside beach fronted by a snorkeling area. Conditions close to shore are suitable for novices while more advanced snorkelers can venture out toward the reef. Depths seldom exceed ten feet. Beyond the reef are several popular surfing breaks. Showers and rest-rooms are across the road.

Directions: From Koloa Town drive south 1.6 miles toward the shore. At the Y intersection bear right toward Spouting Horn. The Beach House Restaurant is on the left almost two miles from the Y intersection, past Prince Kuhio Park.

KE'E BEACH

Occupying the western end of Hā'ena State Park on the north shore, Kē'ē Beach is one of the most beautiful spots in Hawai'i. The fairly large lagoon is deep enough for beginning divers as well as snorkelers. Swimming here is usually safe from May to September. Experienced divers venturing outside the lagoon will find caves and interesting rock formations but sparse coral due to the pounding this coast takes in the fall and winter. Dive beyond the lagoon only when the sea is calm and be careful of currents. Expect depths up to 20 feet inside the lagoon and about 30 feet beyond.

The marine life of Kē'ē Lagoon may not be as profuse as that of Koloa Landing, but above water the scenery cannot be bettered. A short walk west of the beach brings you to an ancient **heiau**, or temple complex, dedicated to Laka, goddess of the **hula**. The famous Na Pali Coast hiking trail begins at the parking lot.

Directions: Kē'ē Beach lies at the very end of the Kuhio Highway (Route 56) — about 32 miles north and west of Līhu'e. Do not leave valuables in your parked car.

LYDGATE STATE PARK

Situated on the east shore north of Līhu'e, Lydgate State Park has a small sheltered swimming area enclosed by a boulder breakwater — an ideal spot for beginning snorkelers and children. Although the variety of fishes is small and the visibility fair at best, unusual species can be seen here including Stripeys and an occasional Morwong. Many beach-goers feed bread to the fishes, which is probably not very good for them.

Directions: Drive north from Līhu'e on the Kuhio Highway (Route 56) about five miles. The park is on the right (ocean) side just before the Wailua River.

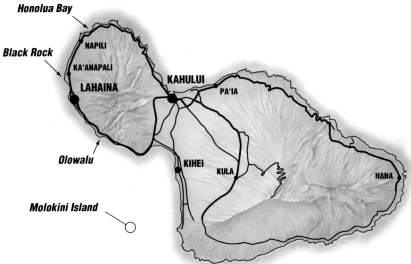

Honolua Bay

Black Rock

NAPILI

KA'ANAPALI

KAHULUI

LAHAINA

PA'IA

Olowalu

KIHEI

KULA

HANA

Molokini Island

ISLAND OF MAUI

Most of Maui's snorkeling and diving sites lie along the leeward shore, from Kā'anapali to La Perouse Bay. The nearby island of Lana'i, regularly visited by charter boats from Maui, offers good diving and fair snorkeling.

MOLOKINI ISLAND

Molokini is an ancient volcanic cone rising out of deep water in the channel between Maui and Kaho'olawe Island. The center of the crater is a prime snorkeling destination; divers can enjoy a variety of locations along the edges of the cone. Visibility is almost always excellent. Molokini is a marine preserve. In addition to the swarms of tame fishes, Whitetip Reef Sharks, Dragon Morays and black coral are featured attractions. Access is only by boat and almost any dive operation on Maui will take you there. Most charters leave early in the morning before the wind comes up.

BLACK ROCK

Popular Black Rock (Pu'u Keka'a) is located right in front of the Sheraton Hotel at Kā'anapali Beach. An ancient cinder cone jutting from the beach forms a protected area that is safe throughout the year. The well-fed fishes here are tame but there is little coral. With a maximum depth of about 20 feet, Black Rock is good for beginning divers. Snorkeling gear can be rented at the hotel.

Directions: Drive north from Lahaina on Route 30 and take the first entrance into the Kā'anapali Resort complex. Follow the signs to the Sheraton. An expensive pay parking lot has convenient access to the beach; if you are staying at a nearby hotel you might prefer to walk over. Otherwise you can park less expensively at the resort shopping center, especially if you buy something and get your ticket validated. The snorkeling area fronts the Sheraton Hotel swimming pool.

HONOLUA BAY

For a little more excitement, try lovely Honolua Bay near the northern tip of the island. This marine preserve features well developed coral on both sides of the bay with a shallow shelf for snorkelers and a modest dropoff for divers. Some of the prettiest coral in Hawai'i is here, home to the exquisitely beautiful Oval Butterflyfish. Schools of **akule** close to shore attract jacks and other large predators. Maximum diving depths are about 35 feet. Snorkelers can follow the left shore to Mokule'ia Bay (Slaughterhouse Beach), also a marine conservation area.

Honolua Bay has a gray sand beach with some shade for picnicking. Chemical toilets are provided but no other facilities. Diving and snorkeling are best from May to September; from October to April big waves pound the area, favored by surfers for its "pipeline."

Directions: From Lahaina drive 11 miles north on the Honoapi'ilani Highway (Route 30) until the road narrows. Almost one mile beyond, where the road descends to the head of Honolua Bay, a dirt track leads to the beach. You can either park here and walk a shady quarter mile to the shore or, if the road is in good condition, drive down. If you drive, the landowner may ask you to pay a few dollars for parking.

OLOWALU

When conditions are poor at Honolua Bay they are likely to be good at Olowalu. The extensive reef fronts a long stretch of beach next to the road. Entry can be made almost anywhere. This is primarily a snorkeling spot featuring beautiful coral formations in shallow water. Although diving is possible, you won't get deeper than about 15 feet unless you swim a long way out. Olowalu is best from May to September. If there is swell from the south the visibility will be poor. This shady, white sand beach has no facilities.

Directions: From Lahaina drive southeast about five miles to the Olowalu General Store. Continue a short way until road and beach converge. Park anywhere that looks good. Mile marker 14 is a favorite spot.

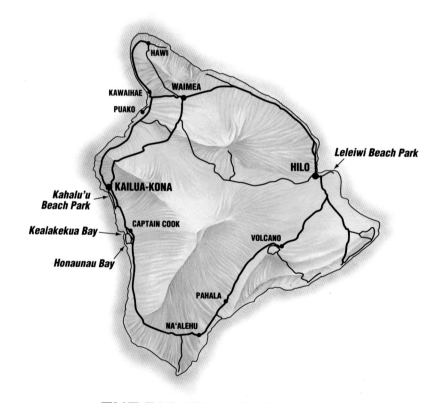

THE BIG ISLAND (HAWAI'I)

Almost all diving and snorkeling on the Big Island is along the Kona Coast, on the west side of the island. Kona means "leeward" in Hawaiian. Sheltered from the prevailing northeast trade winds by enormous mountains, these inviting waters are typically calm and clear. Steep dropoffs often lie close to shore. Because of these unusual conditions, Kona's marine life differs noticeably from that of the rest of the State.

Below are just a few of the diving and snorkeling sites along the Kona Coast. Actually, just about anywhere in Kona is good. Just pick a spot that looks nice. A snorkeling spot on the Hilo side is included for the convenience of visitors to that part of the island.

KAHALU'U BEACH PARK

Located on Ali'i Drive next to the Keahou Beach Hotel about four miles south of Kailua-Kona, Kahalu'u Beach Park, lies on a shallow bay, well protected by the remains of an ancient breakwater. It is ideal for novices. Experienced fish watchers will also enjoy Kahalu'u because of the great variety of tame fishes in residence. Unusual species, such as the Reticulated Butterflyfish and Scribbled Filefish, can be seen here. Surprisingly, Kahalu'u Beach Park is not a marine sanctuary. It is possible to make a shallow dive here. Enter at the small beach next to picturesque St. Peters Church.

KEALAKEKUA BAY

Probably the best marine park on the Big Island is historic Kealakekua Bay, where Captain James Cook anchored his ships in 1779 and was later killed. Diving and snorkeling here are outstanding, but to reach the best sites you will have to arrive by boat or hike 2.5 miles down from the town of Captain Cook. If you hike, take plenty of water and be prepared for a 1500-foot climb back. Your reward will be seclusion and the best snorkeling spot in Hawai'i. Where the trail meets the shore, under a large **keawe** tree, a small memorial plaque marks the spot where Cook was killed (not to be confused with the monument further on). Beyond is a shallow, clear lagoon ideal for beginning snorkelers. Further out the coral-covered bottom drops off abruptly to a depth of 90 feet. If you don't want to hike, any hotel can recommend a sightseeing boat which will bring you to the Captain Cook Monument nearby. As part of the tour you are allowed about 45 minutes of snorkeling. Dive charters also visit the area. The southern part of the bay is accessible by car at Nāpō'opo'o Beach Park, where you can snorkel or dive off the boat ramp. Be careful of boat traffic.

Directions: Drive south from Kailua-Kona about 12 miles to the town of Captain Cook. A prominent sign on the right marks the turnoff to Kealakekua Bay. Hikers can park about 500 feet beyond the sign and follow an old overgrown road 2.5 miles down to the bay. Others bear right and continue four miles down to the shore at Nāpō'opo'o.

HŌNAUNAU

Adjacent to Pu'uhonua-o-Hōnaunau National Historical Park (the "City of Refuge") lies sheltered Hōnaunau Bay offering both shore diving and snorkeling. Conditions here are almost always excellent. To the right of the boat ramp several lava ledges provide exceptionally easy entry and exit. Lush coral carpets the bottom. Snorkelers will enjoy the shallows close to shore; divers can make a 100-foot dive along the dropoff. While in the area don't miss the historical park next door. In addition to its cultural significance, it is a place of quiet beauty.

Directions: Hōnaunau is about four miles south of Nāpō'opo'o Beach Park along a bumpy coastal road. It is also accessible directly from the main highway (Route 11). Drive south from Kailua-Kona about 20 miles until you see the well-marked turnoff onto Route 160. From there drive about four miles down to the coast. Just beyond the park entrance is a small road on the left leading to the boatramp. There are no public facilities.

RICHARDSON OCEAN CENTER
(LELEIWI BEACH PARK)

Situated near the Hilo airport at the end of Kalaniana'ole Avenue, "Richardson's" is the most popular snorkeling spot on the east side of the Big Island. A point of land creates protected conditions and there is a moderate amount of marine life, including beautiful coral in quite shallow water. Enter the water next to the lifeguard tower in front of the Ocean Center building.

Directions: From the Hilo Airport turn right on Route 11. At the next light turn right again on Kalaniana'ole Avenue and follow it about four miles to the far end of Leleiwi Beach Park.

Hawai'i is a wonderful place to watch fishes, not only because of the warm, clear water but because at least 25 percent of the species are endemic — they occur nowhere else. Few locations compare with Hawai'i in number of unique fish species, and none has more. Why? How did our fishes originally get here? Where did they come from? Let us take a closer look.

DISPERSAL

The Hawaiian Islands are the tops of a dramatic undersea mountain range stretching 1500 miles from Kure Atoll in the northwest to the island of Hawaii. This range rises from great depths and (discounting tiny Johnston Island 450 miles to the south) is separated from all others by distances of more than 1000 miles. Sometime in the past the ancestors of all Hawaiian shallow-water marine species must have crossed this gap, far greater than the distances between any other Pacific islands and their nearest neighbors.

Many scientists believe that most tropical marine life originated near what is now Indonesia and the Philippines. More marine species are found in these ancient seas than anywhere else and the number decreases markedly as one moves away. Shallow-water animals and plants spread slowly from this "center of dispersal," moving from island to island or along the shores of continents. When they reached great oceanic gaps, some managed to cross. Even the coral reef animals of the remote Caribbean are believed to have originated from Indo-Pacific species, before the Isthmus of Panama rose to isolate the Atlantic Ocean from the Pacific.

While large ocean-going fishes can swim these distances, how do small reef fishes cross them? They do not swim, they drift. Most fishes begin life as minute larvae that are carried varying distances by ocean currents before settling in a suitable habitat to mature. If there is no suitable habitat, they perish.

The ancestors of Hawaii's shore and reef fishes drifted in as larvae. But only species with long-lasting larval stages made it; those with short larval stages died before they arrived. Ocean currents simply did not move them fast enough. Distance is a natural filter.

One group of fishes that never reached Hawai'i, for example, are the colorful anemonefishes, found almost everywhere else in the tropical Indian and Western Pacific oceans. Anemonefishes have never arrived here because their larval stage lasts only about a week. Surgeonfishes, on the other hand, drift as larvae for months and are here in abundance.

Of course, it is not enough for a species to arrive; local conditions must be suitable for growth and reproduction. If anemonefish larvae did somehow reach Hawai'i they would find no suitable anemones in which to live. Either the anemones themselves are unable to bridge the gap or, in turn, the local environment does not suit them. Hawaii's waters are cooler than many other reef areas of the Pacific. This, as well as other factors, limits the number of organisms that can survive here.

As might be expected, the number of fish species in Hawai'i (about 680) is considerably less than the number found in other Pacific locations such as Micronesia (1,400), or the Philippines (2,000). Out of these 680 Hawaiian fishes, about 420 are inhabitants of coastal waters down to about 200 feet. This book covers those most likely to be seen by snorkelers and divers.

Fish descriptions indicate the known range of each species. Usually this is given simply as "Indo-Pacific," meaning the tropical Indian Ocean and the Western and Central Pacific. Thus, an "Indo-Pacific" fish might be found anywhere from Hawai'i to the coast of East Africa. The tropical Eastern Pacific (off Central and South America), being further from the center of dispersal than Hawai'i, has even fewer species and is considered by scientists to be a separate faunal region.

ENDEMISM

About 25 percent of Hawaiian fish species are unique to the islands. Few places have a comparable percentage. Easter Island — also greatly isolated — is one of these; the Red Sea region — isolated not by distance but by geology — is another. Isolation encourages endemism because species populations are small, localized, and easily affected by genetic changes. Favorable mutations quickly become established in the gene pool, the organism becomes better adapted to its environment and, given enough time, may evolve many characteristics distinct from those of its ancestors.

In isolated regions like Hawai'i endemic species are often the most successful and abundant representatives of their families, probably because they are almost perfectly adapted to local conditions. Examples are the Milletseed Butterflyfish and the Saddle Wrasse, two of our most numerous reef fishes.

A few Hawaiian endemics, however, are uncommon around the main islands. Examples are the Yellowbar and Regal Parrotfishes and the Lined Coris. The Masked Angelfish, another notable example, is extremely rare. Fishes such as these probably evolved in the Northwestern Hawaiian Islands at a time when the main islands we know today did not exist. Adapted to cool temperatures, they have not done well in warmer waters further south. This theory is born out by their relative abundance at the northwestern end of the chain. It is also possible that some now uncommon endemics have been partly displaced by late arriving competitors. Because endemism is such an interesting and important phenomenon in Hawai'i, the names of endemic fishes in this book are marked with a dot. ●

Another characteristic of Hawaiian reefs is the abundance of a few species that are uncommon elsewhere in their range. Hawai'i, for example, is famous for Yellow Tangs. Only here do great schools of these golden fishes grace the reefs, although the species occurs also in Japan and the Mariana Islands. Hawaii's abundance of moray eels may be a variation of this phenomenon, which could result when species become established here leaving their competitors behind.

The Indo-Pacific Sergeant *(Abudefduf vaigiensis),* the probable ancestor of the endemic Hawaiian Sergeant, occurs throughout most of the Indo-Pacific. Before about 1990 it was unknown in Hawai'i, but during the past ten years it has firmly established itself in the Islands, perhaps carried here with drifting fishing debris. It has broader, more conspicuous bars than the Hawaiian species, and bright yellow on the back. Will the invader displace the resident? Will the two species mingle, or coexist indefinitely? Only time will tell.

ENVIRONMENT AND HABITAT

Coral reefs in Hawaii are poorly developed in comparison to other parts of the tropical Pacific. Water temperatures are too low to favor vigorous coral growth, and the factors which have limited the number of fish species have also limited the number of corals. (Actually, most "coral" limestone in Hawaii was formed by limestone-depositing coralline algae, rather than by true corals, which are animals.) The reefs of the main islands are fringing reefs, built up directly on the sides of the volcanoes. The enormous barrier reefs found elsewhere in the Pacific occur in Hawai'i only in the northwestern atolls.

Hawaiian shores offer a variety of habitats. The surge zone where sea meets land is characterized by cliffs or large smooth boulders and scanty coral growth. There is ample algae and seaweed here for fishes agile enough to survive the turbulence and crashing waves. Surge zone specialists include some algae-eating surgeonfishes, damselfishes and blennies.

Further from shore is the shallow reef, extending to a depth of about 30 feet. Here, turbulence is not so severe, coral is more abundant, and variety of life is greater. Colorful wrasses, triggerfishes and butterflyfishes feed on small crustaceans and invertebrates, and schools of parrotfishes and surgeonfishes graze on algae. Hawkfishes perch within branches of coral, ready to strike, while goatfishes probe for food in sandy patches and channels. The dominant corals in the shallow reef zone are Cauliflower Coral *(Pocillopora meandrina)* and Lobe Coral *(Porites lobata)*. This is the realm of the snorkeler; at least half of the fishes described in this book can be seen in this zone.

The deeper reef, starting at about 30 feet and subject to little wave action, is home to more delicate Finger Coral *(Porites compressa)* and, occasionally, Plate Coral *(P. rus)*. Pygmy angelfishes, juvenile surgeonfishes and small, colorful wrasses seek refuge here, while plankton-eating damselfishes hover in the water above and schools of goatfishes hang motionless, like curtains suspended in midwater, waiting for nightfall. Under ledges and in caves, big eyed squirrel and soldierfishes also wait for darkness, as the mysterious sticklike Trumpetfish stalks its prey and the Longnose Butterflyfish swims upside down on the ceiling. Up above, Hawaiian Cleaner Wrasses set up stations near coral heads where fishes, large and small, line up to be serviced, some coming in from deep water. This is the realm of the scuba diver and advanced snorkeler.

The dropoff zone, characterized by steep slopes and perpendicular walls, is a habitat preferred by plankton eaters, such as Pyramid and Pennant Butterflyfishes and anthias, or fairy basslets. Many of the other reef fishes can also be found along the walls, but the excitement along the dropoff comes from the occasional visits of large pelagic or open-ocean fishes, such as manta rays, large **ulua** (jacks), and sharks. At the base of the dropoff a rubble zone is home to yet other interesting fishes, such as the Flame Wrasse and the Indigo Dartfish. The dropoff and rubble zones are almost exclusively the domain of the diver, although occasionally the top of a wall is accessible to snorkelers.

Other habitats include shallow, protected lagoons, home to mullets, ladyfishes, stripeys and gobies, and lava tubes where unusual, deep-water creatures accustomed to perpetual darkness can sometimes be found.

Hawaii's underwater landscape, while not offering the lush exuberance of Micronesia or the Caribbean, has a spare beauty of its own in which unique and colorful fishes are the prime attraction.

CLASSIFICATION AND NAMES

CLASSIFICATION

The world probably has more than 20,000 fish species. They are classified into a hierarchy of evolutionarily related groups known as **classes, orders, genera** and **families.** Families have then been separated into individual **species**.

The **class** is the broadest grouping. Of the four classes of living fishes only two are of interest here: the primitive cartilaginous fishes (sharks, rays, skates and chimaeras) and the more modern bony fishes.

One level down, the **order** is a grouping of broadly similar fishes. All eels, for example, belong to the order Anguilliformes. Most reef fishes belong to the perchlike Perciformes. Other examples of orders are: all scorpionfishes *(Scorpaeniformes)* or all tubemouthed fishes such as pipefishes, seahorses and cornetfishes *(Syngnathiformes).* Note that the names of orders usually end in "...formes." There are 29 orders of living fishes, of which the perchlike Perciformes is by far the largest.

Families are composed of closely related fishes within an order. For example, all moray eels *(Muraenidae),* or all goatfishes *(Mullidae).* This book is organized alphabetically by families. The names of families always end in "...dae."

Within families are even more closely related groups known as **genera** (singular: **genus**). Finally, each genus is divided into **species**, the lowest unit of classification. (Occasionally, however, specialists divide one species into two or more subspecies.)

NAMES

The formal, scientific names of fishes consist of two parts: the genus and the species. This "binomial nomenclature," invented by the great Swedish naturalist Linnaeus (1707-1778), is used in the naming of all animals and plants. In print, the genus is always capitalized while the species is entirely in lower case, as in *Gorgasia hawaiiensis*. Both are italicized.

Binomial names are often, but not always, composed of descriptive Latin or Greek words. *Gorgasia* (named for the Gorgons, mythical Greek monsters with hair of snakes) is a genus of garden eels within the conger eel family *Congridae*. The species name *hawaiiensis* indicates precisely which garden eel we mean, in this case, the Hawaiian Garden Eel. Following the two-part name is the name of the biologist or biologists who first formally described the species and the year in which the description was published. Thus we have: **Gorgasia hawaiiensis Randall and Chess, 1979.** The authorship is considered part of the full scientific name. Parentheses around the author's name indicate that the genus originally assigned by the author has been changed.

It has often happened (especially in the last century) that two or more scientists, working in different parts of the world, each "discovered" and named fishes of the same species. Confusion has resulted, with some fishes receiving a dozen or more published scientific names. The rules of scientific nomenclature state that, within certain limits, only the first published name for a species is valid. Later names are known as "synonyms." Great progress has been made in recent years toward sorting out synonyms and valid names. That work is still going on, and some of the scientific names in this book will undoubtedly be revised in the future. Similarly, older books may use a scientific name different than the one given here. If you need to correlate an older name with the current one, see the Table of Invalid Names at the back of the book.

Scientific names can be intimidating to nonscientists. They look difficult and hard to pronounce, and they frequently do not connect in any obvious way with the actual plant or animal. Nevertheless, if one wants to communicate precisely about plants and animals, scientific names have no substitute. This book tries to make the scientific names more meaningful by providing translations whenever practical.

Common or popular names present another dilemma. A single fish species can have half a dozen popular names, varying from country to country or even region to region. If popular names are not controlled, there is no way to be sure exactly to which fishes they refer; if they are, they might cease to be "popular." There has been some effort by scientists to stabilize the English names of fishes, as has been done for birds and molluscs. This is a worthy goal, yet it sometimes results in names which few people actually use.

Should common names in a fish book reflect common usage, or should the author prescribe a more "correct" name? This volume leans toward established usage, generally preferring not to introduce new names where old ones suffice. In any case, alternate names are provided when appropriate.

In the Hawaiian language fish names are rich and detailed. Fishing was an important part of life in old Hawaii, with many connections to other activities. Different varieties of sugar cane, taro, or sweet potato, for example, often shared names with fishes. The Hawaiians had as many as four or five different names for a single fish species, designating different stages of its growth. Sometimes fish names had parallel meanings important in ceremony and magic.

Hawaiian fish and plant names were often in two parts, a general name coupled with a specific descriptor (similar to the genus and species of a scientific name). Thus **humuhumu** (triggerfish) and **'ele'ele** (black) join to form **humuhumu-'ele'ele**, the Black Triggerfish *(Melichthys niger)*. Unfortunately, by the time anyone thought to record Hawaiian fishing lore much of the old culture and knowledge had been lost. In many cases only the general name has survived. Although secondary descriptive names have been recorded, we often do not know exactly to which species they refer. Many Hawaiian names remain in common use, especially for the more important food fishes. Translations have been provided wherever practical.

FISH ANATOMY

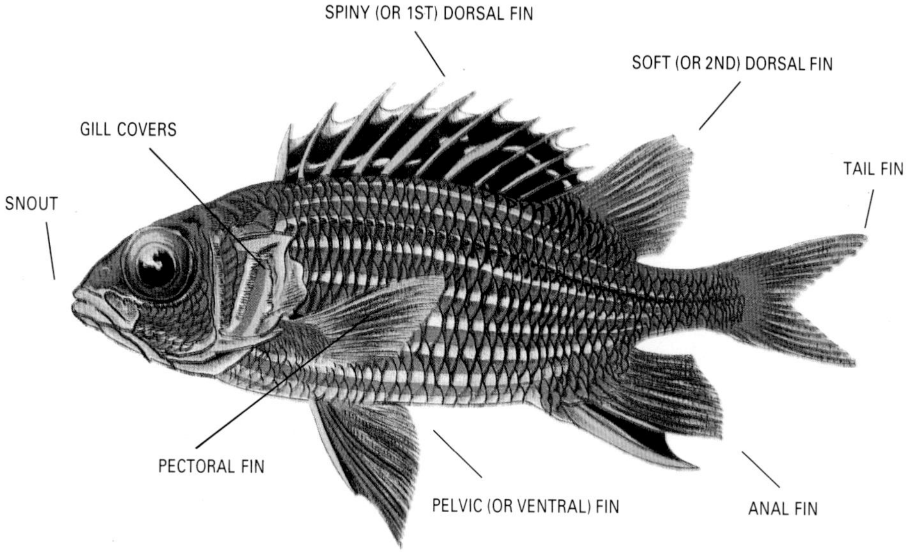

SPINY (OR 1ST) DORSAL FIN

SOFT (OR 2ND) DORSAL FIN

GILL COVERS

TAIL FIN

SNOUT

PECTORAL FIN

PELVIC (OR VENTRAL) FIN

ANAL FIN

Ichthyologists usually work from preserved specimens and perform their identifications in the laboratory, typically by counting fin spines, scale rows, teeth and the like, and by examining the structure of other parts such as the gills. For the purposes of this book, such refinements are not necessary. The shapes, sizes and color patterns of live fishes are usually enough for identification in the field.

It is difficult, however, to describe the characteristics and colors of fishes without elementary knowledge of fish anatomy. One must at the very least know the names and locations of the principle fins, such as the dorsal or pectoral fins. For this purpose a self-explanatory diagram is included. Wherever possible common rather than scientific words are used, i.e. "tail fin" for "caudal fin" and "base of tail" rather than "caudal peduncle." Another distinction is useful: in this book "stripes" are horizontal while "bars" are vertical. For more detailed information on the anatomy of fishes, see the publications listed in Source Materials on page 163.

ANGELFISHES
(POMACANTHIDAE)

Bandit Angelfish *(Desmoholacanthus arcuatus)* Palea Point, O'ahu. 50 ft.

Colorful and appealing, angelfishes are enduring favorites of divers, snorkelers and aquarists. In much of the Indo-Pacific and in the Caribbean, a close encounter with a big, showy angelfish can be a high point of a dive. Often unafraid, these fishes will turn to face their admirers, displaying to full advantage their gorgeous fins and colors. Unfortunately, large angelfishes do not occur in Hawai'i, although small, shy "pygmy angels" are common.

Pygmy angelfishes spend most of their lives in the coral, seldom venturing far from cover. Unlike the conspicuous butterflyfishes, they are rarely seen by snorkelers and easily overlooked by divers. One species, Potter's Angelfish, is common enough, but most divers have probably never seen a Fisher's Angelfish or a Flame Angelfish. Fewer still have seen the exquisite Japanese Pygmy Angelfish *(Centropyge interrupta)*, that occurs in our area only in the Northwestern Hawaiian Islands.

Not all Hawaiian species are pygmies. The larger Bandit Angelfish swims in the open and is so striking in appearance that it can be spotted immediately, even from a distance. The Masked Angelfish also swims openly, but is common only in the Northwestern Hawaiian Islands. Finally, the large and fantastically patterned Emperor Angelfish *(Pomacanthus imperator)* is known in Hawai'i from only one specimen, evidently a stray.

In captivity, angelfishes are delicate (requiring excellent water quality) and are often hard to feed. Aquarists planning to maintain them should have both experience with other marine fishes and familiarity with the symptoms and treatment of fish diseases. Fortunately, Hawaiian pygmy angelfishes are relatively trouble-free in comparison with many of their relatives. They have two requirements: plenty of hiding places and a diet rich in algae or plant material, preferably tank or ocean grown. Frozen preparations that meet these specifications are commercially available. As an alternative, finely minced spinach or other greens may also be tried. (These should have been previously frozen or else dipped in boiling water for about 15 seconds to break down the tough cellulose fibers which fishes can't digest.) Pygmy angelfishes will quickly consume any algae growing in the tank; their little mouth marks will soon appear all over smooth rocks or glass where even a thin film of algae has been allowed to grow. This preference makes them useful, as well as decorative. (For further tips on feeding angelfishes see the section on butterflyfishes.)

13

Because angelfishes are territorial, similar species placed together in a small aquarium will often fight. It is possible, however, to keep mated pairs; under excellent conditions they will even spawn.

Angelfishes were for many years classed in the same family as the butterflyfishes. Anatomically, they differ from butterflyfishes by having a large backward-pointing spine on the gill cover. Their scientific family name combines *poma* ("cheek") and *acanthus* ("spine"). Of the approximately 80 angelfish species worldwide, only five occur in the main Hawaiian Islands, four of them endemic. None have Hawaiian names.

FISHER'S ANGELFISH ●
Centropyge fisheri (Snyder, 1904).
    These small, orange brown angelfishes are quite abundant in finger coral and rubble at depths of about 80 feet or more, but are rarely noticed. On O'ahu look for them on the deeper Wai'anae dives. On Maui they are common at Molokini Island, sometimes as shallow as 30 feet. On the Big Island they can be seen on steep outer slopes at Hōnaunau and many other sites. In captivity their small size is a plus and they eventually lose much of their shyness. The species is named for California zoologist Walter K. Fisher, who was active in Hawai'i around the turn of the century. To about 3 in. Endemic. Photo: Hōnaunau, Hawai'i. 90 ft.

FLAME ANGELFISH
Centropyge loricula (Gunther, 1874).

These beauties are bright red, with dark vertical bars on the body and blue trim on the rear fins (more pronounced in males). The bars evidently reminded someone of a lady's corselet, for that is the meaning of the species name. They prefer dense stands of finger coral at depths of 60 feet or more, but may also be seen in shallower, rockier habitats. They are rare in Hawai'i, but if one is located it can be counted on to stay in the same location, where it can be visited repeatedly. Although spectacular fishes often do poorly in aquariums, the Flame Angel is a happy exception; it is small and peaceful, soon loses its shyness, and eats almost anything that is offered. Specimens sold as "Hawaiian Flames" are usually not from Hawai'i but probably come from the Marshall, Line, or Cook Islands. True Hawaiian Flames (brighter red between the bars) command a higher price, but few aquarists can tell the difference. To 4 in. Pacific Islands, from the Great Barrier Reef to Hawai'i. Photo: Magic Island, O'ahu. 30 ft.

POTTER'S ANGELFISH ●
Centropyge potteri (Jordan & Metz, 1912).

The only truly common angelfishes in Hawai'i, Potter's Angels are rusty orange on the front and back, shading to blackish below, with many irregular vertical grayish to deep blue lines. (Males have more blue.) They are usually seen in clear water at depths of at least 15 feet peering from the coral and darting from one hiding place to the next. On O'ahu, adventuresome snorkelers may glimpse them off the cliffs at Kawaihoa (Portlock) Point, where for some reason they are frequently in the open. Big Island snorkelers can find them at Hōnaunau or Kealakekua Bay in only a few feet of water. Divers, of course, will see them almost anywhere. A beautiful species, they do well in captivity if given peaceful tankmates and plenty of time to adjust. Like many angelfishes they are slow to begin feeding. Named for Frederick A. Potter, director of the Waikīkī Aquarium from its founding in 1903 until 1940. To 5 in. Endemic. Photo: Magic Island, O'ahu. 30 ft.

Masked Angelfish - male ∧   female ∨

MASKED ANGELFISH ●
Genicanthus personatus Randall, 1975
Native to the northwestern Hawaiian chain these angelfishes are extremely rare on the main islands, usually at depths exceeding 200 feet. They feed on plankton in open water near dropoffs. Underwater, the more numerous females appear almost snow white with a black "mask" over the eyes; males, white rimmed in orange, have a yellow mask and tail streamers. When they can be obtained, Masked Angelfishes command over a thousand dollars apiece in the aquarium trade. They are picky eaters which seldom do well in captivity and prefer temperatures of about 70 F. — cooler than most other tropical marine fishes. The species name means "mask." To about 10 in. Endemic. Photos: Midway Island, 90 ft.

BANDIT ANGELFISH ●
Desmoholacanthus arcuatus (Gray, 1831).
White and gray, with a bold black band like a robber's mask passing through the eyes and extending the length of the body, these friendly angelfishes will actually swim over to investigate divers. On Kaua'i they are so common they can sometimes be seen by snorkelers. On the other islands they are encountered most frequently at depths of about 100 feet. Feeding heavily on sponges, they fare poorly in captivity. Their color pattern is unlike that of any other known angelfish. The name means "bent like a bow," referring to the slightly arched black band. This species is sometimes placed in the genus *Apolemichthys*. To 7 in. Endemic. Photo: Palea Point, O'ahu. 50 ft.

BARRACUDAS
(SPHYRAENIDAE)

Lean, fast, and powerful, barracudas have reputations as predators second only to sharks. They are elongated and almost cylindrical in cross section, with a pointed, protruding lower jaw, two dorsal fins spaced widely apart and a large forked tail. The mouth, often held slightly agape, is full of sharp teeth. One species, the Great Barracuda, reaching six feet in length with a weight of about 100 pounds, is reported to strike at speeds of almost 40 feet per second.

Some barracudas hunt in schools, others are solitary. When they feed, they often cut their prey in two then circle back to eat the pieces. Sharks do the same thing. Both lack the expandable mouths common to other fish predators, such as groupers, that facilitate swallowing prey whole.

The reputations of dangerous marine predators rise and fall. Sharks, for example, were downplayed in the early 1900s when many scientists thought them stupid and cowardly. At the same time barracudas were widely regarded as fearless and liable to strike without warning. Barracudas were even stated by one authority to be responsible for most "shark" attacks. Today the pendulum has swung to the other side: sharks are treated with respect and caution, while barracudas are seldom considered a threat.

Barracuda attacks, although rare, can cause serious injury. At least two incidents have been recorded in Hawaiian waters, both to Maui fishermen and both in the 1960s. One man, repeatedly slashed on the leg by a six foot barracuda while throw-net fishing, subsequently underwent five hours of surgery. The other required 255 stitches to close his wounds.

A study of 29 reported barracuda attacks in the United States between 1873 and 1963 confirmed nineteen. Most occurred in murky water or as a result of deliberate provocation. Reasons advanced

GREAT BARRACUDA · **kākū**
Sphyraena barracuda (Walbaum, 1792).

    The largest of the barracudas and the one most frequently implicated in attacks on humans, this species is silvery, often with small black blotches irregularly placed on the lower side. The large tail fin is black except for the tips, which are pale. Smaller specimens may have about 20 indistinct bars. They occur alone or in small groups and are often found in shallow water close to shore, frequently near the hot water outfall at Kahe Point Beach Park, O'ahu. Both common and species names originate from South America. To almost 6 ft. Indo-Pacific and Atlantic. Photo: Mōkōlea Island, O'ahu. 20 ft.

for unprovoked strikes include splashing about in the water and the presence of bright, flashing jewelry on the victim (which the barracuda may interpret as the flash of silver scales). The author was skeptical of this until a jack struck at his shiny camera strobe while he was swimming in murky water close to shore. Nearby was a medium-size Great Barracuda. The author promptly left the water.

Actually, there is more danger in eating barracudas than in being eaten by them; high on the food chain, these fishes often accumulate high levels of ciguatera fish toxin, which causes abdominal pain, nausea, vomiting and strange neurological symptoms such as reversal of hot and cold.

A remarkable partnership has long existed between Hawaiian fishermen and certain large barracudas, tamed by hand-feeding and carefully trained to help catch **'ōpelu**, or Mackerel Scad. The fisherman summons his barracuda, or **'ōpelu mama**, by pounding rhythmically on the bottom of his wooden canoe. Rising from the deep, the barracuda follows the canoe until a suitable school is found. Next, the fisherman lowers a large, circular net and chums the **'ōpelu** with cooked grated squash while the barracuda circles the canoe, driving the fishes into a tight ball underneath where they can easily be caught. Before carefully raising the bulging net, the fisherman tosses his helper a well-earned reward. This remarkable tradition continues on the island of Maui, although fishermen complain that their valuable **'ōpelu mama** are sometimes caught by commercial fishing charters. "Please write about the **mama**," implored one fisherman to a newspaper reporter, "and tell people that they should be respected."

Divers frequently encounter barracudas, either in schools or as individuals. The fishes usually keep their distance and soon disappear into the gloom. Sometimes they show curiosity by circling at a respectful distance. Baby barracudas are abundant at some of O'ahu's north shore snorkeling sites in very shallow water. At least two species are known from Hawai'i.

HELLER'S BARRACUDA • kawele'ā
Sphyraena helleri Jenkins, 1901.

The Hawaiian name means "long and bright," an apt description. Slender and silvery, these barracudas have a broad blue stripe running the length of the body. They hunt by night and frequently form beautiful, tight schools above the reef by day. The ancient Hawaiians used to say of a confusing situation: "The kawele'āhave taken the bait and tangled the lines." Named for Stanford zoologist Edmund Heller who studied the fishes of the Galapagos Islands in the late nineteenth century. To about 2 ft. Western Pacific. Photo: Puakō, Hawai'i. 20 ft.

Bigeyes are red or silvery nocturnal fishes, somewhat similar in behavior to the more common squirrelfishes and soldierfishes, with which they are sometimes confused. However, they are unrelated to squirrelfishes and differ from them considerably, being oval in outline with narrow (compressed) bodies, fine scales and upturned mouths.

During the day bigeyes often remain under ledges and in caves, seemingly asleep, at which time they are are easy to approach and even to touch. At night they emerge to feed on planktonic animals. They are said to occasionally school in enormous numbers close to shore, an event regarded in ancient times as foretelling the death of a chief.

Hawaii's two shallow reef species, almost identical in appearance, are both known as **'āweoweo**. To identify them underwater look at the tail fins — rounded in one, concave in the other. Several other species are known from deep water. Although not often kept in aquariums, small bigeyes do well in captivity.

BIGEYE • **'āweoweo**
Heteropriacanthus cruentatus
(Lacepède, 1801).
(GLASSEYE; GOGGLE-EYE)

Bright red to silvery, or displaying a blotchy mixture of the two, these fishes can switch colors rapidly when alarmed. The back edge of the tail fin is slightly rounded. There are often faint dark spots on the dorsal, anal and tail fins. The species name means "bloody," the Hawaiian name "glowing red." To the ancient Hawaiians, red was a royal color. According to contemporary newspapers, in late January of 1891 (about the time when King Kalakaua died in San Francisco) a multitude of red fishes was observed schooling in Pearl Harbor. They might have been this species. To about 12 in. Found in all tropical seas. Photo: Kawaihoa (Portlock) Point, O`ahu. 30 ft.

HAWAIIAN BIGEYE • **'āweoweo** ●
Priacanthus meeki Jenkins, 1903.

Hawaiian Bigeyes have a tail fin with a slightly concave trailing edge. Their color varies from silvery to red and there is often a series of faint dark spots along the lateral line. They usually occur in deeper water than the common Bigeye and sometimes school in the open outside their shelters. Named after American zoologist S.E. Meek. To about 12 in. Endemic. Photo: Kawaihoa (Portlock) Point, O'ahu. 30 ft.

19

Scarface Blenny • **pāo'o** *(Cirripectes vanderbilti)* Pūpūkea, O'ahu. 30 ft.

Blennies are small, elongated fishes typically seen in tidepools or peering from holes in the reef. Their alert eyes, doleful expressions, and curious antenna-like filaments (cirri), make them favorite close-up subjects of underwater photographers. They also make entertaining and comical aquarium pets and, for marine biologists, interesting subjects of study.

Blennies may be divided into two broad categories: bottom-dwellers and free swimmers. The former subsist mostly on algae scraped from the rocks with their wide mouths. They are poor swimmers, lack air bladders, and sink as soon as they stop moving. When out of their holes they prefer to rest on rock or coral.

The free-swimming or saber-tooth blennies are carnivorous, swim openly, and retreat to their holes only at night or when threatened. Their lower jaws bear a set of curved fangs used primarily for defense. If taken by a larger fish, a saber-tooth blenny will bite the inside of its captor's mouth and be spat out unharmed. In some non-Hawaiian species the fangs are venomous. These venomous species are often mimicked by yet other blennies.

Many saber-tooth blennies feed exclusively on mucus or bits of scale scraped or nipped from the sides of larger fishes. These tiny predators make sneak attacks on their larger hosts, sometimes relying on mimicry to approach within striking distance. One of the most remarkable mimics is the False Cleaner Wrasse Blenny *(Aspidontus taeniatus)*, an almost exact double of the common Indo-Pacific Cleaner Wrasse *(Labroides dimidiatus)*; it even swims with the cleaner's curious up-and-down dancing motion. When a large fish approaches the blenny to have its parasites removed, it loses a bit of skin or scale instead. Although no mimic of the adult Hawaiian Cleaner Wrasse is known, the Ewa Fang Blenny sometimes resembles juveniles of that species.

With over 300 species, the blennies form a large family. The ancient Greeks knew them as *blennos*, the source of our modern name. The general Hawaiian name is **pāo'o**. Of the 14 blennies known from Hawai'i, five are described below. Because of this family's short larval stage, many Hawaiian species are endemic. One (pictured on p. 179) is the Gargantuan Blenny (*Cirripectes obscurus*), a wary and seldom seen shallow water endemic which grows to at least seven inches. It may be recognized by its size and by the many small bright spots, like pinpoints of light, on the head.

Except for the scale eaters, blennies do well in captivity and make amusing pets. Shoreline species should be kept in covered tanks as they are likely to jump out at night.

SCARFACE BLENNY • **pāo'o** ●
Cirripectes vanderbilti (Fowler, 1938).
Very common in areas such as O'ahu's north shore, these blennies can easily be seen peering from crevices or resting in the open on the coral. They probably make excellent aquarium fishes but are not usually offered for sale. The red "scars" on the face are not always as bright as pictured here. Named for Mr. and Mrs. George Vanderbilt, of Philadelphia, sponsors of a scientific expedition to the Pacific in 1937. To almost 4 in. Endemic. Similar to the Red-Speckled Blenny *(C. variolosus)* of Micronesia and the South Pacific. Photo: Pūpūkea, O'ahu. 30 ft.

SHORTBODIED BLENNY • **pāo'o kauila**
Exallias brevis (Kner, 1868).
(Spotted Coral Blenny; Leopard Blenny)
Common wherever coral grows, these large, appealing blennies are frequently seen by both divers and snorkelers. They are densely covered with spots (reddish in males, brown to yellow in females) and have a sail-like dorsal fin which they raise when alarmed. These blennies are unusual in that they feed exclusively on living coral, leaving small mouth marks all over the reef. Males clear a small patch of coral upon which the females lay their bright yellow eggs. The male guards them until they hatch. Species name means "short." Not suitable for aquariums because of their feeding habits. To 6 in. Indo-Pacific. Photo: Hanauma Bay, O'ahu. 20 ft.

ZEBRA BLENNY • pāo'o ●
Istiblennius zebra (Vaillant and Sauvage, 1875).
(ZEBRA ROCKSKIPPER, JUMPING JACK)

Anyone who pokes about the rocky seashore is familiar with these **pāo'o**. Abundant in even the shallowest tidepools, they feed on algae and detritus. When disturbed they can slither and skip a surprising distance over the rocks, somehow knowing in advance the location of the next pool. The color varies from a smart blue black to brownish gray with indistinct bars. Some large individuals develop yellowish white cheek patches. They adapt well to the aquarium and make a fun pet. Be sure the tank is well covered. To 7 in. Endemic. A similar shoreline species, probably the Marbled Blenny *(Entomacrodus marmoratus),* sleeps at night on ledges several inches above the water line, safe from aquatic predators. Photo: Marjorie L. Awai. Waikīkī Aquarium.

EWA FANG BLENNY ●
Plagiotremus ewaensis (Brock, 1948).

This colorful blenny varies from black to orange or red, usually with vivid blue horizontal stripes. It feeds on the scales, skin and mucus of larger fishes; its mouth, underslung like that of a tiny shark, contains two long fangs which are used only for defense. Specimens that are black with blue stripes look somewhat like juvenile Hawaiian Cleaner Wrasses and probably use the resemblance to advantage. Many divers have been nipped by these little fishes (usually on the leg) but they do no harm. If chased, the blenny usually backs tail first into an abandoned worm hole, leaving only its colorful head sticking out. Look closely and you will see it grinning at you. Very similar to the Bluestripe Blenny *(P. rhynorhyncos),* widespread elsewhere in the Indo-Pacific. Named for a district on O'ahu. Not recommended for aquariums. To 4 in. Endemic. Photo: Mākua, O'ahu. 25 ft.

SCALE-EATING FANG BLENNY ●
Plagiotremus goslinei (Strasburg, 1956).

Smaller than the Ewa Fang Blenny and not as colorful, these are greenish yellow on the back and light underneath. The habits of the two are similar. Named in honor of ichthyologist William A. Gosline, for many years a professor at the University of Hawai'i. Closely related to the Piano Blenny *(P. tapeinosoma)* common elsewhere in the Indo-Pacific. Not recommended for aquariums. To 2.5 in. Endemic. Photo: Pūpūkea, O'ahu. 25 ft.

BOARFISHES
(PENTACEROTIDAE)

Boarfishes, or armorheads, are a small family of unusual fishes with narrow, deep bodies and heads encased in bone. About eleven species are known; two occur in Hawai'i. Only one is likely to be seen by divers.

WHISKERED BOARFISH
Evistias acutirostris (Temminck & Schlegel, 1844).
    Rarely seen except on Kaua'i and the Northwestern Hawaiian Islands, these odd fishes are dark brown with five yellowish white vertical bars and a yellow, sail-like dorsal fin which is always extended. The snout projects forward. There are bristles or whiskers under the "chin." The forehead is steep with a lump in front of the eyes. Boarfishes typically shelter in small groups near overhangs or caves at depths of 60 feet or more and are exceptionally easy to approach. Species name means "sharp snout." To about 20 in. Japan, Hawai'i, Australia. Photo: "Fish Bowl," south shore Kaua'i, 60 ft.

Spotted Boxfish • **moa** *(Ostracion meleagris)* male. Pūpūkea, O'ahu. 25 ft.

Boxfishes, as their name implies, are completely encased in rigid armor plate; only their fins, eyes and mouths are movable. Sometimes called trunkfishes, they are immediately recognizable by their shape, usually square in cross-section, but sometimes triangular, pentagonal, hexagonal or even round. Like the pufferfishes, to which they are related, boxfishes propel themselves primarily with their dorsal and anal fins. Also like puffers, they rely in part on poisonous qualities to deter predators. When boxfishes are disturbed their skin secretes a toxin. Captured boxfishes, kept in a small container, are capable of poisoning themselves as well as any other fishes held with them. The poison (ostracitoxin) is not known to affect humans. Boxfishes eat algae, sponges, tunicates, worms and other invertebrates found on the sea bottom. In many species, males and females are differently patterned, males being more colorful. Most species begin life female, with some individuals reversing sex later. This explains why small males are never seen.

In the aquarium, boxfishes are almost irresistible. Their little mouths are perpetually puckered, as if to kiss, and they may become tame enough to surface at feeding time, squirting feeble jets of water in anticipation. (Some species feed in nature by squirting water at the sandy bottom to uncover small creatures.) Shy at first, they sometimes take days or weeks to accept food. Once adjusted, they are hardy and will eat almost anything offered. Small specimens should be given live brine shrimp. Boxfishes can be kept with other fishes, but there is always the danger of wiping out the entire tank if they become upset for any reason. Unlikely as it may seem, they are excitable and can jump out of uncovered aquariums.

Boxfishes belong to the order Tetraodontiformes, which includes such other odd creatures as porcupinefishes and triggerfishes. Their family name comes from the Greek *ostrakon* ("shell" or "potsherd"). In old Hawai'i they were known as **pahu** ("box"). Of the five species occurring regularly in Hawai'i, the three described below are the only ones likely to be seen by snorkelers or divers.

THORNBACK COWFISH • **makukana**
Lactoria fornasini (Bianconi, 1846).

This species has two horns on the head, a thornlike spike on its back and two hornlike projections on the rear. It is light tan with light blue lines or spots, which intensify in males during spawning. As in all boxfishes, the carapace is formed of hexagonal or pentagonal plates fused together; these plates can be seen clearly in the cowfish. To about 5 in. Indo-Pacific. Photo: Kawaihoa (Portlock) Point, O'ahu. 30 ft.

SPOTTED BOXFISH • **moa**
Ostracion meleagris Shaw & Nodder, 1796.

Females are black, densely covered with white spots. The colorful males have dark blue sides with black spots and markings; their tops are black with white spots; their heads and tails are adorned with gold trim. Everywhere but Hawai'i males have gold spots on the sides. Lacking these, the Hawaiian population is regarded as a subspecies, *camurum* (although males with scattered gold spots on their sides are occasionally observed here). Boxfishes are common in shallows where the water is calm and may be seen by waders at the beach as well as by pedestrians walking along sea walls. Species name means "guineafowl" (a bird native to Africa covered with light spots). To about 6 in. East Africa to the Americas. Photo: female. Hanauma Bay, O'ahu. 15 ft. male: see family photo page 24.

WHITLEY'S BOXFISH
Ostracion whitleyi Fowler, 1931.

The blue males of this species are rare in Hawai'i but small females, although uncommon, can be found regularly. They are golden brown with cream spots and a wide cream band along the side (which may contain brown spots or markings). Remaining under ledges, they seldom venture into the open. How these fishes reproduce in Hawai'i with so few males is a mystery. Named after Australian ichthyologist G.P. Whitley (1903-1975). To about 5 in. Restricted to the Central Pacific and most common in the Marquesas Islands. Photo: female. Kawaihoa (Portlock) Point, O'ahu. 30 ft.

25

BUTTERFLYFISHES
(CHAETODONTIDAE)

Milletseed Butterflyfishes • **lau-wiliwili** *(Chaetodon miliaris)*. Hanauma Bay, O'ahu. 30 ft.

If there were a typical coral reef fish, it would probably be a butterflyfish. Brightly colored (often in yellow) pairs of these delicate creatures are a common sight as they flit among the undersea gardens. Their disklike bodies, like artists' palettes, display colors and patterns that are obviously meant to be noticed.

While most other fishes have evolved to blend with their environment, the butterflyfishes have done the opposite. What advantage do they gain? They are spiny and make a prickly mouthful — is their appearance a warning? They travel in pairs and may mate for life — is it for recognition? Whatever the reason — if there is a reason — these fishes delight and inspire all visitors to their undersea realm.

With their disk-shape bodies, butterflyfishes are well suited for maneuvering through narrow spaces; though they might seem easy targets for predators, they can quickly move out of reach. To further confuse their foes, most species have a dark bar through the eye, effectively disguising it. Some go one step further, displaying a false eyespot near the tail. Depending on the species, butterflyfishes feed on small invertebrates, plankton, coral polyps and occasionally algae, often using their snouts to probe into crevices. Although they have long-term, possibly permanent mates, butterflyfishes offer no parental care to their young. As with most fishes, eggs are released into the water; after hatching, the larvae drift with the plankton for weeks or months.

In old Hawai'i, butterflyfishes had several general names. Those called **kīkākapu** ("strongly prohibited") are described in several chants as sacred. Others were **lau-hau** ("leaf of the **hau** tree") or **lau-wiliwili** ("leaf of the **wiliwili** tree"). There were specific names as well, but it is no longer clear to which species they referred.

Anatomically, butterflyfishes are characterized by small, brushlike teeth. The family name, Chaetodontidae, is a combination of *chaeto* ("hair") and *dentis* ("tooth"), the first syllable rhyming with "key." Of the approximately 115 butterflyfish species, 24 occur in the Hawaiian Islands and 20 are pictured here. Omitted are two deep water butterflyfishes (never seen by sport divers) and two shallow-water Indo-Pacific species very rare in Hawai'i. The latter two include the Double-Saddle Butterflyfish (*Chaetodon ulietensis*), known from only two specimens, and the Chevron Butterflyfish (*C. trifascialis*) found at French Frigate Shoals in the Northwestern Hawaiian Islands. Juvenile Chevron Butterflies are occasionally seen around the main islands but are unable to mature because adults of the species feed exclusively on *Acropora*, a type of coral found abundantly in Hawai'i only at French Frigate Shoals.

Aquarists, of course, are fascinated by butterflyfishes. Many recall becoming "hooked" on their hobby upon first seeing one in a dealer's tank. A responsible dealer, however, should probably not sell butterflyfishes to beginners. They are fussy eaters and particularly susceptible to disease. Some are too shy to ever adjust well. The most heartbreakingly beautiful of them feed only on living coral and are therefore impossible to maintain in ordinary home aquariums. Butterflyfishes are unsuitable for "mini-reef" aquariums as they will pick at the live coral and eat the very organisms the aquarist is trying to culture.

For those who cannot resist keeping one, several of our Hawaiian species can be recommended— but only after some experience has been gained with easier fishes such as damselfishes. Milletseed, Threadfin, Raccoon and Pennant Butterflyfishes are hardier than most and adjust well to tank life, eventually accepting flake food right from your fingers.

Recently captured specimens of any butterflyfish species may not eat for days or even weeks. Various techniques can be used to get them to feed. The easiest is to offer live food such as brine shrimp (*Artemia*) or mosquito larvae. Fishes which have been indifferent to the finest prepared fishfoods will perk up when these little wrigglers are added to their tank. After several feedings they will usually begin pecking experimentally at frozen fishfood or even flakes. A second technique is to prepare a feeding stone. (This is only useful if you notice your butterfly pecking at the rocks and coral.) Remove a stone from the tank, press some high-quality frozen fishfood into the cracks, and replace it. When your butterflyfish next pecks at that rock it will get a happy surprise. It is always helpful to have other fishes in the tank which are feeding well, as they will set an example for the newcomer. Be aware, though, that butterflyfishes might not tolerate new tankmates of their own or similar species. If you want to keep a pair of butterflyfishes introduce both at the same time.

For long term success, water quality and temperature control must be excellent. Sudden temperature changes especially weaken their resistance. Familiarity with the symptoms and treat- ment of protozoan parasite diseases, such as Cryptocaryon, is an absolute must for anyone attempting to keep these fishes. Butterflyfishes will live only a few months if not well cared for; given ideal conditions they will survive for years. A Longnose Butterfly at the Nancy Aquarium in France lived 18 years. A Saddleback at the same institution lived 14 years, a Pyramid 10, and a Raccoon nine. Please do not remove these fishes from the reef if you cannot invest in the time and equipment to keep them healthy.

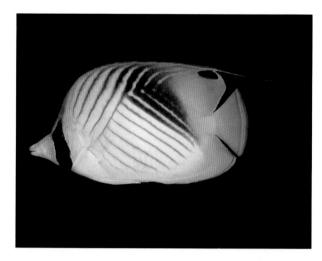

THREADFIN BUTTERFLYFISH
Chaetodon auriga Forsskål, 1775.
The whitish body, shading to gold in back, is marked with sets of fine right-angled diagonal lines. One of the soft dorsal spines is prolonged into a thread-like filament; below it is a black spot. Juveniles lack the filament and have a larger black spot. Like many of their family, pairs hold home territories within which they roam freely. Other species of butterflyfishes are tolerated but those of the same species are driven away. The Threadfin is one of the easiest butterflyfishes for the aquarist. The species name means "charioteer," probably because of the whiplike dorsal filament. To about 8 in. Indo-Pacific. Photo: "Yellow Brick Road," south shore Kaua'i, 30 ft.

SPECKLED BUTTERFLYFISH
Chaetodon citrinellus Cuvier, 1831.
This seldom-seen fish is light yellow with a black margin on the anal fin and the usual dark bar through the eye. It should not be confused with the very common Milletseed Butterfly, which has a black spot at the base of the tail. A shallow water fish, it is rare in Hawai'i; pairs may sometimes be seen by snorkelers off Kahe Point Beach Park or Waikīkī, O'ahu. Elsewhere in the Pacific is one of the commonest butterflyfishes. Species name means "citrus." To about 5 in. Pacific Ocean. Photo: Kahe Point, O'ahu. 15 ft.

SADDLEBACK BUTTERFLYFISH
Chaetodon ephippium Cuvier, 1831.
Among the most striking of their family, these are gray with a bold black saddle rimmed in white. They have an orange snout and a dorsal filament similar to that of the Threadfin Butterflyfish. Not common. Seen in pairs, often in shallow, somewhat turbid water. Unfortunately, these very beautiful fishes often refuse to eat in captivity. Species name means "saddled." To 8 in. Western and Central Pacific. Photo: Hanauma Bay, O'ahu. 20 ft.

BLUESTRIPE BUTTERFLYFISH ●
• kīkākapu
Chaetodon fremblii Bennett, 1829.

Found only in Hawai'i, this attractive fish is yellow with eight narrow blue stripes running diagonally along the body. When alarmed it becomes a darker, dirty yellow. Single individuals are common in shallow water, especially around patches of sand or smooth bottom between boulders and coral. Hawaiian endemics usually resemble species found elsewhere, but the Bluestripe Butterflyfish has no close relatives and is truly unique. Unfortunately, it is shy in captivity, taking on protective coloration and seldom regaining its bright yellows and blues. It will eat the tentacles of any featherduster worms in the tank. To 6 in. Endemic. Photo: Koloa Landing, Kaua'i. 5 ft.

BLUEHEAD BUTTERFLYFISH
Chaetodon kleinii Bloch, 1790.
(Blacklip Butterflyfish; Klein's Butterflyfish)

This small species is dull golden brown, somewhat speckled in appearance. The dark bar through the eye becomes bluish on the forehead, especially in strong light. It is most often encountered well off the bottom feeding on plankton. Relatively hardy in captivity. To 5 in. Indo-Pacific. Photo: *Mahi* wreck, O'ahu. 60 ft.

LINED BUTTERFLYFISH • kīkākapu
Chaetodon lineolatus Cuvier, 1831.

As large as dinner plates, these striking fishes are occasionally seen in areas of rich coral growth, almost always in pairs. The numerous dark, vertical lines on the body are distinctive. Uncommon and difficult to approach, they are encountered most regularly along the Kona Coast of the Big Island and in Kāne'ohe Bay, O'ahu. Relatively hardy in captivity. Species name means "lined." The largest of all butterflyfishes, they grow to 12 inches. Indo-Pacific. Photo: Hōnaunau, Hawai'i. 40 ft.

29

RACCOON BUTTERFLYFISH • kīkākapu *Chaetodon lunula* (Lacepède, 1803).

The face of this fish, with its masked eyes and white crescent-shape mark resembles that of its namesake, a nocturnal North American mammal. Curiously, it may be the only nocturnal butterflyfish; by day it is orange yellow, at night dull brown. During the day Raccoon Butterflyfishes typically rest motionless in midwater, sometimes in large schools that frequent the same locations year after year. Juveniles, seen in tidepools, are brighter in color and have a large false eyespot. Raccoon Butterflies do well in captivity. They relish algae or chopped frozen spinach and will eagerly devour the small sea-anemones (*Aiptasia sp.*) that sometimes multiply out of control in "mini-reef" aquariums. They are definitely incompatible with anemone bearing crabs. Small specimens from tidepools can be difficult to feed — try newly hatched brine shrimp. Species name means "crescent." To 8 in. Indo-Pacific. Photo: Kaiwi Point, Hawai'i. 30 ft.

MILLETSEED BUTTERFLYFISH • lau-wiliwili ●
Chaetodon miliaris Quoy & Gaimard, 1824.
(LEMON BUTTERFLYFISH)

Every diver and snorkeler in Hawai'i is familiar with these bright yellow characters; it is impossible to dive in some areas without being mobbed by them. Even where they have not been fed, schools of them will approach humans, curious for a closer look. In nature, they will descend in a great yellow swarm upon the egg patches of the Sergeant Major, totally overwhelming the defenses of this otherwise aggressive damselfish. They are common at all depths attainable by divers. Although these gluttons are reasonably easy to keep in an aquarium, they tend to lose their yellow color, possibly as a result of an artificial diet. The Frenchmen who named them thought their spots resembled seeds of millet. To 6.5 in. Endemic. Photo: Pūpūkea, O'ahu. 50 ft.

MULTIBAND BUTTERFLYFISH ●
Chaetodon multicinctus Garrett, 1863.
(PEBBLED BUTTERFLYFISH)

These small sedate butterflies almost always occur in pairs, probing and picking at the coral upon which they feed. They are light tan covered with brown dots which coalesce to form four or five vertical bars. In nature they feed almost exclusively on live coral but in captivity soon adjust to an omnivorous diet. Common throughout the islands. Species name means "many bands." To 4 in. Endemic. Photo: Hanauma Bay, O'ahu. 20 ft.

ORNATE BUTTERFLYFISH • **kīkākapu**
Chaetodon ornatissimus Cuvier, 1831.

Among the most beautiful of butterflyfishes, these are cream color with black bars on the face and graceful orange lines running diagonally along the body. Most of the body is rimmed in black. Feeding exclusively on live coral, they are totally unsuitable for aquariums and should never be taken from the reef. To 8 in. Indo-Pacific. Photo: Honolua Bay, Maui. 15 ft.

FOURSPOT BUTTERFLYFISH • **lau-hau**
Chaetodon quadrimaculatus Gray, 1833.

Despite both common and scientific names only two white spots are visible on these fishes. (To make four, the spots on both sides must be counted.) Their bodies are are dark above, becoming orange yellow below, with a yellow tail and a yellow head and the usual dark stripe through the eye. Pairs are often seen resting under ledges. This delicate species is not recommended for aquariums. To 6 in. Known only from the Pacific islands. Photo: Kahe Point, O'ahu. 15 ft.

RETICULATED BUTTERFLYFISH
Chaetodon reticulatus Cuvier, 1831.
   Combinations of white, cream, and gray with black markings give these elegant fishes a quiet beauty all their own. They travel in pairs and are quite approachable. Uncommon in the Hawaiian Islands, this species is seen most often off the Kona coast in relatively shallow water. On O'ahu a pair or two are sometimes encountered near the entrance to Hanauma Bay. Both the common and scientific names mean "netlike" or "meshlike," referring to the pattern on the sides. Very difficult to maintain in captivity. To 7 in. Central and Western Pacific. Photo: Hanauma Bay, O'ahu. 15 ft.

TINKER'S BUTTERFLYFISH
Chaetodon tinkeri Schultz, 1951.
   Both rare and beautiful, Tinker's Butterflies are a treasured find for divers in Hawai'i. They are boldly patterned in white, gold and black and prefer depths of 150 feet or more, although they are occasionally seen at about 100 feet. Tinker's Butterflies are unafraid by nature and can sometimes be hand-fed by divers. Valuable as an aquarium export and easy to catch, they are now rare at sport-diving depths. Enlarging our system of marine parks might ensure that more divers could enjoy these fishes. Tinker's Butterflyfish has long been considered endemic to Hawai'i, but is now known to occur with minor variations in the Marshall Islands and probably elsewhere. Other deep-dwelling species, similar in appearance, are found in Guam, the Marquesas, Palau and the Philippines. The name honors marine biologist Spencer Wilkie Tinker, director of the Waikīkī Aquarium for 32 years and author of the classic *Fishes of Hawaii*. To 5.5 in. Hawai'i and the Marshall Islands. Photo: South Point, Hawai'i. 140 ft.

OVAL BUTTERFLYFISH

Chaetodon lunulatus Quoy & Gaimard, 1824. (REDFIN BUTTERFLYFISH; MELON BUTTERFLYFISH)

These exquisite and richly colored fishes are apricot gold, set off with purple gray lines and tinges of red on the anal fins. Their scarcity in Hawai'i only enhances the delight of finding a pair. Like many other butterflyfishes, they probably mate for life. They eat polyps of living coral, hence cannot be maintained in a home aquarium. Commercial trade in such species is inexcusable. Honolua Bay, Maui is a good place to see them. Species name means "three bars." To 5.5 in. Pacific Ocean. Photo: Ke'ei, Hawai'i. 10 ft. (An Indian Ocean species, *C. trifasciatus,* is very similar.)

TEARDROP BUTTERFLYFISH
• **kīkākapu**

Chaetodon unimaculatus Bloch, 1787.

These are immediately recognizable by the large upside-down "teardrop" on the side. In larger specimens the lower part fades, leaving a round black spot. The large, blunt mouth, unusual for a butterflyfish, is capable of nipping off bits of hard coral. They occur in pairs or small groups. Although this species adjusts quickly to captivity it seldom lives for long. Species name means " one spot." To about 8 inches but usually smaller. Indo-Pacific. Photo: Palea Point, O'ahu, 15 ft.

COMMON LONGNOSE BUTTERFLYFISH
• **lau-wiliwili-nukunuku-oi'oi**
Forcipiger flavissimus Jordan & McGregor, 1898.
(FORCEPSFISH)

Probably more than any other fish (except the Moorish Idol), Longnose Butterflyfishes have come to symbolize the exotic beauty of the coral reef. Their long probing snouts, bristling dorsal spines and solid yellow color are unmistakable. They frequent walls and ledges and often swim upside down on the roofs of caves. Of the two almost identical species of *Forcipiger* (see below), this has the shorter snout. It is also the most widespread of all butterflyfishes, ranging from Mexico to the Red Sea. Somewhat surprisingly, Longnose Butterflyfishes of both species adapt readily to aquarium life, greedily accepting almost any food, including flakes. They sometimes stick their snout out of the water and squirt at their owner. Species name means "yellow." Longnose Butterflies have the longest of all Hawaiian fish names. **Nukunuku** means "beak" and **oi'oi** means "best," or "sharp." To 7 in. East Africa to the Americas. Photo: *Mahi* wreck, O'ahu. 65 ft.

RARE LONGNOSE BUTTERFLYFISH • **lau-wiliwili-nukunuku-oi'oi**
Forcipiger longirostris (Broussonet, 1782).
(BIG LONGNOSE BUTTERFLYFISH; LONGNOSE BUTTERFLYFISH)

With a longer snout than the Common Longnose Butterflyfish, this species differs further by having lines of fine dots on the chest. In Hawai'i it is rare everywhere except the Kona Coast of the Big Island. Individuals occasionally turn very dark brown, a color phase that does not seem to be related to sex or reproduction. Although black and yellow fishes sometimes pair, those of like colors are more often seen together. Common in Kona, the dark phase is quite rare in other areas of the world. Both the Hawaiian and scientific names mean "long-beaked." French literature buffs will appreciate the now invalid scientific name, *F. cyrano*. Originally collected during Cook's third voyage, this was the first of many new fish species to be described from Hawai'i. To 7 in. Indo-Pacific. Photos: Hanauma Bay, O'ahu. 30 ft. Dark phase. Hōnaunau, Hawai'i. 20 ft.

34

Rare Longnose Butterflyfish • **lau-wiliwili-nukunuku-oi'oi** *(Forcipiger longirostris)* dark phase.
(See preceding page)

PYRAMID BUTTERFLYFISH
Hemitaurichthys polylepis (Bleeker, 1857).
     This handsome schooling species is found near steep dropoffs, preferring depths of 40 feet or more. The body has a solid white triangle rimmed with yellow; the head is dark brown. At night they rest near the bottom and the white pyramid darkens to gray leaving a bright white spot in the center. Big Island snorkelers can see these in shallow water at Hōnaunau, on the Kona Coast, toward the right side of the bay. Like most plankton eaters, the species adapts well to captivity; accustomed to lots of space, it is best suited to public aquariums. Species name means "many scales." To 6 in. Western and Central Pacific. Photo: Hanauma Bay, O'ahu. 60 ft.

35

THOMPSON'S BUTTERFLYFISH
Hemitaurichthys thompsoni Fowler, 1923.
(BUSINESSMAN BUTTERFLYFISH)

Neatly clad in conservative gray, these unusual schooling butterflyfishes with their pointy, upturned snouts are surprisingly friendly. They aggregate in midwater near dropoffs and are easily mistaken for more ordinary fishes until they swim over in a group to investigate you. They sometimes form mixed schools with the Pyramid Butterflyfish. The scientific name honors John W. Thompson, a technician and artist at the Bishop Museum from 1901 to 1928, who prepared beautifully colored casts of many Hawaiian fishes. To 6 in. This somewhat rare butterflyfish is found in only a few scattered Pacific locations, including Hawai'i. Photo: Hōnaunau, Hawai'i. 20 ft.

PENNANT BUTTERFLYFISH
Heniochus diphreutes Jordan, 1903.
(BANNERFISH; PENNANTFISH)

Immediately recognizable by their bright white pennants, these butterflyfishes are boldly patterned with white and black vertical bars; their soft dorsal and tail fins are yellow. As they grow the pennant increases in length. Rare specimens have a double pennant. They school along dropoffs, usually at depths of 40 feet or more, but occasionally enter shallow enough water to be seen by snorkelers. Peaceful and relatively easy-to-keep, Pennantfishes in the aquarium trade are sometimes called the "Poor Man's Moorish Idol." To about 8 in. Indo-Pacific. *H. acuminatus*, an almost identical larger species not known in Hawai'i, remains near the bottom and rarely schools. Photo: D.R. Schrichte. Hanauma Bay, O'ahu. 50 ft.

CARDINALFISHES
(APOGONIDAE)

Iridescent Cardinalfish • **'upāpalu** *(Apogon kallopterus)* at night. Pūpūkea, O'ahu. 30ft.

Small to mid-size carnivores, usually nocturnal, cardinalfishes are common in all warm seas. They have two dorsal fins, large eyes and a large mouth. Most Hawaiian species are plain, although many Indo-Pacific species are quite attractive. Some of the first cardinalfishes to be scientifically described were red, hence the common name.

During the day cardinalfishes usually rest quietly under ledges and in other dark places — behavior typical of nocturnal fishes. At night they disperse to hunt for zooplankton, small crustaceans or fishes. During spawning, females lay globular masses of eggs. Males take the eggs in their mouths, holding them until they hatch. During this time their mouths appear full and unable to close completely.

Because of their dull colors, cardinalfishes from Hawai'i are not prime candidates for home aquariums. Should anyone wish to keep them, however, they would not be difficult to capture or maintain.

Although cardinalfishes are a large family with about 250 species worldwide, they are represented in Hawai'i by only eleven. Four are included here. Their Hawaiian name is **'upāpalu**.

RUBY CARDINALFISH ●
Apogon erythrinus (Snyder, 1904).
Rarely seen by day, this small, cryptic cardinalfish is frequently encountered on night dives. Its organs and vertebrae are clearly visible through the translucent, reddish body. This is one of several similar Indo-Pacific species that for many years have been lumped together under the name *A. coccineus* (still a valid name, but now confined to an Arabian cardinalfish). The Hawaiian Ruby Cardinalfish differs enough to be considered a separate species. The name is from the Greek *erythros*, meaning "red." To about 2 in. Endemic. Photo: Pūpūkea, O'ahu. 30 ft.

IRIDESCENT CARDINALFISH • 'upāpalu
Apogon kallopterus Bleeker, 1856.
At night these drab, light brown fishes show considerable blue green iridescence. By day they can be identified by a darkish stripe running through the eye and ending in a black spot on the base of the tail. The stripe may be indistinct. The first dorsal fin often has a yellowish tinge. This is the most abundant shallow water cardinalfish in the main Hawaiian Islands and a common species throughout much of the Indo-Pacific. To 6 in. Photo: Kawaihoa (Portlock) Point, O'ahu. 30 ft.

SPOTTED CARDINALFISH • 'upāpalu
Apogon maculiferus Garrett, 1863. ●
Many rows of dark spots identify this cardinalfish. It is not common around the main islands but, like many endemic species, is abundant in the cooler waters of the northwestern chain. Species name mans "spotted." To 5.5 in. Endemic. Photo: Kawaihoa (Portlock) Point, O'ahu. 30 ft.

BANDFIN CARDINALFISH • 'upāpalu
Apogon taeniopterus Bennett, 1835.
Named for the smart dark bands on the leading edges or bases of the dorsal, anal and tail fins, this cardinalfish shows some iridescence at night, when it is most likely to be seen. Species name means "banded fin." To 7 in. Indo-Pacific, but common only in Hawai'i. The Hawaiian population is regarded by some authorities as endemic (under the name *A. menesemus*). Photo: Hanauma Bay, O'ahu. 25 ft. (at night).

Gray Chubs • **nenue** *(Kyphosus bigibbus)*. The yellow individual is a color variant. At bottom center is a lowfin Chub *(K. vaigiensis)*. Photo: Hanauma Bay, O'ahu. 20 ft.

Sea chubs are typically medium-size, gray, heavy-looking fishes with oval bodies, small pointed mouths and large tails. Also called rudderfishes or **nenue**, they school in shallow rocky areas where they feed on algae. In the days of sailing ships they would congregate around the rudders of ships in harbor, feeding on algae and perhaps wastes thrown overboard. The common Gray Chub loves handouts. When fish feeding was allowed at Hanauma Bay, O'ahu, Gray Chubs would swarm around snorkelers and waders, sometimes becoming pushy and aggressive. If food was not offered quickly enough they would sometimes bite anyway, earning them the nickname "Hanauma Bay piranhas." However, these fish are strictly herbivores. The family Kyphosidae includes about 45 species worldwide; five occur in Hawaii, although only three are common. They look similar and often occur together. The Gray Chub is illustrated on the next page, the Lowfin Chub *(Kyphosus vaigiensis)* and the Highfin Chub *(K. cinerascens)* appear on p. 180.

Stripeys, although related to sea chubs, are far smaller and have high, compressed bodies and brushlike teeth much like those of butterflyfishes. Ichthyologists have from time to time placed stripeys in the butterflyfish family, the chub family, the family Scorpididae, and finally their own small family, Microcanthidae. Out of five species, one occurs in the Islands. Any Hawaiian name it may have had has been forgotten.

GRAY CHUB • **nenue**
Kyphosus bigibbus Lacepède, 1801.
[BROWN CHUB]

　　Hawai'i's most common chub, this fish is usually dull gray to silvery, often with a pale line following the curve of the back. Occasional individuals are bright yellow, white, or multicolored. (In old Hawai'i a yellow or white **nenue** was regarded as "queen" of the school.) Sometimes, especially when in groups, Gray Chubs darken the rear half of their bodies, appearing half light, half dark. They often roam the shore in schools and are abundant at many snorkeling and diving locations, including Hanauma Bay, O'ahu, and Molokini Island, Maui, (where one popular dive site, Enenue, has been named after them). The species name means "two humps." To 2 ft. Indo-Pacific. Photo: Hanauma Bay, O'ahu. 5 ft. (See p. 180 for two additional Hawaiian chub species.)

STRIPEY
Microcanthus strigatus (Cuvier, 1831).

　　With their deep, laterally compressed bodies and bold diagonal stripes, Stripeys could easily be mistaken for butterflyfishes. They prefer quiet murky lagoons, fishponds, or harbors and are almost never seen at the usual diving and snorkeling sites. They are sometimes abundant in the swimming area at Lydgate State Park, Kaua'i (near the mouth of the Wailua River) and also occur near canal entrances on O'ahu and in Kāne'ohe Bay, O'ahu. Stripeys are among the easiest marine fishes to maintain in captivity. Like many of Hawai's unusual fishes, they prefer cool, subtropical waters on either side of the equator, occurring also in Japan, Taiwan, Australia and New Caledonia— —a pattern of distribution known as anti-tropical or anti-equatorial. In Australia juveniles occur in tide pools; in Hawai'i this is not the case. To almost 8 in. Photo: Kāne'ohe Bay, O'ahu. 8 ft.

Mixed school of Oval Chromis and Hawaiian Sergeants • Note the Indo-Pacific Sergeant at middle right.
Palea Point, O'ahu. 30 ft.

The often colorful damselfishes are abundant in most shallow, tropical habitats. A coral reef without them would seem empty. In Hawai'i, small to medium-size fishes congregating above coral heads or swarming in midwater off dropoffs are almost sure to be damsels. So are the small, drab, aggressive fishes common on reef flats or in the rocky shallows. The ubiquitous sergeant majors are members of this family, as are the clownfishes which inhabit stinging sea anemones in other parts of the Indo-Pacific. Many damselfishes are brightly colored, others are plain. Some are social, others are solitary. Few species exceed six inches and most are considerably smaller. All possess one nostril instead of two, a primary characteristic of the family.

Although some species are omnivorous, damselfishes fall into two broad categories: plankton eaters and algae eaters. The former usually hover in groups above the reef, picking their minute prey from the water. The latter are typically solitary, inhabiting shallow, rocky areas where algal growth is heaviest, and protecting their territory from competitors such as surgeonfishes or other damselfishes. All damselfishes attach their eggs to the bottom and guard them until they hatch. Juveniles of some species are more brightly colored than their parents.

Some damselfishes have an immunity to the stinging cells of sea-anemones. The most famous of these are the clown or anemonefishes so popular among aquarists. The only example is the Hawaiian Dascyllus, which when small will seek refuge in large sand anemones.

In captivity damselfishes are hardy and often begin feeding minutes after being introduced to the tank. Colorful and easy to keep, they are one of the mainstays of the marine tropical fish trade. One drawback is their aggressive nature. When two or three of a similar species are kept, the strongest will often pick mercilessly on the others, nipping their fins and driving them into the upper corners of the tank. The trick with aggressive damsels is to procure fishes of the same size, introduce them at the same time, and to keep six or more of the same species. In a school the pecking order becomes unclear and they leave each other alone.

Hawai'i lacks the brilliantly colored damselfishes common elsewhere in the Pacific; the only species regularly collected here is the Hawaiian Dascyllus. Cute while young, they grow rapidly and soon become belligerent. Adults are probably best kept alone. Unless you can easily put them back in the ocean when they get too big, think twice before buying these fishes.

The damselfishes are one of the largest fish families, with about 345 species. Seventeen occur in Hawai'i; twelve are described here. Few damselfishes have Hawaiian names, probably because most are not significant sources of food.

HAWAIIAN SERGEANT • **mamo** ●
Abudefduf abdominalis (Quoy & Gaimard, 1824).
    It is not even necessary to enter the water to see these common and attractive damselfishes. The young, bright yellow with five black bars, abound in tidepools and are easily caught in a dipnet. They are ideal for beginning aquarists, although they become scrappy unless kept in a large group. As they grow, the yellow fades to greenish white, and it soon becomes time to return them to the sea. Underwater, adults are a common sight swarming high in the water column. **Mamo** are omnivorous, eating algae, plankton and anything else they can find. They spawn throughout the year; males temporarily take on a paler bluish "nuptial coloration" to attract females and warn off rival males. Males guard the eggs, which form large purplish patches on rocks. Discovery of the eggs by wrasses, butterflyfishes and others results in colorful feeding frenzies in which the attackers overwhelm the frantic parent. The Hawaiian name is from **ma'oma'o** ("green"). The species name means "abdomen" or "belly." To almost 10 in., but usually smaller. Endemic. Several similar Indo-Pacific and Atlantic species exist. One, the Indo-Pacific Sergeant *(A.vaigiensis)*, has recently established itself in Hawai'i (see p. 9 and 41). Photo: Kahe Point, O'ahu. 15 ft.

BLACKSPOT SERGEANT • kūpīpī
Abudefduf sordidus (Forsskål, 1775).

These large, common damselfishes are drab yellowish gray with six black-ish brown bars that can lighten or darken. Males aggressively guarding eggs are almost black with striking white bars. Sub-adults have indistinct bars and a yellow wedgelike mark on the back. A black spot on the upper base of the tail, always present, confers their common name. These damsels are algae eaters inhabiting the shallow surge zone around rocks and boulders. Juveniles, common in tidepools and easily captured, become territorial and aggressive in a small aquarium. To about 9 in. Indo-Pacific. Photo: Hanauma Bay, O'ahu. 3ft.

AGILE CHROMIS
Chromis agilis Smith, 1960.
(REEF CHROMIS)

Brown with a lavender tinge and a large dark spot at the base of the pectoral fin, this common species hovers several feet above the coral picking plankton from the water. It is particularly abundant along the Kona Coast of the Big Island. To about 4.5 in. Indo-Pacific. Photo: Hanauma Bay, O'ahu. 60 ft.

CHOCOLATE DIP CHROMIS ●
Chromis hanui Randall & Swerdloff, 1973.

The popular name perfectly de-scribes this fish. It is a small species frequenting ledges, walls and the sides of coral heads from which it seldom stays. It may be solitary or in small groups. If threatened it retreats into the coral. The species name, a Hawaiian word, origi-nally applied to a fish whose identity has since been lost. To 3.5 in. Endemic. Photo: Hanauma Bay, O'ahu. 30ft.

43

adult ∧

OVAL CHROMIS ●
Chromis ovalis (Steindachner, 1900).

Like Hawaiian Sergeants, these damselfishes may be seen either swarming after plankton high in the water or guarding their nests near the bottom. Adults are a plain, brassy, yellow green. During the spring spawning season, however, males may darken and develop two broad blue white bars and a blue white tail. The same pattern is sometimes adopted at night. Juveniles, common in the summer months, are silvery blue with a bright yellow dorsal fin. Because there are few blue fishes in Hawai'i, a school of young Oval Chromis is an especially pretty sight. Abundant in most areas. To 7.5 in. Endemic. Photos: Magic Island, O'ahu. 30 ft.

adult - breeding colors ∧   juveniles ∨

BLACKFIN CHROMIS
Chromis vanderbilti (Fowler, 1941).
These small, attractive damselfishes congregate above coral heads, at depths of 15 feet or more, disappearing into crevices if approached. They are yellow with gray blue stripes and a blue black anal fin. Although not often kept in aquariums, a group would make a nice display. Named for Mr. & Mrs. George Vanderbilt, sponsors of a 1937 scientific expedition to the Pacific. To 2.8 in. Restricted to the Pacific islands. Photo: Pūpūkea, O'ahu. 30 ft.

THREESPOT CHROMIS ●
Chromis verater Jordan & Metz, 1912.
Usually found below 30 feet (and becoming more abundant at greater depths), these large damselfishes are dark gray or black with three white spots: one above, one below, and one on the base of the tail. They can lighten or darken their spots. Like all *Chromis,* they are plankton eaters. During spawning season (late November to June) they make large, saucerlike depressions in the sand inside caves or in other protected areas where they lay and guard their eggs. To 8.5 in. Endemic. Photo: Hanauma Bay, O'ahu. 40 ft.

HAWAIIAN DASCYLLUS • 'ālo'ilo'i ●
Dascyllus albisella Gill, 1862.
(HAWAIIAN DOMINO DAMSELFISH)

Juveniles are jet black with a porcelain-white spot on each side and a neon-blue spot on the forehead. They are almost always found in and around heads of branching coral. As they grow they leave the coral to live in loose aggregations, often in deeper water. As adults they lose the forehead spot, their black bleaches out to grayish, and the white side spot becomes less distinct. They can lighten or darken their color; while spawning they become almost entirely white. As with all damselfishes, the females lay eggs on the bottom while the males follow closely behind to fertilize them. When disturbed they make a chirping sound. Snorkelers can see these perky little fishes only in very sheltered, shallow locations, such as Kāne'ohe Bay, where they sometimes live in association with sand-dwelling anemones. In places exposed to even moderate wave action one must dive to 20 or 30 feet to find them. The Hawaiian species is closely related to the Threespot Damselfish (*D. trimaculatus*) found elsewhere in the Indo-Pacific. Species name is from *albus* ("white"). The Hawaiian name means "bright and sparkling." To 5 in. Endemic. Photos: juvenile. Pūpūkea, O'ahu. adults spawning. Kahe Point, O'ahu. 25 ft.

juvenile ∧   adults spawning ∨

BRIGHT-EYE DAMSELFISH
Plectroglyphidodon imparipennis (Vaillant & Sauvage, 1875).

These tiny grayish yellow damsels defend very small territories, usually in small depressions along the top of the reef in shallow water. Although their eyes contain a large dark bar, they nevertheless appear bright yellow white. Species name from *impar* ("unequal") and *penna* ("fin"). To about 2.5 in. Indo-Pacific. Photo: Pūpūkea, O'ahu. 5 ft.

BLUE-EYE DAMSELFISH
Plectroglyphidodon johnstonianus
Fowler & Ball, 1924.
(JOHNSTON ISLAND DAMSELFISH)

These are yellowish gray, with bright blue eyes and blue margins on the dorsal and anal fins. The rear of the body is darker on some individuals. Larger than Bright-Eye Damselfishes, they dwell in deeper water, often among the branches of live coral. They feed in part on coral polyps and do poorly in captivity. To almost 5 in. Indo-Pacific. Photo: Hōnaunau, Hawai'i. 40 ft.

HAWAIIAN ROCK DAMSELFISH ●
Plectroglyphidodon sindonis (Jordan & Evermann, 1903).

These uncommon endemics are dark purplish brown with two narrow light bars. They inhabit the shallow surge zone, hence will be seen only by snorkelers. Juveniles have a dark spot edged in white on the soft dorsal fin and are sometimes found in tidepools. Named for Mr. Michitaro Sindo, who discovered this fish for science near Kailua, O'ahu in 1901. To 5 in. Endemic. Photo: Pūpūkea, O'ahu. 3 ft.

PACIFIC GREGORY
Stegastes fasciolatus (Ogilby, 1889).

This is a drab blackish or brownish gray fish very common on reef flats, where it boldly defends a small territory against other algae-eating fishes and intruding divers. Like similar Indo-Pacific and Caribbean damsels, it may actually "farm" its algae patch by removing undesirable growths. This widespread species has a very slightly different color pattern in Hawai'i. Species name means "banded." Juveniles are bluish black with a pale yellow tail. To almost 5 in. Indo-Pacific. Photo: Kahe Point, O'ahu. 15 ft.

EELS

Whitemargin Moray *(Gymnothorax albimarginatus)*. Magic Island, O'ahu. 20 ft.

Eels are a specialized group of fishes adapted to life in crevices and holes. Their long, snakelike bodies typically lack scales and paired fins, which would only impair movement in narrow spaces. Eels form the order Anguilliformes which contains about 15 families and many hundreds of species. Only moray eels, conger eels and snake eels are likely to be encountered by divers or snorkelers in Hawai'i; all were known to the Hawaiians as **puhi**. Many secondary names are recorded but it is no longer always clear to which species they apply.

In old Hawai'i some eels were relished as food and considered "choicer than wives." Others were revered as **'aumakua**, the physical embodiment of certain family gods. Fierce warriors were sometimes compared to "sharp-toothed eels" and when trouble was brewing thoughts were said to "wiggle like an eel."

CONGER AND GARDEN EELS
(CONGRIDAE)

Congers are large nocturnal eels, unusual in possessing well-developed pectoral fins. Remaining in the reef during the day, they swim openly at night in search of sleeping fishes and other prey. They have very small teeth. Congers are also known locally as White Eels. There are two species in Hawai'i; the endemic *Conger oligoporus*, not pictured, is a deep water eel unlikely to be seen by divers.

Garden eels belong to the same family but have an entirely different lifestyle. Dwelling in burrows, they colonize sandy areas where there is a strong current. There are a number of Indo-Pacific species, with at least one in Hawai'i.

Another member of the family common in some shallow areas is *Ariosoma marginatum*, a small silvery eel with unusually large eyes that lives in the sand, emerging only at night.

MUSTACHE CONGER • **puhi ūhā**
Conger cinereus Rüppell, 1830.
(WHITE EEL)

Plain brownish gray by day, these large eels are marked with broad dark bands at night when they forage for food. A fold of skin along the mouth looks somewhat like a mustache. Congers are seen most often during the evening, although at some popular sites they have been tamed to accept food at any time. Occasionally their daytime hiding places may be betrayed by a bladelike tail protruding from a hole in the reef. Because they differ slightly from others of their species, Mustache Congers in Hawai'i have been given the subspecies name *marginatus*. Species name means "ash-color." To about almost 4 ft. Indo-Pacific. Photo: Hanauma Bay, O'ahu. 40 ft. (night).

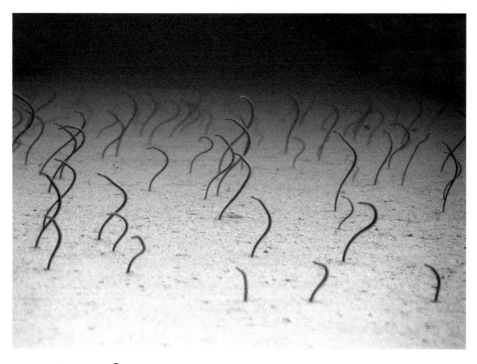

HAWAIIAN GARDEN EEL ●
Gorgasia hawaiiensis Randall & Chess, 1979.

These strange eels are seen beyond the reef at about 80 feet or more at a number of sites, such as Ke'ei, Kealakekua, or Puakō on the Kona Coast of the Big Island, Molokini Island off Maui, and the Corsair wreck in Moanalua Bay, O'ahu. They live by the thousands along steep sandy slopes, stretching up out of their holes and facing into the current to feed on drifting plankton. When approached, they sink into the sand. Cautious, slow-moving divers, however, can enter a garden of waving eels, along a mysterious slope that beckons temptingly down into the blue abyss. Watch your time and your depth while visiting the garden eels. To about 1.5 ft. Endemic. Photo: Moanalua Bay, O'ahu. 100 ft.

VIPER MORAY • **puhi kauila**
Enchelynassa canina (Quoy and Gaimard, 1824).

These large morays vary from reddish brown to dark gray. Their hooked jaws (containing some of the longest, sharpest teeth in the moray family) meet only at the tips, giving the appearance of a perpetual snarl. Like many morays, they sometimes occur in pairs. Nocturnal and relatively uncommon, Viper Morays are seldom encountered by divers and snorkelers, which is perhaps just as well: they grow to a length of at least five feet and are one of the largest and potentially most dangerous of Hawaii's eels. The species name means "dog-like," in reference to the sharp teeth. Indo-Pacific. Photo: "Manta Ray Bay," Kona Coast, Hawai`i. 50 ft.

Great favorites of divers, morays are among the most easily observed members of the reef community. They peer from the coral watching the underwater world go by, while their thick, muscular bodies remain securely hidden. Most morays open and close their mouths rhythmically, displaying needle-sharp teeth; their necks swell and pulse alarmingly with each gulp. To humans this appears menacing, but the eels are only pumping water over their gills — their way of breathing. In the late afternoon or twilight some morays emerge to hunt, undulating across the sand or twining and turning among the rocks and coral. They will also enter tidepools or slither across wet rocks. But for every moray seen, many more remain hidden; most species spend almost all of their lives within the recesses of the reef. Morays are usually dull in color, marked with blotches and speckles. Some, however, such as the Snowflake, Dragon and Zebra Morays, have attractive patterns.

Morays are perhaps best known for their sharp teeth and supposedly nasty dispositions. (The Roman emperor Nero was said to have thrown rebellious slaves into special pools containing these eels.) Writers, however, disagree on the danger they pose. Alarming eel stories are common in older books, but recent authors agree that almost all documented attacks occurred after the eel was hooked, speared or otherwise molested. Left alone, eels pose little threat. It is foolish, however, to stick hands into crevices and holes that may contain eels. Even small morays can inflict considerable damage; their backward-pointing teeth make extraction of a hand or finger difficult. If you are bitten, don't jerk your hand back in alarm but wait for the eel to let go by itself—admittedly easier said than done!

A tip for lobster hunters: "bugs" showing only one antenna are said to be pointing the other back to keep track of an eel. Spearing morays is risky; when attacked they can fight back aggressively, sometimes wriggling right up the spear to bite their tormenter. Dangerous or not, moray eels are often hand-fed by divers, and grow tame enough to be stroked and handled. If you do not know your eels, however, it is best to leave feeding to dive guides. Some species, and even some individuals, are more friendly than others.

Not all morays have sharp teeth; some, such as the Snowflake and Zebra Morays, possess grinding plates or blunt pebblelike teeth which they use to crush invertebrates. (They can do the same to a human finger.) These are the best species for the aquarium as they pose no threat to other fishes in the tank. A weekly feeding of shrimp or crab is usually sufficient. Fish eating eels can be offered live guppies. Eels do best when they have a good hiding place. A length of plastic pipe does nicely.

Morays are well represented in Hawai'i, with about 40 species. Their relative abundance here has been attributed to the lack of native groupers and snappers that elsewhere in the world compete with them. Ten species are described below. One of the more interesting morays omitted (because it is rare in Hawai'i) is the Giant Moray *(Gymnothorax javanicus)*. Nearly eight feet in length, with unconfirmed reports to ten feet, it is the largest of all morays. Steindachner's Moray, an endemic eel most commonly seen in the Northwestern Hawaiian Islands, is pictured on page 181. The rare and possibly venomous Whitemargin Moray *(G. albimarginatus)* is pictured on page 48.

SNOWFLAKE MORAY • puhi-kāpā
Echidna nebulosa (Ahl, 1789).
   The white snout is usually enough to identify this eel. The body is light brown with black speckles and several indistinct rows of irregular dark blotches, which usually have white or yellowish centers, producing a sort of tie-dyed effect. Snowflake eels do not possess sharp teeth. They are attractive and do well in captivity but are not common. The species name means "misty" or "cloudy." The Hawaiian name presents a dilemma: although early physical descriptions of **puhi-kāpā** do match the Snowflake, records emphasize that it was an aggressive fighter eel. In fact, the great warrior, King Kamehameha I, was nicknamed **puhi-kāpā**. However, a more docile eel than the Snowflake can probably not be found. To almost 30 in. East Africa to the Americas. Photo: Makapu'u, O'ahu. 30 ft.

51

DRAGON MORAY • **puhi-kauila**
Enchelycore pardalis (Schlegel, 1847).
(LEOPARD MORAY)

Most remarkable for its appearance, the Dragon Moray's snout has long nasal tubes like horns. The jaws, full of teeth, are so curved they cannot close completely. Vivid spots and streaks complete the picture of this unusual, secretive creature. It feeds primarily on fishes and is most often encountered at night. After dark, unfortunately, it becomes brownish and less striking. Dragon Morays are more common in the Northwestern Hawaiian Islands than in the main group, where they are rare. Species name means "leopard." To about 3 ft. Indo-Pacific. Photo: Mike Severns. Pu'u Olai, Maui. 30 ft.

ZEBRA MORAY • **puhi**
Gymnomuraena zebra (Shaw, 1797).

One of the easiest morays to identify, its blackish brown body is encircled by yellow white stripes. Zebra morays often swim in the open. They have blunt, pebblelike teeth and feed chiefly on crabs. Their striking appearance makes them popular aquarium eels, but they can take weeks to begin eating. Although lacking sharp teeth, they are not harmless; a Honolulu aquarist bitten on the finger describes the experience "painful, like a vice." To 5 ft., but usually smaller. East Africa to the Americas. Photo: Kahe Point, O'ahu. 10 ft.

STOUT MORAY • **puhi**
Gymnothorax eurostus (Abbott, 1860).

Extremely variable in color, this species ranges from brown, covered with irregular light spots and marks, to white with a few dark spots and marks. It is one of the most common morays in Hawai'i. In its darker form it could be confused with the Whitemouth Moray (below) but lacks the bright white inner mouth. Species name means "stout," "strong." To almost 2 ft. Indo-Pacific. Photos: Magic Island, O'ahu. 25 ft.

YELLOWMARGIN MORAY • **puhi**
Gymnothorax flavimarginatus (Rüppell, 1830).

Easily tamed, these large eels are featured attractions at many dive sites. They are finely mottled in yellow and brown, with a dark blotch over the gill opening. The tail is edged in yellow green. This is one of Hawaii's largest morays, growing to four feet, and also one of the boldest. The name **puhi-paka** ("fierce eel") may refer to this species. Hawaiians of old were very careful where the **puhi-paka** was concerned. Species name means "yellow margin." East Africa to the Americas. The rare Giant Moray *(G. javanicus)* is similar; it lacks the colorful margin and grows to eight feet in length. Photo: Hālona Blowhole, O'ahu. 30 ft.

Stout Moray - dark form ∧   light form ∨

∨

DWARF MORAY • puhi
Gymnothorax melatremus Schultz, 1953.
Fully grown, this tiny moray attains a length of only about half a foot. It is yellow to yellowish brown. Because of its secretive nature it is seen infrequently. To 7 in. Indo-Pacific. Photo: Pūpūkea, O'ahu. 60 ft.

WHITEMOUTH MORAY • puhi
Gymnothorax meleagris (Shaw & Nodder, 1795).
This is probably the most commonly seen moray in Hawai'i. It is brown, covered with white dots. The inner mouth is entirely bright white. They occasionally hold their mouths wide open in a threat display, making for easy identification. Species name means "guineafowl" or "spotted." The Hawaiian name **puhi-'ōni'o** ("spotted eel") may refer to this species. To 3.5 ft. Indo-Pacific. Photo: Magic Island, O'ahu. 25 ft.

YELLOWMOUTH MORAY • puhi
Gymnothorax nudivomer (Gunther, 1866).
Once they open their mouths these eels are unmistakable—the interior is bright orange yellow. The color may be a warning to potential predators as their skin contains a poison. Their brown bodies are covered with fine white spots that become larger and more conspicuous toward the tail. In Hawai'i they prefer depths of over 100 feet. Species name from *nudi* ("bare") and *vomer* (a bone on the roof of the mouth). To 6 ft. Indo-Pacific. Photo: Gulf of Oman, Indian Ocean. 20 ft.

YELLOWHEAD MORAY • **puhi-'ou**
Gymnothorax rueppelliae (McClelland, 1845).

The brown body is usually encircled with broad bands of gray; the top of the head is yellow. This nocturnal species is occasionally seen during the day. Very large individuals lose most of their color. The more common Undulated Moray (below) also has a yellowish head but lacks the bands on the body. The name honors German naturalist and explorer Eduard Rüppell (1794-1884). To almost 3 ft. Indo-Pacific. Photo: Hālona Blowhole, O'ahu. 15 ft.

UNDULATED MORAY • **puhi-lau-milo**
Gymnothorax undulatus (Lacepède, 1803).

This moray has narrow jaws full of long sharp teeth, including a row down the center of the mouth. The top of its head sometimes has a greenish yellow tinge. The body color varies from dark brown with light speckles and irregular vertical lines or net-like markings, to the reverse — almost white with irregular brown blotches. It could be confused with the Yellowmargin Moray but is usually smaller, has a narrower snout, and lacks the dark blotch on the gill opening. It could also be confused with the Yellowhead Moray, but it has no encircling bands. This is perhaps the commonest Indo-Pacific moray and one of the nastiest. Do not attempt to play with or feed it. Hawaiian name means "leaf of the milo tree." To 3.5 ft. East Africa to the Americas. Photo: Kawaihoa (Portlock) Point, O'ahu. 30 ft.

TIGER MORAY • **puhi**
Scuticaria tigrinus (Lesson, 1828).

A secretive, nocturnal eel, its light gray or brown body is covered with round, dark spots of varying size. Despite its name it has no stripes. Rarely seen during daylight, it is often caught in traps and thus turns up occasionally in aquariums. To 3 ft. or more. East Africa to the Americas. Photo: Hanauma Bay, O'ahu. 80 ft.

**SNAKE EELS
(OPHICHTHIDAE)**

As might be expected, many of these eels are slender and could be confused with sea snakes, which are rare in Hawai'i. Unlike sea snakes, most snake eels have a long low dorsal fin running the length of the body and a pointed (rather than paddle-like) tail. They typically live in burrows in the sand or mud, sometimes made by wriggling backwards into the substrate with their stiff tail tip. There are hundreds of species worldwide with about 16 known from Hawai'i. Snake eels are more secretive in general than moray eels and only one is described below. Two additional snake eels seen on sand or rubble bottoms, Henshaw's Snake Eel *(Brachysomophis henshawi)* and the Freckled Snake Eel *(Callechelys lutea)*, are pictured on p. 181.

MAGNIFICENT SNAKE EEL · **puhi lā'au** ●
Myrichthys magnificus (Abbot, 1861)
White, with large, dark round or oval spots, these striking but uncommon eels typically emerge in the late afternoon or evening to nose about the bottom, probing into holes along the reef for crustaceans, small fishes, or carrion. Occasionally several hunt together. Honolulu's Magic Island is a good place to see them. Long lumped together with the similar Spotted Snake Eel *(M. maculosus)* of the Indo-Pacific, the Hawaiian species, originally described in 1861, has recently been re-recognized as a valid endemic. The name means "magnificent, splendid." The Hawaiian name means "stick," "pole" or "male erection." To about 2.5 ft. Photo: Magic Island, O'ahu. 15 ft.

**CUSK EELS
(OPHIDIIDAE)**

Cusk eels, or brotulas, belong to the order Ophidiiformes and are thus not true eels. Characteristic of the group are long dorsal and anal fins that converge at the tail, which is pointed. Many have barbels on the snout and chin, making them look like a cross between an eel and a catfish. Although a number of Hawaiian species exist, only one is encountered by divers.

BEARDED CUSK EEL · **puhi palahoana**
Brotula multibarbata Temminck & Schlegel, 1846.
(Large-Eye Brotula)
This is the most common cusk eel, or brotula, in Hawai'i. It is wary and seldom seen except at night when it emerges to feed. The body is dark reddish brown with long dorsal and anal fins that meet at its pointed tail. Sets of white sensory barbels sprout from the snout and chin. The chin has white markings. Species name means "many-bearded." To about 2 ft. Indo-Pacific. Photo: Pūpūkea, O'ahu. 20 ft. (at night).

Fantail Filefish • **ʻōʻili-ʻuwī ʻuwī** *(Pervagor spilosoma).* Kealakekua Bay, Hawaiʻi. 20 ft.

Closely allied to the triggerfishes, filefishes have narrower, more compressed bodies and lack the "trigger" mechanism on their first dorsal spine. Many rely on camouflage for protection and are able to change color quickly to match their surroundings. The popular name comes from the rough texture of their skin. The Hawaiian name, **ʻōʻili** ("sprout" or "come up"), probably refers to their frequently raised dorsal spine. Like triggerfishes, filefishes move by rippling their soft dorsal and anal fins and can swim backward or forward with equal ease. They lack pelvic fins entirely. In general, these fishes are omnivorous.

Filefishes belong to the order Tetraodontiformes, which includes other odd reef fishes such as boxfishes and puffers. Seven species are found in Hawaiʻi; six are described below. The family name means "one spine."

The only Hawaiian filefish commonly kept in home aquariums is the beautiful little Fantail Filefish. It does well, but often at the expense of other creatures in the tank. For example, it will unfailingly nibble the antennae of Banded Coral Shrimps down to stubs. Filefishes require very little time to adjust and will eat almost anything.

SCRAWLED FILEFISH • **loulu** • *Aluterus scriptus* (Osbeck, 1765) • (Scribbled Filefish)
Thin as a board, covered with short blue lines like scribblings, and with a tail fin fully a third the length of its body, this is one of those fishes often called "bizarre." Its hairlike dorsal spine is scarcely visible even when raised, and the body can rapidly darken to a mottled camouflage pattern. Scrawled Filefish occur in the open ocean as well as close to shore and are more abundant in some years then in others. They eat jellyfish, zoanthids (colonial anemones), fire corals (which don't occur in Hawai'i), and other noxious or poisonous animals. The Hawaiian name refers to a group of endemic, greenish white fan-palms *(Pritchardia sp.)* similar in color to the fish. **Lou** means "to hook," and the fish was used in sorcery to cause death. The species name means "written upon." To over 3ft. All warm seas. Photo: Molokini Islet, Maui. 60 ft.

YELLOWTAIL FILEFISH • **'ō'ili**
Pervagor aspricaudus (Hollard, 1854).
(Lacefin Filefish)
Extremely shy, this small filefish is gray black with a yellow or orange tail. It retreats into a hole or crevice when approached, usually before a diver even sees it. More common in some years than in others. To 7 in., but usually smaller. Sub-tropical Indo-Pacific. Photo: Magic Island, O'ahu. 30 ft.

FANTAIL FILEFISH • **'ō'ili-'uwī'uwī** ●
Pervagor spilosoma (Lay & Bennett, 1839).
In some years abundant, in others only moderately common, Fantail Filefishes are yellow, marked with black spots, and have bright orange, fanlike tails. Blue markings about the mouth and throat further adorn these beautiful little fishes. They frequently pair off in a head-to-tail position, raising and lowering their spines, and spreading their colorful tails in some sort of territorial or sexual display. During years of peak population they die off by the thousands, washing up on beaches. In old Hawai'i this was said to portend the death of a chief; their dry bodies were sometimes used as fuel. If removed from the water they make a small noise, hence the Hawaiian name **'uwī'uwī**, meaning to squeal. Species name means "spotted." To 7 in. Endemic. Photo: Lana'i Lookout, O'ahu. 35 ft.

SHY FILEFISH • 'o'ili ●

Cantherhines verecundus (E.K. Jordan, 1925).

This plain, light color filefish usually darkens rapidly to a blotchy mottled pattern when approached. Its skin is covered with short, hairlike appendages. Appropriately named, it seldom strays far from cover. Species name means "bashful," "shy." To about 5 in. Endemic. Closely related to the Indo-Pacific *C. fronticinctus*. Photo: Kawaihoa (Portlock) Point, O'ahu. 20 ft.

BARRED FILEFISH • 'ō'ili

Cantherhines dumerilii (Hollard, 1854).

These deep-bodied filefishes are brownish gray with faint vertical bars on the side. A tuft of orange spines (longer in males) sprouts at the base of the tail, also orange. Equipped with powerful jaws and strong teeth, they can sometimes be heard crunching rock and coral, much like parrotfishes. They often travel in pairs, warily tilting their backs toward divers as they swim. Juveniles are covered with white spots. Named for French naturalist Auguste Duméril (1812-1870). To about 15 in. East Africa to the Americas. Photo: Hōnaunau, Hawai'i. 30 ft.

HAWAIIAN FILEFISH • 'ō'ili-lepa ●

Cantherhines sandwichiensis (Quoy & Gaimard, 1824).

(SQUARETAIL FILEFISH)

Immediately recognizable, this dark gray filefish has a prominent white spot at the top of the tail base. The Hawaiian name, **lepa** ("flag-bearer" or "flagpole"), refers to the particularly long dorsal spine. The tail is not rounded, as in other Hawaiian filefishes. Hawai'i was once called the Sandwich Islands, hence the scientific name. To about 7 in. Endemic. Closely related to the widespread *C. pardalis* found elsewhere in the Indo-Pacific. Photo: Hanauma Bay, O'ahu. 30 ft.

FLAGTAILS
(KUHLIIDAE)

Flagtails are a small family of silvery, perchlike fishes with a single dorsal fin. In many species the tail fin is banded, but in Hawai'i bands occur only on juveniles. Nocturnal feeders, they rest during the day, either in caves or in areas of heavy surge. Known in Hawaiian as **āholehole**, flagtails have long been prized as food. According to an 1893 Hawaiian newspaper, when a chiefess in Hilo yearned for the "fat **āholehole**," runners brought them to her from Puna, still alive in their wrappings of seaweed. "Because the chiefess had a craving," it reported, "the distance was as nothing."

In old Hawai'i names were often significant on several levels. For example, the word **hole** means "to strip away" and the **āholehole** was prepared for eating by gripping the dorsal fin with the teeth and pulling the body away. These fish were sometimes used in ceremonies for the "stripping away" of evil spirits. Early Caucasian settlers, with their white skins, were sometimes called **āhole** (not to be confused with **haole**, meaning "foreigner").

Of the two flagtail species in Hawai'i, the most common is shown below.

HAWAIIAN FLAGTAIL · **āholehole**   ●
Kuhlia xenura (Jordan & Gilbert 1882)
These common endemic fish form dense schools by day, often in areas of heavy surge where they are safe from predators. A second Island species, *K. sandvicensis*, aggregates in dark caves. Regardless of species, flagtail schools are almost stationary and tend to remain in the same location year after year. (They sometimes disappear for a few weeks or months, but generally return.) At night individual fish disperse to feed on plankton. The young, which have banded tails, are abundant in tidepools. They will enter brackish and even fresh water and do well in a beginner's aquarium. You will have to catch them yourself, however, as they cannot be taken commercially at such a small size. In old Hawai'i the young were called **āholehole** while adults were simply **āhole**. To 1 ft. *Kuhlia xenura* is endemic; *K. sandvicensis* is widespread in the Central Pacific. Photo: Hanauma Bay, O'ahu. 10 ft.

FLATFISHES
(BOTHIDAE AND SOLEIDAE)

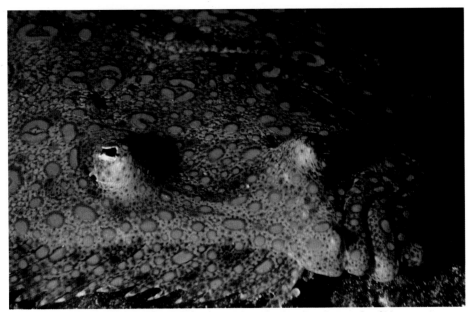

Peacock Flounder • **pākiʻi** *(Bothus mancus)*. Photo: D. R. Schrichte. Hanauma Bay, Oʻahu.

Every habitat has its specialists, and flatfishes are masters of the sandy or gravelly seabed. Their greatly flattened, oval bodies lie almost flush with the bottom. Virtually invisible to predator or prey, they wait patiently for the small crustaceans or fishes on which they feed. Flatfishes begin life as normal fishes, with eyes on either side of the head. As they grow, one eye actually migrates over the top of the head, eventually joining the other on the opposite side. As this happens, the fish starts leaning over, eventually ending up flat on the sand with the blind side down.

The underside of most flatfishes is white; the upper side is usually speckled or mottled to match the substrate. They are able to fine tune this pattern for an almost perfect blend. To make doubly sure they are not seen, they can partially cover themselves with sand, the eyes protruding like little periscopes.

Flatfishes are so strange and different that they constitute their own order, the Pleuronectiformes. There are many species, including the enormous Barn-Door Halibut of northern seas which can grow to seven feet in length and weigh hundreds of pounds. Most flatfishes dwell in temperate waters or on deep muddy bottoms and are unlikely to be encountered by snorkelers or divers. Of the seven flatfish families, only the left-eyed flounders (Bothidae), right-eyed flounders (Pleuronectidae) and the soles (Soleidae) are seen regularly in reef environments.

Flounders have eyes on the left, whereas soles have eyes on the right. The easiest way to distinguish between the two is to look for the fish's mouth. If it is on the left, with the eyes above it, the fish is a flounder. If the mouth is on the right, with the eyes above it, it is a sole. Unfortunately, this is not a perfect test; there exists a family of right-eyed flounders, a few of the left-eye species are actually right-eyed, and some species are variable.

An old story relates that Moses once tried frying a sole in oil. He browned one side nicely, but the oil ran out and he threw the half-cooked fish back into the sea. Miraculously, it sprang back to life. Ever since flatfishes have been brown on one side and white on the other. A Red Sea species *(Pardachirus marmoratus)*, still called the Moses Sole, secretes a milky fluid containing a remarkably effective shark repellent. The active ingredient has been found to be similar to household detergent.

61

Hawai'i has thirteen left-eyed flounders, at least two right-eyed flounders, and at least two small soles. Because they are quite similar, only one is described below. The Hawaiian name for flatfishes is **pāki'i** ("fallen flat" or "spread out").

Underwater, flounders can be closely approached. If disturbed, a flounder will take off rapidly in a cloud of sand. It typically swims ten feet or so in a straight line, lands, then flutters backward into the settling sand, which partially covers it. Thus the wily creature ends up well-hidden several feet from where you expect it.

Small flounders, which might make interesting aquarium specimens, can sometimes be found in the canal entrances at Kailua Beach, Windward O'ahu.

PEACOCK FLOUNDER • **pā ki'i**
Bothus mancus (Broussonet, 1782).
(MANYRAY FLATFISH)

Probably the most common flatfish on Hawaiian reefs, the Peacock Flounder is pale to light brown, with spots and blue flowerlike markings. The eyed side has three unequal dark blotches in a row, the one nearest the tail smaller. The eyes of males are further apart than those of females and males have a greatly elongated pectoral fin. The species name means "wounded," or "hurt." To 19 in. Indo-Pacific. The similar Panther Flounder (*B. pantherinus*) prefers sandy bottoms. Photo: "Black Rock," leeward O'ahu. 20 ft.

FROGFISHES
(ANTENNARIIDAE)

Commerson's Frogfish *(Antennarius commerson)*. Photo: Bob Owens. Kona, Hawai'i.

Frogfishes, or anglerfishes, are the ultimate sedentary predators. Barely recognizable as fishes, they sit for long periods in one spot, either blending in perfectly with the reef or mimicking brightly colored sponges and other growths. Their pectoral fins grasp the coral like hands or feet, and can be used (with the help of a joint) to clamber about. One of their dorsal spines resembles a fishing pole; a lure at the end is dangled over an enormous mouth. Fishes, large or small, attracted to the waving lure soon find themselves inside the frogfish, whose innards can expand twelve-fold to accommodate guests of any size. With a reflex measured in milliseconds, frogfishes swallow their prey far too quickly for the eye to follow.

Most remarkably, these awkward fishes are jet propelled. Although poor swimmers in the normal sense, some (if not all) species can gulp water through their large mouths and eject it under pressure through small, round gill openings set far back on the body. By this means, perhaps aided by currents and surge, they can "fly" considerable distances. A Commerson's Frogfish perched on an outcrop can spread its pectorals like small stiff wings, drop its pelvics like landing gear, and glide about 20 feet to a perfect touchdown.

Frogfishes rely almost entirely on camouflage for protection; they can inflate with water when molested, but have no sharp spines and are not poisonous. Preferring deeper water, they are unlikely to be seen by snorkelers. Small specimens make fascinating aquarium fishes and several Hawaiian species are available in the fish trade. Frogfishes must be fed live food initially, but may eventually learn to accept whole frozen shrimps or fishes (thawed before feeding, of course). Needless to say, they are best kept alone or with much larger tankmates; they have been known to swallow prey longer than themselves, including other frogfishes.

Frogfishes are a primitive group, belonging to the order Lophiiformes. Nine species inhabit Hawaii's reefs. Most are small and rarely seen. A tenth, the pelagic Sargassumfish *(Histrio histrio)* inhabits floating seaweed.

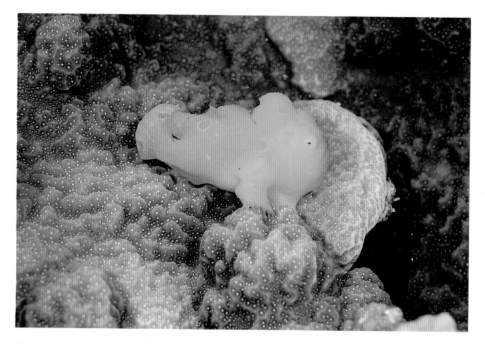

COMMERSON'S FROGFISH
Antennarius commersoni (Latreille, 1804).
(GIANT FROGFISH)

Larger than most other frogfishes, this species can be bright yellow, orange, red, brown or blackish and is often covered with spots, scab-like patches and small growths. In captivity it has been observed to change color over a period of days or weeks. Younger specimens are often the brightest, mimicking sponges or other organisms. The name honors French biologist Philibert Commerson (1727-1773), who first described this fish. To 12 in. East Africa to the Americas, but absent from many Pacific islands. Photos: juvenile. Hōnaunau, Hawai'i; adult. Kawaihoa (Portlock) Point, O'ahu. 30 ft.

GOATFISHES
(MULLIDAE)

Whitesaddle Goatfish • kūmū *(Parupeneus porphyreus)* Honolua Bay, Maui. 20 ft.

Goatfishes are often the first fishes seen by a snorkeler finning over the sandy bottom. They are easily recognized by their barbels, reminiscent of a goat's beard, with which they busily "taste" the sand for worms, molluscs and other invertebrates. When not feeding they tuck their barbels up out of sight. All goatfishes have a forked tail and two dorsal fins. Many can change color dramatically in seconds, and their resting colors may differ from their active colors. Variable, yet looking much alike, goatfishes are sometimes difficult to identify underwater. Most are bottom dwellers, but several of the most abundant species school in midwater during the day.

Despite the obvious similarity between all members of the family, there is no general Hawaiian name for goatfishes. Species with one or more body-length stripes are known as **weke** ("to open") and were sometimes used in religious ceremonies when an "opening" or "releasing" was required. **Weke** under seven inches are called **'oama**. Some goatfishes are known as **moano**. Others have individual names. All are prized as food. In the words of an old chant: "Delicious, delicious is the fish of the sea, the **moano** of the yellowish sea, delicious, delicious."

Goatfishes are sometimes called "surmullets," the family name coming from the Latin *mullus* ("mullet"). Nine native species inhabit shallow Hawaiian waters; one is endemic. A tenth, the uncommon Yellowbanded Goatfish (*Upeneus vittatus*), was accidentally introduced from the Marquesas Islands in 1955. Goatfishes are not good aquarium pets, being highly susceptible to shock. Although small specimens might be kept, they tend to stir up the bottom, keeping the water cloudy.

WHITE GOATFISH • **weke'ā**
Mulloidichthys flavolineatus (Lacepède, 1801).

The **weke'ā** and the **weke'ula** (below) are very similar. This species has a squarish black spot on the side embedded within a yellow stripe running from head to tail. The black spot, often intense while the fish is feeding, sometimes disappears. The body is whitish; the fins are whitish to yellowish. **Weke'ā** are occasionally encountered in schools off the bottom, but are more likely to be seen in pairs or small groups foraging or resting on the sand. Species name means "yellow striped." Hawaiian name means "staring **weke**." To 16 in., but usually smaller. Indo-Pacific. Photo: Bob Owens. Pūpūkea, O'ahu. 30 ft.

YELLOWFIN GOATFISH • **weke-'ula**
Mulloidichthys vanicolensis (Valenciennes, 1831).

Similar to the species above but lacking the black rectangular spot, **weke-'ula** have yellow fins as well as a yellow stripe from eye to tail. The yellow stripe may be bordered faintly with blue. They rest during the day in tight schools, hanging motionlessly in midwater or hiding under ledges. The Hawaiian word **'ula** means "red" and **weke-'ula**, usually whitish, can turn pink or red (including yellow stripe and fins). Species name is from Vanikoro Island in the Solomon Islands. To 15 in. Indo-Pacific. Photo: Hanauma Bay, O'ahu. 25 ft.

ORANGE GOATFISH • **weke-'ula**
Mulloidichthys pflugeri (Steindachner, 1900).

When foraging on the bottom these goatfishes display a pattern of broad light bars on their reddish orange bodies. When resting their red becomes more uniform, but when swimming high off the bottom they become gray. At such times, because of their color, forked tails and large size, they can resemble Gray Snappers. This species prefers deeper water, but is sometimes seen in as little as 20 feet. To at least 24 inches. Indo-Pacific. Photo: Hanauma Bay, O'ahu. 40 ft.

DOUBLEBAR GOATFISH • munu
Parupeneus bifasciatus (Lacepède, 1801).
   Two widely separated dark bars (the first often narrower) give this fish its common and scientific names. The gray body can become reddish overall, losing its dark bars almost completely. The tail is usually dark with a thin light blue margin. This solitary goatfish, deeper bodied than many others, is perhaps most easily identified underwater by its profile, thick lips, and the slightly rounded margins of its tail fin. To 13 in. Indo-Pacific. Photo: Hōnaunau, Hawai'i. 30 ft.

BLUE GOATFISH • moano ukali-ulua
Parupeneus cyclostomus (Lacepède, 1801).
(YELLOWSADDLE GOATFISH)
   With its bluish body and yellow saddle this is probably the easiest Hawaiian goatfish to identify. It is one of the few that does not change to red. An all-yellow color phase, fairly common elsewhere, is rare or absent in Hawai'i. These goatfishes are unusual in that they eat small fishes. As a feeding strategy, juveniles will closely follow a similar size wrasse. Because most wrasses do not eat fishes, small fishes do not seek cover when they see the wrasse approaching. Adults of this species are sometimes followed by **ulua** (jacks) which feed on organisms stirred up by their foragings. The Hawaiian name **ukali-ulua** means "**moano** with **ulua** following." Species name means "round mouth." To 20 in. Indo-Pacific. Photo: Kahe Point, O'ahu. 15 ft.

67

MANYBAR GOATFISH · moano
Parupeneus multifasciatus (Quoy & Gaimard, 1824).

A dark stripe through the eye and three unequal black bars on the rear half of the body distinguish this fish. The ground color may be whitish to reddish, or some of each. The pelvic and anal fins are sometimes beautifully colored in shades of magenta and blue. In color, this is one of the most highly change-able goatfishes. The two photographs of the same individual were taken several seconds apart, a camera flash triggering the change. However, these are only two of several possible patterns. Very common. Species name means "many bars." Hawaiian name means "pale red." **Moano** were said to become red by eating the red blossoms of the **'ohi'a lehua** tree. To 11 in. Pacific Ocean. Photos: Hanauma Bay, O'ahu. 10 ft. Magic Island, O'ahu. 30 ft.

SIDESPOT GOATFISH • **moano**
Parupeneus pleurostigma (Bennett, 1830).

This goatfish has an oval white area on the upper side (between the two dorsal fins) with black markings in front and behind. Usually gray, it can blush to a lovely pink. Younger fishes are often seen in schools. They are among the easiest of the family to identify. Species name means "side spot." Hawaiian name means "pale red." To 13 in. Indo-Pacific. Photo: Kahe Point, O'ahu. 15 ft.

WHITESADDLE GOATFISH • **kūmū** ●
Parupeneus porphyreus (Jenkins, 1903).

The **kūmū** can be grayish purple, greenish or red but almost always has a small white spot (or saddle) above the base of the tail. Light streaks along the body above and below the eye are another identifying feature. The species name means "purple." Highly valued, this fish was sometimes used in offerings calling for a pig, when a pig was unobtainable. It was forbidden to women, as was pork. The name **kūmū** also means master; when a student attained full mastery in any endeavor a **kūmū** was often offered. To 15 in. Endemic. Photo: Hanauma Bay, O'ahu. 25 ft.

BANDTAIL GOATFISH • **weke pueo**
Upeneus taeniopterus Cuvier, 1829.
(NIGHTMARE WEKE)

This is the only native Hawaiian goatfish with a banded tail. Two stripes run the length of the body, one brown and one yellow. The barbels are bright lemon yellow. It inhabits shallow sandy bottoms near the shoreline and can often be seen in only inches of water. The brain is sometimes toxic; if eaten it can cause disturbed sleep and hallucinations. Offerings to Pahulu, King of Ghosts were believed to prevent ill effects. For this reason the fish was sometimes called "**weke-pahulu**." The 5-6 tail bands resemble those of the **pueo** or Hawaiian owl, hence the Hawaiian name "owl **weke**." Species name means "banded fin." To about 12 in. Indo-Pacific. The similar Yellowbanded Goatfish (*Upeneus vittatus*), an accidental introduction, has only 2-4 bands on the lower lobe of the tail fin. Photo: Honolua Bay, Maui. 5 ft.

69

GOBIES AND DARTFISHES
(GOBIIDAE AND MICRODESMIDAE)

Shoulder-Spot Goby (Gnatholepis cauerensis). Mākua, Oʻahu. 50 ft.

Although few gobies are seen by snorkelers and divers in Hawaiʻi, the family Gobiidae is by far the largest of all fish families, with approximately 1600 species worldwide. The typical goby is a small, blunt headed, somewhat elongated fish, often dwelling in a burrow or hole—but gobies have adapted to many other habitats, including tidepools, exposed mudflats, and branches of living coral. The pelvic fins of most gobies are fused into a single appendage resembling a suction cup with which they can cling or perch. In general, they are omnivores. Bottom-dwelling species sift mouthfuls of sand for small animals, algae or detritus. The free swimmers and coral-dwelling gobies probably pick plankton from the water.

Many gobies construct their own homes by digging burrows or excavating spaces under stones, using their large mouths to carry rocks and sand. Some species, including the endemic Mainland's Goby, inhabit burrows excavated by snapping shrimps. These shrimps, which are nearly blind, rely on gobies to warn them of predators. The gobies perch at the entrance to the hole, while the shrimps labor underground clearing or extending the passages. Occasionally a shrimp appears at the surface, pushing a load of rubble like a little bulldozer. While near the surface, it keeps contact with the tail fin of its partner with one of its antennae. If approached too closely, both disappear instantly into the hole.

There are other unusual gobies: One Hawaiian freshwater species, **oʻopu-alamoʻo** (Lentipes concolor), scales the rocky sides of 1000-foot waterfalls to reach the headwaters above. The mudskipper gobies of Asia have adapted to life on exposed mudflats and can remain out of the water for hours. Two gobies with adult lengths of less than one centimeter vie for the title of smallest fish in the world.

The blue-striped Neon Goby of the Tropical Atlantic picks parasites from the bodies and gills of larger fishes, filling the role of the Indo-Pacific cleaner wrasses. (Their coloring is similar; Indo-Pacific fishes placed in an aquarium with a Neon Goby will pose to be cleaned.)

Gobies are known in Hawaiian as **'o'opu**. In addition to the **'o'opu-kai** (marine gobies), there are a number of **'o'opu-wai** (freshwater gobies). Once abundant, they were highly regarded as food. Today they inhabit only the few remote streams which remain relatively unchanged. The word "goby" is from the Greek *kobios*.

Dartfishes (family Microdesmidae), a closely related group, hover some distance above the bottom but retreat into burrows when approached. Formerly classified in the Gobiidae, they were for many years known popularly as "hover gobies." Dartfishes lack the fused pelvic fins of gobies. The similar wormfishes belong in the same family.

Two species of dartfishes, one wormfish and about 28 species of gobies are known in Hawai'i. Many of the gobies inhabit sandy or silty bottoms rarely explored by snorkelers and divers. Others, abundant in tidepools, are seldom encountered in deeper water. A few of the smaller, more secretive species can only be found by cracking open coral heads.

Although not illustrated, the following gobies might be seen by observant divers and snorkelers: Taylor's Goby *(Trimma taylori)*, a tiny yellow orange species occurring in small groups under ledges and along walls, often at depths of 50 feet or more; the Halfspotted Goby *(Asterropteryx semipunctatus)*, dark with small blue spots, and the Noble Goby *(Priolepis eugenius)*, brownish black with vertical bands, both of which thrive in dead coral rubble; and Mainland's Goby *(Psilogobius mainlandi)* which is commensal with two species of snapping shrimps. The last three species may be found in Kāne'ohe Bay, O'ahu. The Eyebar Goby *(Gnatholepis anjerensis)*, which lives over sand at the bases of ledges and coral heads is similar to the Shoulder-Spot Goby illustrated on page 70.

Gobies make excellent aquarium fishes and require no special care. The bottom dwellers spend much of their time shifting stones and sand to and fro, improving and adjusting their little homes, and providing their keepers with hours of entertainment. Unfortunately, most Hawaiian gobies are drab, but colorful species from other parts of the Pacific are available. The two dartfishes described below are attractive and make good pets.

COCOS FRILL GOBY • **'o'opu-'ohune**
Bathygobius cocosensis (Bleeker, 1854)
   The dark mottlings of this goby blend well with Hawaii's black volcanic rock but it can lighten to match other backgrounds. Occurring mainly in tidepools, it might be mistaken at a distance for the abundant and active Zebra Blenny. To about 3 in. Indo-Pacific. Photo: Marjorie L. Awai, Waikīkī Aquarium.

WIRE-CORAL GOBY

Bryaninops yongei (Davis & Cohen, 1969).

Wire corals are solitary whiplike relatives of black corals. They usually grow off rocky walls in areas with some current. Many wire corals harbor a pair of these minute fish, which scoot up and down the single branch, probably never leaving it. (Juveniles and a pair of small shrimps may be present as well.) If you find a wire coral colony, look near the tip for a band cleared of living tissue where the gobies lay their eggs. The species name honors pioneer Australian zoologist, Sir Charles Maurice Yonge (1899-1986). In addition to this species, two similar gobies occur in Hawai'i: the larger but less common *Bryaninops amplus* lives on wire corals and also buoy lines and other man-made objects; *B. tigris* inhabits the black coral *Antipathes dichotoma.*) To about 1.3 in. Indo-Pacific. Photo: Mākua, O'ahu. 80 ft.

GOLDEN GREEN GOBY ●

Priolepis aureoviridis (Gosline, 1959).

This goby dwells in crevices and holes, often clinging upside down to the ceiling. The entire fish is yellowish to brownish green (usually contrasting nicely with its surroundings) but only its head may be visible, peering out at the underwater world. To about 5 in. Endemic. Photo: Mākua, O'ahu. 40 ft.

FIRE DARTFISH
Nemateleotris magnifica Fowler, 1928.

Beautiful and unusual, these little fishes were unknown in Hawai'i until 1975 when collectors encountered a few off Wai'anae, O'ahu. They are white in front, becoming pink and then red near the tail, and have a very long dorsal spine which they flick up and down. Preferring rubble bottoms at depths of at least 50 feet, they are rare in Hawai'i, but are often imported in the aquarium trade from other regions of the Pacific. In captivity they should be provided with a place to construct a burrow. Territorial, they will fight with their own kind unless a mated pair is obtained. They are not fussy eaters and are peaceful toward other species. To about 3 in., but usually smaller in Hawai'i. Indo-Pacific. Photo: Mike Severns. Molokini Island, Maui. 80 ft.

INDIGO DARTFISH
Ptereleotris heteroptera (Bleeker, 1855).

These small, pencil-thin fishes hover a few inches to several feet over patches of sand or rubble, frequently in pairs or small groups. Over sand they are bright blue, over rubble darker. When approached they dive headfirst into their burrows, usually under a piece of rock. Seen most often at depths greater than 60 feet, but occasionally in as little as 20, they prefer areas with some current. Indigo Dartfishes do well in captivity, especially if provided with a flat stone or large overturned shell under which to make their home. Keep them in a small group. They will hide at first and can take several weeks to adjust. Species name from *hetero* ("different", "other") and *pteros* ("fin"). To almost 5 in. Indo-Pacific. Photo: George K. Stender. Kea'au Ledge, O'ahu. 50 ft.

CURIOUS WORMFISH
Gunnellichthys curiosus Dawson 1968

Except for the prominent spot on the tail, these slender, sinuous fishes look much like the common Scale-Eating Blenny. They live over rubble bottoms, usually in groups, and when threatened dive headfirst into their holes. (Blennies, by comparison, wriggle in tail first.) To about 3 in. Indo-Pacific. Photo: Mākua, O'ahu. 50 ft.

Hawaiian Black Grouper • hāpu'u *(Epinephelus quernus)* Midway Island. 40 ft.

The groupers are heavy-bodied, large-mouthed, bottom-dwelling predators, usually solitary in nature. The social anthias, by contrast, are small, delicately colored plankton eaters. Both belong in the same family.

Groupers occur from shallow water to depths of many hundreds of feet. Some grow to enormous size. They have a protruding lower jaw and their tail fin is usually rounded. Most groupers are blotched, spotted and dull in appearance, but a few are brightly colored. Many species are of commercial importance. Often known as sea basses, they form the subfamily Epinephelinae.

Groupers do not chase their prey but rely on ambush or careful stalking to get within striking distance. Their method of ingestion is common to many other fish predators, such as hawkfishes or scorpionfishes. When the prey is sufficiently close, the grouper merely opens its large expandable mouth. Water rushes in, carrying with it the grouper's meal. This operation takes only a fraction of a second and is surprisingly effective. The stomachs of large groupers have been found to contain lobsters, stingrays, porcupinefishes and sea turtles. At least one species, the Giant Grouper *(Epinephelus lanceolatus)*, is capable of swallowing a man. It can weigh almost 900 pounds and attains a length of nine feet.

Large groupers are known for their curiosity and intelligence. On reefs where they have not been speared or molested they often approach human visitors and may learn to accept food or stroking. They have even been known to identify individual divers. Unfortunately, large groupers have been speared or fished out from many of the world's diving areas.

An enormous species does, or did, exist in Hawai'i, as evidenced by fishing records. In 1956 a 354-pound specimen was speared at a depth of 110 feet in Honokahua Bay, Maui, and in 1958 a 350-

pounder was taken at 120 feet off the south shore of Kaua'i after a four-hour fight involving three divers. It exceeded seven feet in length. More recently, in 1989, a 554-pound monster was caught on a handline in Kihei, Maui. These rare fishes are said to be found between 40 and 200 feet, usually in caves. Judging from their size, they are probably Giant Groupers (*E. lanceolatus*). Let us hope that somewhere in the islands a few remain.

At the other end of the scale are the delicate and brightly colored anthias, or fairy basslets (subfamily Anthiinae), which live in schools and seldom exceed four inches in length. In the Red Sea and other parts of the tropics these graceful little fishes swarm around shallow coral heads in enormous numbers. In Hawai'i they occasionally occur near dropoffs at about 60 feet, becoming more abundant at depths greater than 150 feet. Anthias are among the most pleasing and attractive of reef fishes, and Hawai'i is home to a number of species. Most divers, however, have probably never observed them.

The reproductive life of groupers and anthias is interesting — all begin life as females. Groupers eventually become male, but most anthias remain female for life, living in "harems" dominated by a single male. If the male dies, the top-ranking female reverses sex and takes his place. Some wrasses and parrotfishes have similar life histories.

Although the groupers and anthias belong to one of the largest fish families, only 17 are native to Hawai'i. Most are anthias, and none are from shallow water. Among the most interesting are three deep-water endemics: the **hā pu'u** (*Epinephelus quernus*), a mid-size grouper (see page 74), the rare, beautiful Sunset Basslet (*Liopropoma aurora*) and the striking Hawaiian Yellow Anthias (*Holanthias fuscipinnis*). The last two are pictured in the appendix.

Shallow water groupers are an important fishery resource in many parts of the world. Their absence in Hawai'i prompted the State Division of Fish and Game in the 1950s to introduce three species from the South Pacific. Only one has survived to reproduce in Hawaiian waters.

Because groupers have a high tolerance of ammonia and nitrite small specimens are excellent for "breaking in" aquariums. Friendly and intelligent, they peer at their keeper through the glass and always seem to know when they are about to be fed. The smaller anthias also make hardy, colorful pets. Plankton eaters, they will not bother invertebrates or pick at coral and are ideal for "mini-reef" tanks. Males placed together tend to fight; a male and several females make a good combination. Anthias will accept almost any kind of food, especially if introduced into the filter current. Unfortunately, because of their deep dwelling habits anthias are difficult to collect and require lengthy decompression.

The word "grouper" (from the Portuguese "garoupa") is, in turn, probably of Native American origin.

PEACOCK GROUPER · **roi**
Cephalopholis argus Bloch & Schneider, 1801.
 Introduced from Moorea, French Polynesia, in 1956 **roi** have become common throughout the Hawaiian Islands. Small individuals are dark and covered with fine iridescent blue spots. In larger speciments the spots fade and a series of light vertical bars may appear on the rear half of the body. These wary fishes are usually encountered sitting on a coral head or on the bottom and always disappear into a crevice when approached. Small ones make good pets if kept with tankmates they can't swallow. Named for the hundred staring eyes of the mythical monster, Argus. To about 16 in. Indo-Pacific. Photo: Hōnaunau, Hawai'i. 40 ft.)

male ∧

BICOLOR ANTHIAS
Pseudanthias bicolor (Randall, 1979).

Of the Hawaiian anthias, these are the most likely to be seen by divers. They are orange yellow on the upper half, lavender below. Males are larger than females, their second and third dorsal spines are elongated, and the front of the dorsal fin is red. Only the third spine is long in females. These fish prefer depths of 60 feet or more, but occur in as little as 15-20 feet off Mākua, O'ahu, where they often share a crevice or hole with a large Yellowmargin Moray. Bicolor Anthias are frequently seen around isolated coral heads in deep water. To about 4.5 in. Indo-Pacific. Photos: male. Pūpūkea, O'ahu. 70 ft.; colony, Puakō, Hawai'i. 120ft.

THOMPSON'S ANTHIAS • *Pseudanthias thompsoni* (Fowler, 1923). ●
   Larger than most other anthias, these are pinkish red on the sides and back with lavender overtones, especially on males. Males develop beautifully extended filaments on their tail fins. As with most anthias, they are larger than females and less numerous. Inhabiting ledges and dropoffs at 60 feet or more, (rarely in as little as 30), Thompson's Anthias become increasingly plentiful at greater depths. They are especially abundant on the wall dives off Niʻihau Island. Named after John W. Thompson, a technician and artist at the Bishop Museum from 1901 to 1928. To 8.5 in. Hawaii and the Ogasawara Islands. Photo: "Black Coral Arch," east shore Kauai, 70 ft.

HAWAIIAN LONGFIN ANTHIAS • *Pseudanthias hawaiiensis* (Randall, 1979). ●
   Very long pelvic and anal fins (especially on males) characterize this small, beautiful, uncommon species. Males have a yellow head and a reddish orange body which becomes violet toward the tail. Females, smaller and more numerous, are mostly yellow on the head and back, with lavender sides. Hawaiian Longfin Anthias prefer depths of 100 feet or more, sometimes living under ledges and often swimming upside down on the ceiling. Originally a subspecies of the Indo-Pacific *P. ventralis,* they are now considered endemic to Hawaiʻi. Although hardy in captivity, they often suffer decompression problems when brought to the surface. It's best to leave them on the reef. To about 3 in. Indo-Pacific. Photo: male. "General Store," south shore Kauaʻi. 100 ft.; female (inset). Hōnaunau, Hawaiʻi. 150 ft.

Stocky Hawkfish • **po'o-pa'a** *(Cirrhitus pinnulatus)* Hanauma Bay. 15 ft..

Hawkfishes are small to medium-size predators that spend most of their time perched motionless among rocks or coral branches. The pectoral fins, which help hold them in place, are typically thick and enlarged. Although not strong swimmers, hawkfishes are capable of descending swiftly on their prey and pursuing it vigorously for short distances. Characteristic of the family are curious tufts of filaments extending from the ends of their dorsal spines. Males maintain harems.

The smaller species make alert, intelligent pets. Sitting on the highest rock in the tank, they watch their keeper's every move, soon learning to eat out of his or her fingers. Hawkfishes are voracious and should not be kept with anything much smaller than themselves. They are also territorial; introduce them last into a community tank.

Out of 35 species of hawkfishes worldwide, six are found in Hawai'i and five are described here. The Hawaiian name for most hawkfishes was **pili-ko'a**, which means "coral clinging."

Morwongs (family Cheilodactylidae) are a small family related to the hawkfishes with one species in Hawai'i. As a family, they prefer cooler temperate waters and are not often found in the tropics.

REDBARRED HAWKFISH • **pili-ko'a**
Cirrhitops fasciatus (Bennett, 1828).

This perky and attractive hawkfish is marked with grayish red to brick red bars on the side, and a black spot on the gill cover. There may be a blackish spot on the base of the tail. Very common. Species name means "barred." To about 5 in. Recorded from Hawai'i, Madagascar and Mauritius. Similar in appearance, the smaller and more secretive Twospot Hawkfish (*Amblycirrhitus bimacula*) has rounder, darker black spots in similar locations. Photo: Pūpūkea, O'ahu. 30 ft.

STOCKY HAWKFISH • **po'o-pa'a**
Cirrhitus pinnulatus (Bloch & Schneider, 1801).

The Stocky Hawkfish blends in well with its environment and is easy to overlook. Preferring exposed rocky areas in shallow water, it wedges its pectoral fins into cracks to stabilize itself in the surge. Its robust, mottled body has three loose rows of white spots on the side. Hawaiian specimens have more colorful markings on the head than those of their Indo-Pacific cousins. This hawkfish can be hand-fed — if it expects food and none is offered it will swim off its perch and nibble your fingers. Species name from *pinna* ("fin"). The Hawaiian name means "hard head." Known to fishermen as "Rockfish", they are easily hooked, but not greatly esteemed. In old Hawai'i it was said, "The fisherman who fools around in shallow water takes home a **po'o-pa'a**." To about 11 in. Indo-Pacific. Photos:

79

LONGNOSE HAWKFISH
Oxycirrhites typus Bleeker, 1857.

An inhabitant of black coral and gorgonians, usually in water over 100 feet, the Longnose Hawkfish is a prized find in Hawai'i, where most black coral was removed in the early days of scuba diving. It is crosshatched in red and, with its long snout, cannot be confused with any other species. Longnose Hawkfishes may be seen on Kaua'i at several popular dive sites in as little as 70 feet. The back side of Molokini Island, Maui is also home to a few. Not as aggressive as other hawkfishes, they make excellent aquarium pets. However, the little black coral still remaining at diving depths in Hawai'i should probably be protected, along with its inhabitants. Species name means "figure" or "shape." To about 5 in. Indo-Pacific, from East Africa to the Americas. Photo: Mākua, O'ahu. 100 ft.

ARC-EYE HAWKFISH • pili-ko'a
Paracirrhites arcatus (Cuvier, 1829).

Although this hawkfish has two color phases, the prominent "U" mark in back of the eye will always serve to identify it. The two patterns are: grayish brown to reddish with a broad white stripe on the side; and brown without the white stripe. This is one of the most common hawkfishes in Hawai'i. In captivity it is "lazy," preferring to sit on the bottom. To 5.5 in. Indo-Pacific. Photo: Pūpūkea, O'ahu. 50ft.

adult ∧   juvenile ∨

BLACKSIDE HAWKFISH • hilu pili-koʻa
Paracirrhites forsteri (Bloch & Schneider), 1801.

The front half of this fish is brown, densely freckled in reddish black; the rear has a very broad black band bordered in white. Juveniles are half white, half black (divided lengthwise) and have a bright yellow back. Very small ones look and act somewhat like juvenile Saddle Wrasses. The species is named for the Forsters, father-and-son naturalists who accompanied Captain Cook on his second voyage to the Pacific and Indian oceans between 1772 and 1775. To almost 9 in. Indo-Pacific. Photos: adult. Hanauma Bay, Oʻahu. 30 ft. juvenile. Kawaihoa (Portlock) Point, Oʻahu. 30ft.

HAWAIIAN MORWONG • kīkākapu
Cheilodactylus vittatus Garrett, 1864.

These odd, rarely seen fishes have bold diagonal stripes which may serve to disrupt their outline or to make them appear extra-large to predators. Morwongs swim freely, often in pairs; sometimes, like hawkfishes, they prop themselves on the bottom with their strong pectoral fins. Common in the Northwestern Hawaiian Islands, they can be seen occasionally on Kauaʻi, and are rare everywhere else. Around the main islands they prefer depths greater than 100 feet, although small specimens may occur in shallow water. For many years this species was thought to be endemic, hence the common name. It shares its Hawaiian name ("strong **kapu**") with several species of butterflyfishes. The species name means "striped." Hardy in captivity. To 16 in. Hawaiʻi, New Caledonia, and Lord Howe Island. Photo: Hanauma Bay, Oʻahu. 5 ft.

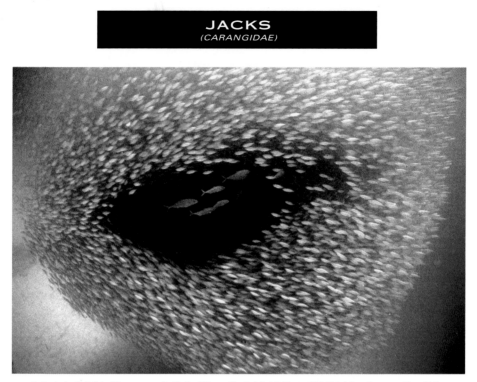

Amberjacks **(kahala)** with enormous baitball of Bigeye Scads **(akule)**. Photo: D.R. Schrichte. Hanauma Bay, O'ahu.

The family Carangidae includes the jacks (or trevallies), rainbow runners, leatherbacks, scads and others. Most are swift, strong-swimming predators which frequent open water near dropoffs or over reefs. They are especially prized by fishermen for their spectacular fighting ability.

Jacks are typically silvery on the sides and undersides, and bluish or greenish on the back. This color pattern, common among ocean-going (pelagic), fishes makes them difficult to see both from above and below. They have deep, narrow, streamlined bodies (varying in shape according to the genus) and deeply forked tails. In most species the base of the tail is slender and reinforced by specially strengthened scales called scutes.

Jacks and their relatives frequently patrol the reef in schools, although single individuals are not uncommon. In the early morning or late afternoon hunting behavior intensifies and schools of jacks may flash by swiftly, making sudden changes of direction to confuse or isolate their prey. Jacks feed primarily on other fishes, relying on superior speed to chase them down. They also forage on the bottom for crustaceans and other invertebrates. Occasionally a jack hovers near a feeding ray or goatfish, ready to dash in and snatch up any tidbits that may be uncovered. Some smaller members of the family, such as the scads, (**akule** and **'ōpelu**), are schooling plankton eaters.

There are about 140 species of jacks worldwide, with at least 24 known in Hawai'i. Pictured here are 11 species commonly seen in the reef environment. Most jacks are known as **ulua** in Hawaiian. Juveniles are **pāpio**. The scientific family name comes from *caranga,* a Native American word.

GIANT TREVALLY • **ulua aukea**
Caranx ignobilis (Forsskål, 1775).
(White Ulua; Giant Ulua)

White Ulua may be seen in pairs or as solitary individuals, sometimes very close to shore. In areas not heavily fished they occur in large schools. Their color ranges from silvery to silvery black. The steep profile of the head and a black spot at the base of the pectoral fin are identifying features. One of the largest of all jacks, they are inappropriately named "low," or "ignoble." The Hawaiian name means "white." In old Hawai'i, when a human sacrifice was called for a large **ulua aukea** was sometimes substituted. The species grows to over five feet with a weight of almost 200 pounds. Indo-Pacific. Photo: D.R. Schrichte. Hanauma Bay, O'ahu.

BLUEFIN TREVALLY • **'ōmilu**
Caranx melampygus (Cuvier, 1833).
(Blue Ulua)

These beautiful jacks are silvery blue, with scattered dark blue spots on the sides and lovely blue fins. They can quickly alter their color, however, becoming almost black. The most commonly seen jacks in Hawai'i, they may be solitary or in small groups. Species name means "black rump." To about 30 in. East Africa to the Americas. Photo: Hanauma Bay, O'ahu. 10 ft.

YELLOWSPOTTED JACK • **ulua**
Carangoides orthogrammus Jordan & Gilbert, 1881.
(Island Jack)

Silvery, like most jacks, these can be identified by a few scattered yellow spots on the side. Small individuals sometimes feed near the bottom in very shallow water. In earlier books this species is misidentified as *C. ferdau*, a jack uncommon in Hawai'i. To 28 in. East Africa to the Americas. Photo: Kahalu'u, Kailua-Kona, Hawai'i. 3 ft.

BIGEYE JACK • ulua
Caranx sexfasciatus Quoy & Gaimard, 1824.

The scientific name means "six-banded" but only **pāpio** (juveniles) display this pattern. The upper edge of the gill cover has a black spot and the point of the second dorsal fin is white. Although they feed primarily at night, individuals may forage during the day in shallow water. When not feeding they often congregate in tight schools. To about 3 ft. East Africa to the Americas. Photo: Indian Ocean. 20 ft.

RAINBOW RUNNER • kamanu
Elagatis bipinnulatus (Quoy & Gaimard, 1824).

These powerful, streamlined jacks are round in cross section with a large forked tail. The back and upper sides are deep blue. A yellow stripe bordered on each side with light blue runs from eye to tail. They are seen adjacent to deep water, or on wreck dives well offshore. Species name from *bi,* "two" and *pinna,* "fin." To almost 4 ft. All warm seas. Photo: Hōnaunau, Hawai'i. 30 ft.

GOLDEN TREVALLY • ulua pa'opa'o
Gnathanodon speciosus (Forsskål, 1775).
(YELLOW ULUA)

Among the most beautiful of all jacks, and probably the easiest to identify, these fishes are golden yellow with five wide black vertical bands. In older adults the black bands fade or are replaced with spots. Adults spend much of their time feeding on the bottom. Juveniles accompany large fishes, such as sharks, in the manner of the well known Pilot Fish *(Naucrates ductor),* also a jack. They appear to lead their host by maintaining a position just a few inches in front of the snout, but their real purpose there is to eat scraps left by the predator when it feeds. The position is safer than it seems; they swim in the predator's blind spot (resulting from eyes placed on either side of the head). The species name means "splendid" or "showy." To about 3 ft. East Africa to the Americas. Photo: Gulf of Oman, Indian Ocean. 30 ft.

84

THICKLIPPED JACK • **ulua**
Pseudocaranx dentex (Bloch and Schneider, 1801)
(PIG ULUA)

Pointed snouts and thick, fleshy lips distinguish these from other Hawaiian jacks. They often have a yellow stripe from eye to tail. Travelling in large schools, they are especially common in the Northwestern Hawaiian Islands. Around the main islands they prefer deep water and are infrequently seen. To 36 in. Subtropical waters worldwide. Photo: Midway Island. 60 ft.

LEATHERBACK • **lai**
Scomberoides lysan (Forsskål, 1775).

Leatherbacks, or queenfishes, have long, slender silvery bodies marked with a series of fairly conspicuous round spots. This species has a double row of 5-8 such spots, the lower larger than the upper. The dorsal fin has a black tip. The skin is very tough and the spines are reported to be venomous. Solitary individuals are not uncommon roving near the surface along dropoffs. Years ago their skins were used for the heads of small drums; today they are used for making fishing lures. To about 28 in. Indo-Pacific. Photo: Hanauma Bay, Oʻahu. 5 ft.

AMBERJACK • **kāhala**
Seriola dumerili (Risso, 1810).

These large predators occasionally come inshore to feed off schooling fishes in shallow water. They are silvery, with a dark diagonal bar through the eye and a yellow stripe along the side. While feeding on **ʻōpelu** or **akule**, several **kāhala** may work together, herding their prey into a tight school to make the pickings easier. Named after French naturalist Auguste Duméril (1812-1870). To almost 6 ft. All tropical seas. Photo: Midway Island. 15 ft

MACKEREL SCAD • 'ōpelu
Decapterus macarellus Cuvier, 1833.

'Opelu are small, schooling fishes of the jack family. Their bodies are round in cross section, tapering evenly at both ends, and they have a dark patch on the gill cover. The tail fins are yellowish. 'Opelu are highly prized as food by humans, larger fishes and seabirds. Frenetically active, they swim high off the bottom picking plankton from the water. Occasionally small groups descend to the reef to be cleaned by wrasses. Large jacks, such as **kāhala**, sometimes herd them into dense schools for their feeding convenience. Fishermen in old Hawai'i trained special barracudas to do the same. The species name translates as "happy," or "fortunate" (perhaps in reference to the humans who catch them). The English word "scads" is synonymous with "many," as in "scads of people." To about 12 in. All tropical seas. Photo: Magic Island, O'ahu. 25 ft.

BIGEYE SCAD • akule
Selar crumenophthalmus (Bloch, 1793).

Resting by day in schools close to shore, silvery **akule** are common at some protected beaches. They are often attacked in shallow water by predators such as **ulua, kāhala** and even small sharks. When the action gets heavy the school takes evasive action, twisting and turning as one, and producing an unusual tearing or ripping sound underwater. Among the most important food fishes of old Hawai'i, **akule** were called **pā'ā'ā** when very small and **halalū** at a size of six or seven inches. Their movements are seasonal and they are sometimes found offshore. **Akule** have large dark eyes and might be mistaken for **āholehole** or Hawaiian Flagtails, which form denser, more stationary schools, usually over rocky reefs instead of sand. They are deeper bodied and less active than **'ōpelu**, which never stay still for long. Species name means "purse-eyed." To about 12 in. All tropical seas. Photo: Honolua Bay, Maui. 5 ft.

LADYFISHES (MEGALOPIDAE), MILKFISHES (CHANIDAE) AND BONEFISHES (ALBULIDAE)

Ladyfishes and Bonefishes belong to the primitive order Elopiformes. Both are slender, silvery fish with a single dorsal fin and a deeply forked tail. They inhabit shallow protected areas with sandy or silty bottoms and are well known as hard-fighting game fishes. The Hawaiian Ladyfish or Tenpounder *(Elops hawaiensis)* is rarely seen except in Hanauma Bay, Oʻahu. For lack of space it is not pictured here. Called **awaʻaua** in Hawaiian, it is similar to the Bonefish but its mouth is at the tip of the head, not underslung. Milkfish belong to the order Gonorhynchiformes. There is a single species. Although quite large, its nearest relatives are believed to be freshwater minnows.

BONEFISH • ōʻio
Albula sp.
Bonefishes have underslung mouths adapted for feeding on sand-and rubble-dwelling organisms. Their flesh is full of small bones, hence the common name. Although typically seen in protected bays, bonefishes will also enter deep water. Do not confuse them with threadfins, which have an underslung mouth but two dorsal fins. The two Indo-Pacific bonefish species occurring in Hawaiʻi *(A. glossodonta and A. argentea)* appear identical in the field. Neither is common in Hawaiʻi, possibly due to habitat degradation and overfishing. Prized for their flavor in olden times, they were known by different names according to the stage of growth. Finger length fish were **pua ʻoʻio**, those of forearm length were **ʻamoʻomoʻo**. The word **ʻoʻio** also meant the soft flesh of the coconut (which resembled the soft mashed flesh of the bonefish), and a kind of braid or plaiting, such as in hatbands, that resembled the backbone of the fish. While feeding, bonefish are sometimes followed by jacks which snatch up tidbits they uncover. To about 3 ft. Photo: Hanauma Bay, Oʻahu. 3 ft.

MILKFISH • **awa** ●
Chanos chanos Forsskül, 1775.
These large silvery fish have a small pointed mouth, a deeply forked tail and a single, almost sharklike dorsal fin. They attain at least 6 ft. (but 3 is more typical) and sometimes enter surprisingly shallow water to nibble on algae. In deeper habitat they often swim with mouth wide open to feed on microplankton, usually blue-green algae. Known in Hawaiian as **awa**, they were once raised in fishponds and were as highly regarded as the **ʻamaʻama**, or mullet. In Southeast Asia they remain one of the most important cultured food fishes. The common name is said to derive from a milky white underside. Both genus and species names mean "open mouth." To about 6 ft. East Africa to the Americas. Photo: Palea Point, Oʻahu, 10 ft.

Like reptilian predators, lizardfishes sit motionless on rocks or sand, often blending in perfectly with their surroundings. Propped on their pelvic fins with head tilted up for a better view, they display a grinning mouthful of teeth as they wait for their next victim to swim by. These nasty customers even have teeth on their tongues. Lizardfishes sometimes wriggle into soft bottoms, partially covering themselves. Confident in their camouflage, they may allow a diver to come surprisingly close before disappearing explosively in a cloud of sand. With their powerful acceleration, some lizardishes are able to strike successfully at prey up to 6 feet away. Out of about 50 species worldwide, 17 are known from Hawai'i. Five are pictured here.

CLEARFIN LIZARDFISH • 'ulae
Synodus dermatogenys Fowler, 1912
This lizardfish lies in sand or rubble, sometimes buried with only the eyes and tip of the snout visible. The series of 8-9 dark blotches along the side usually have pale centers and may even be ringlike. The spaces between the blotches are wider than the blotches themselves. Six tiny black spots mark the tip of the snout. Pelvic and anal fins have no dark markings, hence the common name. This species is very similar to the one below. Differentiate them by noting the width of the blotches relative to the spaces between the blotches. To about 9 in. Photo: Kahe Point, O'ahu. 30 ft.

HAWAIIAN LIZARDFISH • 'ulae
Synodus ulae Schultz, 1953.
These lizardfish have a series of 8-9 blotches along the side that tend to have pale centers and may be shaped somewhat like an hourglass. The blotches are the same width or greater than the spaces between. Like the similar Clearfin Lizardfish (above), these fish inhabit sand and rubble bottoms near rocks or coral. They are often paired. Courtship activities include the male chasing the female and flaring his gill covers or circling her. Sometimes the two fight. Afterwards they rest side by side, or the male may lie across the female. The species name is the Hawaiian word for lizardfish. To about 13 in. Hawai'i and Japan. Photo: Lāna'i Lookout, O'ahu. 20 ft.

TWOSPOT LIZARDFISH • **'ulae**
Synodus binotatus Schultz, 1953.
　　Lizardfishes of the genus *Synodus* have no teeth on the lips. This small species has a pair of black spots on the tip of the snout. (The larger Clearfin Lizardfish has six). Blotchy greenish gray or, in deeper water, reddish, it often displays an almost iridescent or metallic sheen and has a slightly striated appearance. Like many other lizardfishes it may have dark smudgy bars along its back below and behind the dorsal fin. It typically rests on rocks or coral in 30 ft. or less. The species name means "two marks." To 7 in. Indo-Pacific. Photo: "Hale'iwa Trench," O'ahu. 20 ft.

REEF LIZARDFISH • **'ulae**
Synodus variegatus (Lacepāde, 1803)
　　This is the lizardfish seen most often by snorkelers and divers in Hawai'i. It prefers rock or coral substrate rather than sand and is splotched with varying shades of red or sometimes greenish or grayish brown. A dark central stripe along the side passes through a series of dark spots, some of which may extend upward as saddles on the back. The lips are often banded red and white. A study performed (appropriately) at Lizard Island on Australia's Great Barrier Reef shows that on average this fish shifts position every 4 minutes and strikes at prey every 35 minutes. It succeeds only 11% of the time, eating about two fish per day. The species name means "marked with differing colors." To about 9 in. Indo-Pacific. Photo: Hīnaunau, Hawai'i. 30 ft. (on Finger Coral).

ORANGEMOUTH LIZARDFISH • **'ulae**
Saurida flamma Waples, 1982
　　Lizardfishes of the genus *Saurida* have thick lips bearing multiple bands of small teeth (scarcely visible in the field). The bright red-orange lips of this species, often barred with white, are distinctive. Three smudgy dark saddles varying in intensity mark the back and sides, the first just behind the dorsal fin, the last at the base of the tail. These fish typically lie at the edge of the reef in crevices or under ledges at depths greater than 15 ft. The species name means "fire." The distribution is antitropical: Hawai'i, Easter Island, and southern French Polynesia. To about 12 in. Photo: Portlock Point, O'ahu. 20 ft.

Mullets were the early Hawaiians' most important food fishes. They occur in shallow, often brackish, coastal waters and are easily raised in fish ponds. Silvery or gray with long bodies that are round or oval in cross section, mullets have blunt snouts, flattened heads and large scales. Like the barracudas, to which they are related, they have two widely separated dorsal fins; unlike barracudas, they lack teeth of any distinction. Mullets feed primarily off the bottom, taking in sand or mud and filtering out the organic material through their gills.

There are three species of mullets in Hawai'i. The common Striped Mullet appears below and the Sharpnose Mullet or **uouoa** (*Neomyxus leuciscus*) is pictured on page 180. The third species, *Moolgarda engeli*, is a small, commercially worthless introduction which is proliferating at the expense of the valuable Striped Mullet.

Threadfins, bottom feeders related to mullets, are also highly esteemed table fishes. Their name derives from the detached threadlike rays of their pectoral fins.

STRIPED MULLET • **'ama'ama**
Mugil cephalus Linnaeus, 1871.
(GRAY MULLET)

This mullet is silvery with faint stripes along the scale rows and has a very blunt snout. The tail fin is often edged in black. Striped Mullets are common inside the reef at Hanauma Bay, O'ahu. They are also at home in brackish water and are easily raised in fish ponds. The ancient Hawaiians gave different names to each stage of growth: **pua'ama** (finger length), **kahala** (hand length), **'ama'ama** (8-12 inches) and **'anae** (full sized). Because mullet were highly valued in Hawaiian society, ambitious persons were sometimes told "Don't strive for the **'ama'ama** fish." (In other words, be satisfied with what you have.) To about 20 inches. Found in tropical seas around the world. Photo: Hanauma Bay, O'ahu. 5 ft.

THREADFIN • **moi**
Polydactylus sexfilis (Valenciennes, 1831).
(KINGFISH)

Threadfins are named for the threadlike rays, or "whiskers," arising from the base of the pectoral fins. When searching for food they fan their whiskers out, trailing them along the sandy bottom. Threadfins have a bulbous snout (like a cartoon character), an underslung mouth, distinctive swept back fins and a deeply forked tail. They are usually found in sandy areas close to shore. Unlike mullets, **moi** do not swim at the surface. In old Hawai'i large schools of **moi** were said to foretell disaster for chiefs. The Hawaiian word **moi** also signified a variety of taro and a variety of sweet potato. Species name means "six threads." To about 12 in. Indo-Pacific. Photo: Hanauma Bay, O'ahu. 3 ft.

NEEDLEFISHES
(BELONIDAE)

Needlefishes are long, slender, surface dwelling carnivores with pointed, needlelike beaks filled with sharp teeth. They prey on small schooling fishes which they catch sideways and swallow whole. Some needlefishes dwell in the open ocean; others live close to shore. They are strong swimmers and can skim the surface or leap out of the water. Lights attract and excite them at night and on rare occasions they have caused serious injuries to night swimmers. After dark, wherever needlefishes are common, dive lights should be left off until one is well submerged. If impaled by a needlefish, do not attempt to remove beak fragments. Seek medical help.

Needlefishes are related to the flying-fishes or **malolo** (family Exocoetidae) which are frequently seen from boats as they skim over the surface to escape underwater pursuers. They can fly for distances approaching a quarter mile. Columbus was branded a liar when he first described this feat to the royal court of Spain. Also related to needlefishes are the halfbeaks (family Hemiramphidae), whose lower jaw only is elongated. Small halfbeaks often swim with schools of needlefishes. They have slightly deeper bodies and remain closer to the surface.

The tail fins of all these fishes have a lower lobe longer than the upper, a modification helpful in propelling them on the surface. Most are silvery below and bluish on top, a color pattern common among open-ocean (pelagic) fishes that makes them hard to see from both above and below.

Hawai'i has at least four species of needlefishes. Known in Hawaiian as **'aha** ("cord"), they look much alike. Juveniles sometimes resemble small twigs floating on the surface. The Gaping Needlefish *(Ablennes hians)* is a large, schooling, open-ocean species which occasionally comes inshore. It usually has a row of dark, square spots on the sides, especially near the tail. Needlefishes and their relatives belong to the order Cyprinodontiformes.

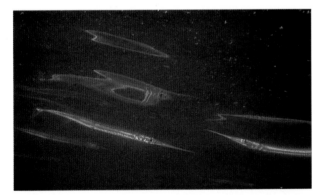

FLAT-TAILED NEEDLEFISH • 'aha
Platybelone argalus (Bennett, 1832).
(KEELED NEEDLEFISH)
    Schools of these are common at many shallow snorkeling areas. Look for them right at the surface. They have a silvery blue stripe along the side, and the base of their tails is flattened. To about 15 in. All tropical seas. Photo: Bruce Mundy, Kahalu'u, Hawai'i. 1 ft.

CROCODILE NEEDLEFISH • 'aha
Tylosurus crocodilus (Peron and LeSueur, 1821)
(HOUNDFISH)
    Large and heavy-set, with stout beaks and deeply forked tails, these powerful fishes grow to more than three feet in length. They swim near the surface along the outer reef but are not usually noticed by divers unless they descend to be serviced by a cleaner wrasse. To 40 in. All tropical seas. Photo: Kahe Point, O'ahu. 10 ft.

Spectacled Parrotfish • **uhu-uliuli** *(Chlorurus perspicillatus).* terminal male. Midway Island. 50 ft.

The heavy-beaked, blue green parrotfishes are aptly named. Like the wrasses, to which they are related, they swim primarily with their pectoral fins and undergo confusing sex and color changes as they mature. Unlike wrasses, parrotfishes are herbivorous. Their teeth are fused into strong, beaklike dental plates which they use to scrape algae from coral limestone or even to bite off chunks of living coral. This scraping and crunching is easily heard underwater. Small wrasses may hover nearby, hoping to catch bits of food dislodged by the giant as it attacks the substrate. Gouge marks on the coral show where parrotfishes have fed. They actually ingest coral rock which they grind into fine sand with special bones in the throat. Organic matter is extracted and the sand expelled in a cloud through the anus. (The Hawaiian name for one species means "loose bowels.") It is said that much of the world's coral sand is produced by these fishes.

Parrotfishes are known for their ability to secrete a thick envelope of mucus around themselves at night. The advantage of this is not clear, and not all parrotfishes do it. Because eels hunt by smell, some biologists believe that this covering protects the sleeping fish from eels during the night. Others suggest that it wards off small crustacean parasites. Parrotfishes are very sound sleepers and often can be gently picked up by divers, photographed, and replaced without waking up.

Parrotfishes are an ichthyologist's nightmare. Anyone who can accurately identify them underwater is a master, for they are fast-moving, shy, and, although extremely variable, often look alike. Color patterns can differ within a species, depending on sex and age, and some species can modify their pattern in seconds. Researchers are still sorting out the names sometimes assigned to male, female and juvenile forms of the same fish. The Bullethead Parrotfish, for example, has had 13 different names in addition to the currently accepted *Chlorurus sordidus.* According to the International Code of Scientific Nomenclature only the earliest published name is valid. It sometimes takes considerable sleuthing in libraries and museums all over the world to determine who first named a species, and when.

In the Hawaiian Islands parrotfishes are known collectively as **uhu**. In old Hawai'i it was said that the behavior of the **uhu** could tell a fisherman what his wife was doing at home. Hawaiian scholar Mary Pukui Kawena writes, "If the **uhu** capered and frolicked in the water it was a sure sign of too much levity.... If two **uhu** seemed to be rubbing noses, it was a sure sign that there was flirting going on at home." A wily person, hard to catch, was called "a slippery **uhu**."

Seven species of parrotfishes, including three endemics, inhabit Hawaiian reefs. Although brightly colored, they are seldom maintained in captivity because of their size and unusual feeding habits.

In the descriptions below references are made to initial and terminal phase fishes. In the initial phase most parrotfish species are drab. Mature initial phase males and females (identical in appearance) sometimes spawn together in large groups, "capering and frolicking." Terminal phase parrotfishes are always male and usually brightly colored. They hold territories and mate with individual females. These "supermales" are always sex-reversed females.

terminal phase ∧   initial phase ∨

STAR-EYE PARROTFISH • uhu
Calotomus carolinus (Valenciennes, 1840).
Magenta lines radiating from the eyes of terminal males provide easy identification. Their bodies are grayish green to dark green, often with a broad pale patch on the side or irregular pale spots along the back. Initial phase adults lack distinct markings. They are gray brown, speckled with lighter marks, especially on the back. In parrotfishes of the genus *Calotomus* the beaks are composed of many separate teeth fused together; in others the beaks are smooth. To 20 in. East Africa to the Galapagos. Photos: Hanauma Bay, O'ahu. 20 ft.

93

YELLOWBAR PARROTFISH • **uhu** ●
Calotomus zonarchus, (Jenkins, 1903).
Terminal males are gray brown with a bright yellow vertical bar on the side, usually containing scattered white spots. The size and shape of this bar varies among individuals. Initial phase adults have scattered white scales in a faint central bar but otherwise look much like initial phase Star-Eye Parrotfishes. Uncommon except in the Northwestern Hawaiian Islands. Species name from *zona* ("belt" or "girdle"). To about 1 ft. Endemic. Photo: terminal ph. Lana'i Lookout, O'ahu. 40 ft.

Regal Parrotfish - terminal ∧   initial ∨

REGAL PARROTFISH • **lauia** ●
Scarus dubius Bennett, 1828.
Terminal males have a crescent-shape tail fin with a prominent bright green band at the end. Their bodies, covered with orange and blue scales, appear grayish or brownish underwater, sometimes with a paler central section. They often swim with their fins extended. Initial adults are reddish, usually with several lighter bars and sometimes a bright green band at the end of the tail. There are several white longitudinal stripes on the belly. More common in Northwestern Hawaiian Islands than around the main islands. The species name means "doubtful" or "wavering." To about 14in. Endemic. Photos: terminal ph. Puakō, Hawai'i. 30 ft. initial ph. Hōnaunau, Hawai'i 40 ft.

SPECTACLED PARROTFISH • **uhu 'ahu'ula** (initial ph.); **uhu-uliuli** (terminal ph.)
Chlorurus perspicillatus Steindachner, 1879. ●
   Terminal males have a blue green body with a conspicuous dark band across the top of the snout (the spectacles). There is a bright yellow mark at the base of the pectoral fin. Initial adults are grâyish brown with a broad white band at the base of the tail (including part of the fin). The fins are red and they can rapidly display a series of pale blotches along the back. Body and fins sometimes become uniform gray. Hawaiian names: female: "feather cape"; male: "dark." Species name means "spectacled." To 24 in. Endemic. Photos: Hanauma Bay, O'ahu. 20-30 ft.

BULLETHEAD PARROTFISH • **uhu** • *Chlorurus sordidus* (Forsskål, 1775).
   A bullet-shape head profile (symmetrical above and below the beak) marks this species. Terminal males are greenish overall, often with cheeks or sides washed with yellow orange. Some are entirely green with pink edges on each scale. Initial adults are grayish in front, shading to dark brown, almost black, often with a broad white bar at the base of the tail, which may contain a large dark spot in the center. There is often a double row of three or more white spots on the side and red around the mouth. The species name (describing the initial phase) means "dirty." To about 15 in. Indo-Pacific. Photos: Hanauma Bay O'ahu. 30 ft.

PALENOSE PARROTFISH • uhu
Scarus psittacus Forsskål, 1775.

Among the most variable of Hawaiian parrotfishes in appearance, terminal males have a green body with lavender tints, sometimes with a large yellow area on the side. Often they have a dark blue black "cap" on the head or a large yellow spot at the base of the tail. Initial adults have no distinguishing marks, being plain gray to brownish, with a few lighter spots. The pelvic fins are often red. Terminal males swim high in the water while patrolling their territories. Initial adults school close to the bottom. Despite the popular name, the snout is not much paler than the rest of the fish. Species name means "parrot." To almost 1 ft. Indo-Pacific. Photos: Hanauma Bay, O'ahu. 10-15 ft.

REDLIP PARROTFISH • uhu pālukaluka (initial ph.); **uhu 'ele'ele** (terminal ph.)
Scarus rubroviolaceus Bleeker, 1849.

The squarish humped snout of this species is unique among Hawaiian parrotfishes. Both initial and terminal phases usually display a distinct bicolor pattern, front half dark, back half light. Terminal males are green (darker in front, lighter in back) and the hump is more pronounced. Their beaks are green. Initial adults are brownish red in front, yellowish grey in back, with numerous short black lines at odd angles on the sides, creating a textured appearance. They may become entirely pale. Their beaks are reddish to white. Hawaiian name: female: "loose bowels"; male: "dark." Species name: "reddish-violet." To 28 in. East Africa to the Americas. Photos: Hanauma Bay, O'ahu. 20 ft.

Redstripe Pipefish *(Doryrhamphus baldwini)*. Photo: Marjorie L. Awai. Waīkīki Aquarium

Most people are familiar with seahorses. Their cousins, the pipefishes, though less well-known, are more numerous in Hawai'i and more often seen. Both have tubular snouts, small toothless mouths, and fairly rigid, armored bodies segmented into rings.

Pipefishes have thin heads and snouts which are directly in line with their long, slender bodies. Seahorses have horselike heads roughly at right angles to the body. They are stockier than pipefishes and have a prehensile tail. Both are weak swimmers. Seahorses use their tails to anchor themselves to plants or other suitable objects while many pipefishes simply rest on the bottom. Other pipefishes swim freely but remain in small protected areas such as under ledges. A few species have been observed "cleaning" other fishes of parasites. Both seahorses and pipefishes feed on tiny crustaceans with their elongated tubular mouths and in aquariums must be provided with suitable live food. Slow feeders, they are best kept alone. Their independently moveable eyes probably assist them in locating their tiny prey.

Because the males regularly get "pregnant," pipefishes and seahorses have been called the answer to a woman's dream. The female places her eggs in a special pouch on the male, then leaves. The male incubates them until they hatch (about 10-50 days). During this time his abdomen is noticeably distended. The young are expelled as free-swimming miniature adults. Newly hatched seahorses immediately rise to the surface for a tiny gulp of air, which helps them stay upright. For this reason, brooding males are usually found in very shallow water. If subjected to the stress of capture, a "pregnant" male will often give birth prematurely.

Pipefishes and seahorses belong to the order Syngnathiformes which includes other tube-mouthed fishes such as Cornetfishes and Trumpetfishes. Forming a large family with several hundred species worldwide, they are small, cryptic or well camouflaged and most are rarely seen. It is possible, for example, to look directly at a foot-long seahorse a few inches away and mistake it for a weedy appendage of the reef. Two seahorses and at least six pipefishes are known from Hawaii; three of the pipefishes are endemic.

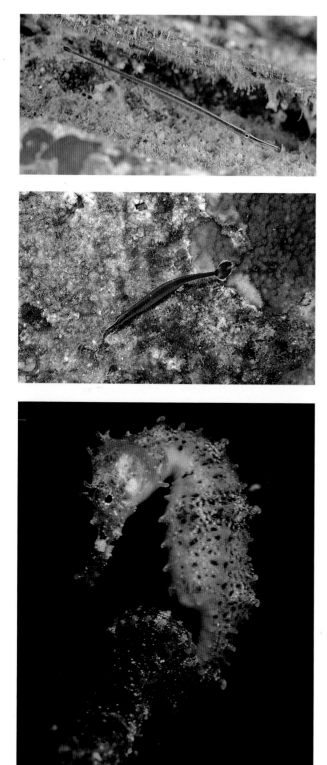

REDSTRIPE PIPEFISH ●
Doryrhamphus baldwini (Herald & Randall, 1972).

Occurring in caves and under ledges at depths of 20 feet or more, these long slender pipefish have a red stripe along the side and an orange-red tail with white edges. They often occur in small groups of mixed adults and juveniles and have been observed cleaning other fishes. (On at least one occasion, a pipefish has attempted to clean a diver's hand.) With pipefishes, as with seahorses, it is the male that carries and incubates the eggs (carried not in a pouch but directly on the male's underside, where they can easily be seen by divers). To about 5 in. Endemic. Photo: David B. Fleetham. Molokini Island, Maui. 80 ft.

BLUESTRIPE PIPEFISH
Doryrhamphus excisus Kaup, 1856.

These tiny, free-swimming pipefishes have a fanlike tail with orange marks and a dark bluish stripe down the body. Almost always in pairs, they remain under ledges where they sometimes clean other fishes. Not uncommon, they are rarely noticed. Aquarium specimens must be carefully fed with live baby brine shrimp and other tiny organisms. To about 2.5 in. East Africa to the Americas. Photo: Pūpūkea, O'ahu. 20 ft.

FISHER'S SEAHORSE
Hippocampus fisheri Jordan & Evermann, 1903.

Seahorses are rare in Hawai'i. Fisher's Seahorse has small sharp spines and may be golden orange, red, pink or yellowish with blackfish mottling. Apparently pelagic, it probably attaches to floating seaweed or other objects and is little known. Seahorses found washed ashore after storms are probably this species. Those occasionally collected in the shallows of Kāne'ohe Bay, O'ahu, may be as well, or could be a variant of the Yellow or Spotted Seahorse (*H. kuda*), a common Indo-Pacific species also recorded from Hawai'i. (*H. kuda* is a "smooth" seahorse without pointed spines that attains about 12 inches.) Captive seahorses initially require live food such as amphipods or baby guppies but can be trained to accept match-head size pieces of frozen supermarket shrimp right from the aquarist's fingers. Live brine are unsuitable as a staple food. Seahorses also need something around which to wrap their tails. Fisher's Seahorse is known with certainty only from Hawai'i but may also occur in New Caledonia and at Lord Howe Island. It attains about 3 in. Photo: Mike Severns, surface trawl, O'ahu. (identification tentative)

Porcupinefish • **kōkala** (Diodon hystrix). Photo: D. R. Schrichte. Hanauma Bay, O'ahu.

When it comes to unusual defensive strategies, few fishes outdo the pufferfishes and porcupinefishes. Although belonging to different families, their techniques are similar. Puffers have bristly skins while porcupinefishes are completely covered with sharp spines. Both, when alarmed, distend themselves with water into prickly balloons to discourage attack and to make themselves difficult, or impossible, to swallow. If removed from the sea, they inflate with air, to the accompaniment of little croaking noises.

Inflating into a spiny or bristly ball is not their only defense; these fishes are also poisonous. The little tobies, or sharpnose puffers, of the genus *Canthigaster*, with limited powers of inflation, secrete a substance from their skin making them immediately unpalatable to predators. But more importantly, most of these fishes accumulate in their internal organs and in other parts of their bodies a poison called tetrodotoxin, one of the most interesting and powerful neurotoxins known. Tetrodotoxin may or may not be dangerous to other fishes, but it is deadly to humans. It causes tingling, numbness and eventual paralysis. Sometimes a curious state of "living death" ensues wherein the victim retains consciousness while unable to move, or even breathe. True death may occur within 24 hours. In spite of this, or perhaps because of it, pufferfishes are delicacies in Japan, where specially licensed *fugu* chefs prepare them safely for the table. The flesh is said to be firm, white and sweet; the small amount of poison left produces a highly prized warmth or "glow."

Like the closely related boxfishes, puffers have chunky, short bodies that lack both scales and pelvic fins. They are comparatively weak swimmers which nevertheless roam freely over the reef and do not appear to have territories. They range in size from the small colorful tobies, which rarely exceed four inches, to large porcupinefishes attaining almost a yard. Equipped with sharp beaks and powerful jaws, they are capable of eating almost anything that doesn't swim away. They are also capable of delivering a painful bite if inexpertly handled. Some puffers are reported to feed by squirting a jet of water at the sandy bottom to uncover buried organisms.

In a sufficiently roomy aquarium, the larger puffers make greedy and amusing pets. At feeding

99

time they often swim in anxious circles at the surface with their snouts out of the water. Better suited to the home aquarium are the cute, colorful little tobies. Although they are shy and can take a week or more to begin feeding, most are subsequently easy to keep. They have two drawbacks: they will attack invertebrates, and some species will nip the fins of other fishes. Needless to say, the good aquarist docs not inflate his puffers to amuse guests. If they accidentally swallow air they may not be able to get rid of it, and will float helpless at the surface.

Both puffers and porcupinefishes belong to the order Tetraodontiformes, which also includes boxfishes and triggerfishes. The Hawaiian names for these fishes are the subject of question. The popular word **makimaki**, a corruption of **make** ("death"), was probably not used in ancient Hawaii. The fishes called **'o'opu-hue** ("stomach like a gourd"), or **kēkē** ("potbelly") were probably puffers. Most of the small tobies, which make up the majority of Hawaii's puffers, have no known Hawaiian names. All told, twelve puffers and three porcupinefishes inhabit our waters. Nine are described below. Among those omitted is the Pelagic Puffer *(Lagocephalus lagocephalus)*, a large open-ocean species that sometimes dies by the thousands, washing up on island beaches.

STRIPEBELLY PUFFER • 'o'opu-hue
Arothron hispidus (Linnaeus, 1758).

Sometimes called the "Stars and Stripes Puffer," this species has white spots on its back and sides and stripes on its belly. The body is light brown. At the base of the pectoral fin is a prominent black area surrounded by white rings. It is the largest Hawaiian puffer, but small aquarium-size specimens may sometimes be caught in the ponds at Ala Moana Beach Park, Honolulu. Species name means "bristly" or "rough." To about 19 in. Indo-Pacific. Photo: Kahe Point, O'ahu. 30 ft.

SPOTTED PUFFER • 'o'opu-hue
Arothron meleagris (Lacepède, 1798).
(GUINEAFOWL PUFFER; VELCRO FISH)

This chunky puffer, usually dark brown or black, is covered with numerous small white spots. Two other color phases occur but are rarely seen: all yellow with a few dark spots, and partly yellow, partly brown, with dark or white spots. It is found near coral, upon which it feeds. The bristly skin feels like velcro, especially when the fish is inflated. Species name means "guineafowl," an African bird covered with white spots. To about 13 in. Indo-Pacific. Photo: Hanauma Bay, O'ahu. 30 ft.

AMBON TOBY
Canthigaster amboinensis (Bleeker, 1865).

In bright light this dark toby displays iridescent blue-green lines and spots. Pairs are frequently encountered in boulder habitat close to shore but may also be seen in the coral environment. They are fast swimmers for tobies, and difficult to approach. Hardy in captivity, but incompatible with small invertebrates. Named for the Indonesian island of Ambon. To about 5 in. Indo-Pacific. Photo: Kahe Point, O'ahu. 15 ft.

CROWNED TOBY • pu'u olai
Canthigaster coronata (Vaillant & Sauvage), 1875.

The three dark saddles on the back of these tobies may have reminded the old Hawaiians of lava flows, for the Hawaiian name means "cinder cone." Their bodies are white with yellow dots; blue and yellow lines radiate from the eyes. Preferring depths of 20 feet or more, they are unlikely to be seen by snorkelers. Usually in pairs. Difficult to feed in captivity. Species name means "crowned." To about 5 in. Indo-Pacific. Photo: Magic Island, O'ahu. 30 ft.

LANTERN TOBY
Canthigaster epilampra (Jenkins, 1903).

Iridescent blue green lines radiate from the eyes and across the top of the head of this beautiful little toby. It is most easily identified at a distance by a large dark mark at the base of the dorsal fin. Common at depths of 80 feet or more, it is occasionally seen in as little as 20 feet. Species name means "shining." No aquarium data available. To about 4 in. Western Pacific. Photo: Pūpūkea, O'ahu. 65 ft.

HAWAIIAN WHITESPOTTED TOBY ●
Canthigaster jactator (Jenkins, 1901).
Covered with white spots and often displaying a slight green fluorescence, these are by far the commonest Hawaiian tobies. They usually occur in pairs. Occasional individuals have irregular black marks on the snout and body. In the aquarium these cute but mischievous puffers will stealthily approach other fishes and nip their fins, leaving perfect semicircular "cookie-bites" along the edges. Although they seem shy by nature, their species name means "boaster," or "braggart." To 3.5 in. Endemic. As with most Hawaiian endemics, close relatives similar in appearance occur elsewhere in the Pacific. Photo: Magic Island, O'ahu. 20 ft.

MAZE TOBY
Canthigaster rivulata (Schlegel, 1850).
This large, uncommon toby prefers deeper water. Its head and back are covered with a maze of blue lines. A dark band runs from above the pectoral fin to the tail, with a fainter one below. There is a black mark under the dorsal fin. Small individuals are reported abundant in shallow water during some years. No aquarium data available. Species name from *rivulus* ("stream"). To almost 8 in. Indo-Pacific. Photo: Hanauma Bay, O'ahu, 40 ft.

GIANT PORCUPINEFISH • kōkala
Diodon hystrix Linnaeus, 1758.
   This is the largest of the porcupinefishes. Its big head makes the flabby, tapering body seem emaciated in comparison. Spines lie flat along the entire body, which is grayish or tan covered with small black dots. Although these fishes typically rest alone under a ledge during the day, loose aggregations regularly hover in midwater at certain locations, such as over the wreck of the Mahi off leeward O'ahu. They are primarily nocturnal, as evidenced by the large eyes and tendency to rest by day. The Hawaiian name means "spiny" while the scientific species name means "porcupine." To 28 in. All tropical seas. Photo: Mākua, O'ahu. 30 ft. (The rare Spotted Burrfish, *Chilomycterus reticulatus*, is similar but has fewer, shorter spines which are permanently erected.)

LONGSPINE PORCUPINEFISH • kōkala
Diodon holocanthus Linnaeus, 1758.
(SPINY BALLOONFISH)
   Frequently resting under ledges by day, these are light tan marked with several large dark blotches and bars on back and sides. The dark makers may be indistinct, but very long spines on top of the head (usually lying flat) help distinguish this fish from the Giant Porcupinefish (above). The large eyes and proclivity to rest quietly by day indicate they are probably most active after dark. Both the Hawaiian and species names mean "spiny." To about 15 in. Found in all tropical seas. Photo: Magic Island, O'ahu. 25 ft.

Spotted Eagle Rays • **hailepo** *(Aetobatus narinari), Mahi* wreck, leeward, O'ahu. 80 ft.

Cousins to the sharks, but totally unlike them in appearance, rays have flattened bodies, great winglike pectoral fins, and often a long thin tail. Like sharks, their skeletons are cartilage, they have gill slits instead of gill covers, and the mouth is usually on the underside. Except for the large plankton-eating manta and devil rays, these animals are carnivores which feed off the bottom. When not foraging for food most species remain motionless on the sea floor, sometimes covering themselves with sand. They swim by rippling their large pectoral fins. The more active eagle, manta, and devil rays, however, use their pectoral fins like wings, "flying" gracefully high in the water and sometimes leaping into the air.

Eagle rays (family Myliobatidae) are the most commonly-seen rays on Hawaiian reefs. They have a distinct head, triangular "wings" and a long, slender tail that often greatly exceeds the length of the body. Of about 24 species, one is in our area.

Manta and devil rays (family Mobulidae) are among the largest of fishes. Mantas attain up to 3100 pounds with a "wingspan" of 23 feet. Devil rays (not ordinarily found in Hawai`i) are similar but not quite as large. The most distinctive characteristic of these harmless plankton eaters, apart from sheer size, is the strange pair of flaps which funnel water into the mouth. They are often hosts to remoras, or suckerfishes, which attach themselves by means of a sucking disk on the top of the head, thereby obtaining a free ride. Seeing a manta is a sought-after experience. Although stories are told of divers stroking or even riding them, Hawaiian mantas are generally shy of humans and easily frightened. There is probably but one species of manta worldwide, but no one is completely sure. Giant rays do not fit easily into museum jars, making comparative studies difficult.

The stingrays (family Dasyatidae) are bottom-dwellers. They bear one or more venomous spines on their tails and can deliver a serious wound if stepped upon. Immersing the limb in hot water rapidly alleviates the intense pain and is the best first-aid treatment. (Most eagle rays also have venomous spines, but a swimmer or diver is unlikely to get close enough to get wounded.) Three species of stingrays inhabit Hawaiian waters. Although uncommon at snorkeling and diving sites in Hawai'i, they are often displayed in Island aquariums.

The Hawaiian language has two general names for rays: **lupe**, which also means "kite", and **hīhīmanu**, "magnificent."

MANTA RAY • hāhālua
Manta birostris Walbaum, 1792.

These graceful giants are black on the back, occasionally with white shoulder patches, and have a white underside with scattered dark spots. As plankton eaters, they are considered harmless, although their enormous size and strength command respect. Any place where mantas appear regularly becomes a mecca for divers. Several such spots occur along the Kona coast of the Big Island, where "Manta Ray night dives" are available. (The rays feed on plankton attracted to lights.) A good place to see mantas by day is Molokini Island, Maui, where they regularly glide in to cleaner wrasse stations in the late afternoon. They occasionally visit many other dive sites as well. *Manta* means "mantle" or "cloak." The species name ("two snouts") and the Hawaiian name ("two mouths") probably refer to the two flaps extended while feeding. The largest manta recorded was 23 ft. from wingtip to wingtip. Most Hawaiian mantas are half that size or less. Photo: Hanauma Bay. 10 ft.

STINGRAY • lupe; hīhīmanu
Dasyatis sp.

Two stingrays occur in Hawaii's coastal waters, the Diamond Stingray *(Dasyatis dipterura)* and the Broad or Brown Stingray *(Dasyatis lata.)* It is difficult to tell which species is pictured here. In each the tail bears a venomous spine near the base. *Dasyatis dipterura* has two folds of skin running much of the tail's length, one above and one below, while *D. lata* has a single fold on the tail's underside. Both animals live on sandy or silty bottoms. Neither is encountered with any frequency except in rarely-dived locations such as Kāne'ohe Bay, O'ahu, and Ma'alea Bay, Maui. Sightings are most likely in the late afternoon when these animals become active, digging for worms, crustaceans and possibly sand-dwelling fishes, leaving large craters in the sand. Photo: D.R. Schrichte. Hanauma Bay, O'ahu. 50 ft. The ray was about 4 ft. wide.

105

SPOTTED EAGLE RAY • **hailepo**
Aetobatus narinari (Euphrasen, 1790).

Light brown with white spots and long thin tails, Spotted Eagle Rays can often be seen from shore as they forage for shellfish in the shallow protected waters of Kāne'ohe Bay or Pu'uloa (Pearl Harbor). Divers are more likely to encounter them patrolling the reef well off the bottom, sometimes in groups. One of the most beautiful of all underwater sights is a formation of eagle rays "flying" together in synchrony. Several Spotted Eagle Rays can almost always be seen at the wreck of the *Mahi*, off O'ahu's west shore. In ancient Hawai'i this species was forbidden to women as food. To over six feet in width. All tropical seas. Photo: Kahe Pt. O'ahu. 20 ft.

SANDPERCHES
(PINGUIPEDIDAE)

Sandperches, like hawkfishes, are ambush hunters which wait for prey perched on their pectoral fins. Whereas hawkfishes prefer rocky or coral environments, the more elongated sandperches are adapted to sand or rubble bottoms. They live in colonies composed of a male and numerous females. Recent research on a Red Sea species reveals that the male regularly visits each of his females every evening. There is only one species in Hawai'i. No Hawaiian name is recorded. They are also known as grubfishes.

REDSPOTTED SANDPERCH
Parapercis schauinslandi (Steindachner, 1900).

These slender, attractive fishes are marked with several rows of dull red spots. The front of the dorsal fin is red with a black spot. They are found on rubble bottoms at depths of 60 feet or more, although common at 30 feet near the hot water vents at Kahe Point Beach Park, O'ahu. Colorful and small, they make alert, attractive pets. A colony would make a fascinating aquarium display as long as no small invertebrates or fishes were kept with them. Named after the German naturalist Hugo Schauinsland (1857-1937) for whom the Hawaiian Monk Seal is also named. To about 5 in. Indo-Pacific. Photo: Marjorie L. Awai. Mākaha, O'ahu. 60 ft.

Titan Scorpionfish • **nohu** *(Scorpaenopsis cacopsis)* Hanauma Bay, O'ahu. 30 ft.

Scorpionfishes are slow-moving or sedentary carnivores, many with venomous spines that can deliver a painful sting. Some, like the dreaded stonefishes, are masters of camouflage almost impossible to detect; others, such as the lionfishes, have conspicuous colors and enlarged fins that enhance visibility.

Most scorpionfishes fall into the hard-to-detect category. They rely on dull, mottled coloration and rough looking spiny, warty or tasseled exteriors to escape notice. If threatened they bring into play the venomous spines on the dorsal, anal and pelvic fins. In some scorpionfishes the spines are connected to a sac of venom at their base. Once a spine enters the victim's flesh, pressure on it causes the venom to flow up through two grooves and into the wound — a self-administered injection. In others the poison glands lie beneath a sheath of skin covering the spines. Punctures can be extremely painful, causing nausea, cramps and, in the case of stonefishes (not found in Hawai'i), prolonged suffering and possibly death. Heat destroys the protein venom; if stung, the best treatment is immediate immersion of the affected area in hot (but not scalding) water for 30 to 90 minutes. Bleeding should be encouraged and the victim taken for medical care.

Stepping on or touching a highly camouflaged scorpionfish is a distinct possibility while exploring the reef. Devil Scropionfishes can look like knobs of rock or coral, perfect to hold on to. Lionfishes lurk upside down on the roofs of caves and ledges where careless divers may brush up against them.

The ornate lionfishes have caught people's fancy and are known by a number of other names, including turkeyfishes, fireworks-fishes, fire-fishes, zebra-fishes and butterfly-cod. The Hawaiians named them **nohu pinao**, after the dragonfly. When a lionfish glides slowly over the reef, its magnificent fins extended, the effect is majestic. These fanlike fins have a very practical purpose: they help corner small fishes or crustaceans. They can also be used to brush the bottom, stirring up the creatures that live there. Despite the obvious risk, lionfishes are popular aquarium pets. They will fearlessly swim up to the glass to observe their keepers and rise on cue to be hand-fed.

Captive lionfishes are attracted initially only to live food such as guppies, small tidepool fishes or crustaceans. It is easy to wean them over to chunks of shrimp or fish. Start by feeding live guppies. When these are accepted readily, skip a feeding or two until your fish is very hungry, then substitute a frozen guppy (thawed). With any luck, your greedy pet will snatch it too fast to notice it wasn't alive. After it has accepted several frozen guppies you can confidently begin feeding chunks of shrimp or fish to your now tame lionfish.

The family Scorpaenidae (one of about 20 families in the order Scorpaeniformes) includes about 350 species worldwide. Twenty-five occur in Hawai'i; six are pictured here. Sharp-eyed divers might also see the endemic Spotfin Scorpionfish (*Sebastapistes ballieui*) or the Decoy Scorpionfish (*Iracundus signifer*) illustrated on page 182. The dorsal fin of the latter, with markings that resemble a fish, is used as lure. The peculiar Flying Gurnard from the related family, Dactylopteridae, is also included in this chapter. The general name for scorpionfishes in Hawaiian is **nohu**, the same name used in the South Pacific for the deadly stonefish. In olden times it was believed that the eggs of some **nohu** hatched into sharks.

Popular names in this family can be confusing. Ordinary scorpionfishes are sometimes called stonefishes, but true stonefishes (genus *Synanceia*) do not occur in Hawai'i. The long-spined fishes of the genera *Dendrochirus* and *Pterois* (pronounced "terr-oh-iss") are popularly called "lionfishes," although some authorities prefer "turkeyfish" for the latter genus. We have followed the popular usage here.

GREEN LIONFISH • **nohu** ●
Dendrochirus barberi (Steindachner, 1900).

This greenish brown species is dull in comparison to its better-known cousin the Hawaiian Lionfish (Turkeyfish), and more difficult to spot underwater. Its pectoral fins, although large and fan-like, lack long showy spines. Well camouflaged, it often sits in the open along the sides or bases of coral heads. It is hardier than the Hawaiian Lionfish in captivity and makes an engaging pet, becoming very tame and accepting food from its keeper's fingers. Be careful of the spines. Named for Captain Barber, who gave a specimen to his scientist passenger, Steindachner, around the turn of the century. Some authorities prefer the name Hawaiian Lionfish for this species and use Hawaiian Turkeyfish for the following species. To 6.5 in. Endemic. Photo: Mākua, O'ahu. 30 ft.

HAWAIIAN LIONFISH • **nohu pinao** ●
Pterois sphex Jordan & Evermann, 1903.

Also called the Hawaiian Turkeyfish, this fantastic creature is striped red and white with long dorsal spines and enormously extended white spines on the pectoral fins. Although similar in appearance to other Indo-Pacific lionfishes, the species is unique to Hawai'i. During the day these fishes remain in caves and under ledges, usually on the ceiling. At night they glide forth, with fins extended, hunting for small crabs or shrimps. Lucky daytime divers may see them swimming openly in the late afternoon or early morning. The spines are venomous; these fishes should not be played with or handled. (An aquarist stung on the hand by a similar species, *P. volitans*, described the sensation as similar to having his fingers slammed repeatedly with a hammer.) Not common, they are seen most often along the Kona Coast of the Big Island. Some dive sites have been stripped of these fishes by over-eager collectors — another good reason to strengthen our system of marine parks in Hawai'i. The Hawaiian name means "dragonfly," the species name "wasp." To about 8 in. Endemic. Photos: Magic Island, O'ahu. 25 ft.

TITAN SCORPIONFISH • **nohu** ●
Scorpaenopsis cacopsis Jenkins, 1901.
(Uglyface Scorpionfish)

This scorpionfish, mottled and reddish, lies motionless on rocks or sand and is easy to overlook. The lower jaw is fringed with orange red flaps or tassels. The body and fins are covered with short appendages which look like algae or other growths. The largest of the Hawaiian scorpionfishes, it is easy to spear and thus no longer common. Its size, its color, the flaps under its chin, and its lack of a hump differentiate it from the common Devil Scorpionfish. Species name from *kakos* ("bad"). To about 20 in. Endemic. Photos: Hanauma Bay, O'ahu. 30 ft.

DEVIL SCORPIONFISH * **nohu 'omakaha**
Scorpaenopsis diabolus Cuvier, 1829.

The Devil Scorpionfish has a hump on its back and pectoral fins that are bright yellow and orange underneath. When disturbed, it moves a few feet, flashing its bright colors. Predators stung while attacking a Devil Scorpionfish will remember the yellow and not repeat the mistake. The body color of these highly camouflaged fishes varies to match the surroundings. The skin may harbor algae or other growths. The Hawaiian name means "streaked," and the species name means "devil." To 12 in. Indo-Pacific. Photos: Magic Island, O'ahu; Pūpūkea, O'ahu. 25-30 ft.

SPECKLED SCORPIONFISH ●
Sebastapistes coniorta Jenkins, 1903.

Look into heads of antler coral and you may see one or more of these small scorpionfishes wedged deep within the branches. Their light bodies are covered with small dark spots. They leave their refuge at night to hunt. Species name means "cloud of dust." To almost 4 in. Endemic. (Another small fish, the Coral Croucher or Velvetfish, *Caracanthus maculatus,* also hides deep in branching coral. Its highly compressed body is gray speckled with red spots.) Photo: Magic Island, O'ahu. 25 ft.

LEAF SCORPIONFISH
Taenianotus triacanthus Lacepède, 1802.

These unusual laterally flattened scorpionfishes perch on the bottom, sometimes waving slightly to and fro like seaweed. They vary from grayish white to yellow, red, brown or black and appear to harbor algae or other growths in their skin. When too "fuzzy," they molt, emerging sharp and clean (sometimes in a new color). Leaf Scorpionfishes frequently occur in pairs, usually near ledges or other shelter. In captivity, most specimens will accept only live foods. Species name means "three spines." To 4 in. Indo-Pacific. Photo: Marjorie L. Awai. Mākaha, O'ahu.

FLYING GURNARD • **loloa'u; pinao**
Dactyloptena orientalis (Cuvier, 1829)
(HELMET GURNARD)

Flying Gurnards do not fly; they crawl along sandy bottoms using the specially modified fingerlike spines of their pelvic fins. When alarmed they spread their "wings" (an enormous pair of pectoral fins) thus blending with the bottom and greatly increasing their apparent size. Ordinarily, the "wings" are kept folded along the side of the armored, boxlike body. Flying Gurnards are occasionally encountered in sandy channels in the reef environment; the lagoon at Honolulu's Magic Island is home to several. Photo: Bob Owens. "Fingers Reef" Waīkīkī, O'ahu. 25 ft.

SHARKS

Sharks, along with the rays, skates, chimaeras and ratfishes, belong to an evolutionary branch of fishes having skeletons of cartilage instead of bone. They perfected their form 60 million years ago, and have changed little since. Instead of the gill covers typical of modern bony fishes they have 5-7 gill slits on each side. Their tough skins lack scales; shark skin is so rough to the touch that it has sometimes been used as sandpaper. This roughness is caused by embedded dermal denticles much like small teeth. Sharks' teeth, in fact, are special dermal denticles enlarged and modified.

Most sharks are active fishes; heavier than water, they will sink if they stop swimming. Some open-ocean species must swim continuously to pass water over their gills, suffocating if they do not. Sharks propel themselves with powerful sweeps of their tails; as they move their stiff pectoral fins add lift, acting somewhat like airplane wings. The pectorals are also used for steering and braking. Sharks lack swim bladders, gaining buoyancy instead from their enormous oily livers. This is an advantage, allowing them to rise or descend in the water column more rapidly than most other fishes.

Sharks' senses are keen. They can home in on the source of a smell, such as blood, from as far as a quarter mile and can "hear" the low frequency vibrations of a wounded and thrashing animal from a mile away. These are detected by a system of special organs corresponding to the lateral line system of bony fishes. At closer range sharks can sense the weak electrical fields emitted by all living organisms.

GRAY REEF SHARK • **manō**
Carcharhinus amblyrhynchos (Bleeker, 1856).

Like many sharks, these are grayish brown on the back and sides, and lighter below. A conspicuous black margin on the trailing edge of the tail fin helps distinguish them from Galapagos Sharks. Although Gray Reef Sharks generally ignore divers, they are territorial and can be aggressive toward perceived intruders. In advance of an attack they usually perform a threat display by humping the back, raising the head, dropping the pectoral fins, and swimming with exaggerated motions. Divers who see a Gray Reef Shark acting strangely should pause and slowly withdraw. Although common around most Indo-Pacific islands, these sharks are sparsely distributed in Hawai'i except in the uninhabited northwestern chain. In the main islands they are most likely to be seen around offshore islets such as Molokini (Maui), Moku Ho'oniki (Moloka'i), Lehua Rock (Ni'ihau), and a few select spots off the Kona coast of the Big Island. Gray Reef Sharks feed on mostly on fishes, but cephalopods are also taken and occasionally crustaceans. To almost 8 ft. Indo-Pacific. Photo: Five Fathom Rock (south of Ni'hau).

GALAPAGOS SHARK • **manō**
Carcharhinus galapagensis (Snodgrass & Heller, 1905)
   Any shark approaching a diver in Hawai'i is likely to be a Galapagos. Bold and inquisitive, these sharks are potentially dangerous, especially to anyone carrying speared fishes. Although similar to Gray Reef Sharks in appearance, they lack the conspicuous black margin on the back edge of the tail fin (although the edge may be dusky). Also, the dorsal fin has an unusually straight trailing edge which forms a right angle with the body. These are probably the most abundant sharks in the northwestern chain; around the main islands they are seldom seen. They eat mostly bottom fishes. A threat display similar to the Gray Reef Shark has been reported. They attain almost 12ft. but most in Hawai'i seem to be half that size. Worldwide in warm seas. Photo: Keoki Stender, Midway Atoll.

   In matters of reproduction sharks and rays are surprisingly advanced. Male sharks use modified parts of their pelvic fins, called claspers, to internally fertilize the female, and in many species the young develop inside the mother's body and are born alive. (Sometimes, true to nature, the largest of the young will eat its smaller siblings while still in the "womb.") Other species lay leathery egg capsules, usually on the sea bottom. In either case, infant sharks are fully formed and do not pass through a larval stage as most bony fishes do.

   With the exception of a few large plankton eaters, such as whale sharks, all are carnivores. While smaller species may subsist on molluscs, shellfish or other less exciting fare, in the main these are swift, sleek, streamlined creatures superbly suited to a predatory life. Few animals, and certainly no other fishes, have so captured the human imagination or excited such admiration and dread.

   Sharks are known as **manō** in Hawaiian. In old days, and even into the present, individual sharks were believed to physically embody the spirits of certain family ancestors. The haunts of these sharks were known, and they were given regular offerings of food. In return, the sharks were said to protect their worshipers. The story is often told of the Pearl Harbor drydock, which, despite warnings from native Hawaiians, was constructed in 1913 over the known home of a sacred shark. When almost complete, the entire structure collapsed. A **kahuna** was brought in to bless the site, and a new dry-dock (this time a floating one) was completed without further trouble. When it was finished the skeleton of a 14-foot shark was found underneath.

   Not all sharks were sacred; the hunting of large man-eaters called **niuhi** (probably Tiger Sharks) was a sport especially reserved for chiefs. Large amounts of bait mixed with **'awa**, a narcotic root,

113

SCALLOPED HAMMERHEAD SHARK •
manō-kihikihi
Sphyrna lewini (Griffith & Smith, 1834)
    The strangely shaped head of this animal probably provides a certain amount of lift as it swims forward; by greatly separating the eyes it might also increase depth perception. Small pits on the underside, sensitive to electric fields, help locate living organisms under the sand. Scalloped Hammerheads regularly enter shallow protected bays in the Islands from April to October to mate and give birth. Adults are believed to feed at sea for much of the year, mostly on squid. Females are 3-4 ft. longer than males. Schools of 50 or more of these animals have been reported on occasion at Moku Ho'oniki, Moloka'i, and at select spots off the Kona Coast of the Big Island. Scalloped Hammerheads occur in all warm seas and attain a length of 13 ft. The Hawaiian name means "curves" "corners" "angular" "zigzag." Photo: Keoki Stender, Sea Life Park.

were fed to the shark from canoes until it became careless enough to be noosed, whereupon the gorged animal was led to shore and slaughtered for its highly prized teeth. The bait is said often to have consisted of human flesh, left to decompose several days to enhance its appeal. King Kamehameha I, who enjoyed this sport, was said to pen up his victims near the **heiau** at Hawi, on the Island of Hawai'i, until he was ready to go fishing.

How dangerous are sharks? The answer can only be: very dangerous... but unpredictably so. Except for the Whitetip Reef Shark, most sharks in Hawai'i avoid people. Divers see them infrequently. Many of the species known to attack humans — the Bull Shark, Oceanic Whitetip Shark, Blue Shark, and Mako Shark — are not encountered around Hawaii's reefs. The Great White Shark *(Carcharodon carcharias)*, probably the best known and most feared of all, is a rare visitor from temperate waters. But the vicious Tiger Shark, not uncommon in Hawai'i, has a reputation almost as bad.

Tiger sharks *(Galeocerdo cuvier)* grow to 18 feet, weigh up to 2000 pounds, and eat almost anything. The stomach of a ten-foot specimen harpooned in Pearl Harbor in 1931 contained the hind leg of a mule, two bathing suits, a belt buckle, a pint of buttons, two horseshoes, the corner of a wooden soapbox, two small anchors, anchor chain and assorted bolts, nails and copper fittings. Recent evidence indicates that sharks rid themselves of such accumulations from time to time by completely everting their stomachs.

Tiger Sharks are believed to remain in deep water during the day and for that reason do not usually threaten humans. Nevertheless, between 1900 and 1991 Hawai'i recorded 91 incidents involving sharks, 37 of them fatal. These numbers include bites sustained by fishermen who had caught sharks and numerous cases where it is impossible to determine whether the attack occurred before or after the victim's death (which may have been by drowning or other accident). Tiger Sharks are believed to have been responsible for many of these incidents, but Scalloped Hammerheads and Great White Sharks have also been implicated. Typical victims have been surfers, fishermen swept off shore by large waves, and spearfishermen. A few well-publicized attacks have also occurred to shallow-water bathers. Even so, considering the number of people in the water each day, Hawai'i remains a generally safe location.

Sharks (along with rays) are often referred to as "elasmobranchs" because they belong to the large subclass Elasmobranchii. There are about 370 living species divided into 19 families. At least 40 are reported from Hawai'i. In addition to the four pictured here, sharks that might be encountered in the islands include the Sandbar Shark *(Carcharhinus plumbeus)*, and the Whale Shark *(Rhincodon typus)*.

The wary Sandbar Shark, which usually disappears at the first sign of divers or snorkelers, is probably the most common inshore shark in the islands. The Whale Shark (*Rhincodon typus*), attains almost 60 feet and is the largest fish in the world. To swim with one of these bus-size giants is a once-in-a-lifetime experience. They are docile and sometimes allow divers to cling to their enormous dorsal fin for a ride.

According to old-timers, sharks used to be a common underwater sight around the main Hawaiian Islands. Today this is not the case. However, in the Northwestern Hawaiian Islands, where they regularly enter shallow water to feed on seabirds and seals, sharks are abundant and dangerous to swimmers. A happy medium is attained around Ni'ihau, southwest of Kaua'i, where shark sightings by divers are routine. To date, these animals have shown little interest in humans. Ni'ihau and its small neighbor, Lehua Island, to the east are the locations of choice for observing sharks in Hawai'i.

The word "shark," from the same root as "shirk," originally meant scoundrel or villain. Due to massive and often senseless predation by human beings, coupled with their own slow rate of reproduction, shark populations around the world are believed to be dwindling.

WHITETIP REEF SHARK • **manō-lālā-kea**
Triaenodon obesus (Rüppell, 1837).
  This is one of the most common Indo-Pacific sharks and the only shark seen with any regularity on the reefs of the main Hawaiian Islands. The body is grayish brown and the tips of the first dorsal and upper tail fins are white. These sharks hunt at night and are adept at nabbing fishes and crustaceans from their hiding places in the coral. By day they usually rest on the bottom in caves or under ledges, probably using the same locations over a period of time. Although they appear lethargic, they are not harmless and should not be trifled with. Divers at Molokini Island, Maui have the best chance of finding Whitetips but they can also be seen at many other sites. The species name means "fat", but it is a comparatively slender shark. To about 6 ft. East Africa to the Americas. Photo: D.R. Schrichte. Palea Point, O'ahu. 40 ft.

SNAPPERS AND EMPERORS
(LUTJANIDAE AND LETHRINIDAE)

Bluestripe Snappers • **ta'ape** *(Lutjanus kasmira).* Photo: D. R. Schrichte

Perchlike carnivores of considerable economic importance, snappers are common on shallow tropical reefs throughout the world. Most snappers native to Hawai'i, however, inhabit depths greater than 200 feet. These include the **'opakapaka, 'ula-'ula** and **onaga,** some of the Islands' best loved food fishes. The two native shallow-water species — solitary predators sometimes known as jobfishes — are not abundant enough to be of major commercial value. To stimulate the fishing industry three species of reef-dwelling snappers from the South Pacific and Mexico were introduced to the State of Hawai'i in the 1950s and early sixties. The **to'au** and the **ta'ape,** described below, have become common; the third *(Lutjanus gibbus)* is rare.

Little thought was given in earlier days to the ecological effects of these introductions. We now suspect that valuable shallow-water food fishes such as **weke** and **kūmū** are being displaced by one of the new snappers, the **ta'ape.** This voracious fish also ranges into deeper waters; when fishermen set their lines for valuable **'opakapaka,** schools of **ta'ape** often steal the bait. Unfortunately, **ta'ape** have a low market price and their introduction has been a commercial failure.

About 100 species of snappers are known worldwide. They vary in length from about 10 inches to 3 feet. The larger snappers are usually solitary while the smaller species typically school by day, dispersing at night to feed on small fishes and crustaceans. Hawaii has thirteen snappers (including two introduced species); only the four below are likely to be seen by sport divers or snorkelers.

The emperors are closely related fishes which, until recently, were classified in the snapper family. Hawai'i has one emperor, the **mū,** which is included in this section.

FORKTAIL SNAPPER • **wahanui**
Aphareus furca (Lacepède, 1802).
(SMALLTOOTH JOBFISH)
Dark silvery gray with a large, slightly downturned mouth and a deeply forked tail, this solitary snapper typically scouts the reef from a position well off the bottom, often near dropoffs. The species name means "fork," the Hawaiian name, "big mouth." To about 12 in. Indo-Pacific. Photo: Kahe Point, O'ahu. 15 ft.

GRAY SNAPPER • **uku**
Aprion virescens Valenciennes, 1830.
(GREEN JOBFISH)
This long, powerful-looking, greenish to bluish gray predator has sharp teeth and a large tail fin. The dorsal fin, when raised, reveals an easily seen series of marks at the base. It usually swims in midwater, individually or in small groups. The species name means "becoming green." To 3 ft. Indo-Pacific. Photo: Hanauma Bay, O'ahu. 20 ft.

BLACKTAIL SNAPPER • **to'au**
Lutjanus fulvus (Bloch & Schneider, 1801).
(FLAMETAIL SNAPPER)
These handsome snappers are grayish yellow with a red dorsal fin and a black tail fin which becomes red at the edges. Adults usually remain close to the bottom and are solitary by nature. Juveniles are abundant among the mangroves of Kāne'ohe Bay, O'ahu. The species was introduced to Hawai'i from Moorea, French Polynesia in 1956 but is not as common around reefs as the **ta'ape** (below). Species name means "tawny." **To'au** is the Tahitian name. To 13 in. Indo-Pacific. Photo: Honolua Bay, Maui. 20 ft.

BLUESTRIPE SNAPPER • ta'ape
Lutjanus kasmira (Forsskål, 1775).

Large schools of these showy snappers are a common sight around wrecks and other popular dive sites, especially where fishes have been hand-fed. Yellow with four narrow, bright blue longitudinal stripes, they provide a colorful thrill to visiting divers as they swarm for a handout. Although introduced to Hawai'i from the Marquesas in 1958 for commercial reasons, they have been a flop in island markets and are sometimes regarded by fishermen as a pest rather than an asset. The Tahitian name, **ta'ape**, has come into common use in Hawai'i. To 15 in., but usually smaller. Indo-Pacific. Photo: *Mahi* wreck, O'ahu. 65 ft.

Bigeye Emperor - adult ∧ juvenile ∨

BIGEYE EMPEROR • mū
Monotaxis grandoculis (Forsskål, 1775).

These lovely fishes have large, dark eyes and blunt snouts. Adults are entirely silvery but can quickly take on a pattern of broad dark bars. Smaller individuals usually show the barred coloration, with some yellow about the head and lips. **Mū** feed at night and hover by day in midwater off the face of the reef, rippling their fins gently to maintain a position facing into the current. Juveniles, usually seen closer to the bottom, have a pointed snout and a more highly contrasting barred pattern. **Mū** have teeth that resemble human molars. Because of this, it is said, a man sent to find victims for live burial beside the body of a chief was also called **mū**. Children, of course, were told that if they were bad the **mū** would get them. To almost 2 ft. Indo-Pacific. Photos: adult. "Ammo Reef," leeward O'ahu; juvenile. Marjorie L. Awai. Honokohau Harbor, Hawai'i.

Hawaiian Squirrelfish • **ʻalaʻihi** *(Sargocentron xantherythrum),* "Black Rock" leeward, Oʻahu. 20 ft.

Squirrelfishes and soldierfishes are medium-size nocturnal fishes, usually red, with big scales and large dark eyes. They rest by day under ledges and in caves, roaming freely over the reef at night. Some are able to make a chattering or chirping sound.

The squirrelfishes (**ʻalaʻihi**) are prickly and spiny, and the spines on the gill covers of some species are venomous. Their bodies are usually marked with horizontal silvery stripes which follow the scale rows. Approached in their shelters, squirrelfishes typically peer out, then dash uneasily to and fro. This nervous behavior, as well as the dark eyes, probably gave them their popular name.

Soldierfishes (**ʻūʻū**) lack stripes, are snub-nosed and have deeper bodies. Less high-strung than squirrelfishes, they often "stand guard" near the entrance to their cave, retreating only when necessary. In Hawaiʻi, soldierfishes are often called by their Japanese name, *menpachi.*

Both these fishes emerge at dusk to feed; the **ʻalaʻihi** seeks out crabs and shrimps near the bottom, while the **ʻūʻū** favors plankton higher up in the water. Their red color is typical of many nocturnal and deep water fishes, actually making them more difficult to see. Red wavelengths are rapidly absorbed by seawater. Thus, in deep water or at night, red becomes equivalent to black.

Despite their ordinary perchlike appearance, squirrel and soldierfishes do not belong to the order Perciformes with the majority of fishes in this book. Due to more primitive anatomy, they are placed in the order Beryciformes and are the only representatives of that order common on coral reefs. The family name Holocentridae means "all spiny" or "all prickly."

About seventeen squirrelfishes and soldierfishes inhabit Hawaiian waters. Most are deep-dwelling or reclusive species seldom seen by divers or snorkelers; ten are pictured here. Others sometimes encountered include the lovely Yellowfin Soldierfish *(Myripristis chryseres),* easily identified by its golden yellow fins, and the chunky Rough-Scale Soldierfish *(Plectrypops lima),* which dwells in the far recesses of caves and crevices. The former prefers depths well over 100 feet but the latter, although secretive, is not uncommon at snorkeling depths, where it is most likely to be glimpsed at night. (See page 183.)

Squirrelfishes and soldierfishes are only occasionally offered for sale in the aquarium trade. They are peaceful, easy to feed and make a colorful addition to a large tank. The Peppered Squirrelfish is well suited to small aquariums. It is easily caught in tidepools at night with a dip net and flashlight. Use as coarse a mesh as possible, as these spiny fishes are extremely difficult to remove from ordinary aquarium nets. Squirrelfishes prey on small invertebrates; do not attempt to keep them with these animals. Chopped shrimp or fish are ideal foods. Their mouths are too big to deal effectively with flakes, although they will occasionally try to accept them. Individual fishes vary remarkably. Out of five Peppered Squirrelfishes captured on one night from the same area, one learned to accept pieces of shrimp within days, two took over a week to begin feeding, and the rest, which never learned to eat, were returned to the sea.

SPOTFIN SQUIRRELFISH • 'ala'ihi
Neoniphon sammara (Forsskål, 1775).
  Most squirrelfishes are red; this one is silvery with brownish red stripes following the rows of scales. A dark red spot is visible on the dorsal fin when it is raised. Shy and retiring, this squirrelfish does not congregate in large groups as often as its relatives and is seen infrequently. At night a red stripe appears on the upper side. To 10 in. Indo-Pacific. Photo: Kealakekua Bay, Hawai'i. 30 ft.

HAWAIIAN SQUIRRELFISH • 'ala'ihi ●
Sargocentron xantherythrum (Jordan & Evermann, 1903).
  This is the squirrelfish seen most often by divers and snorkelers in Hawai'i. It is red with silvery stripes. Its dorsal fin is deep red except for the spine tips, and there may also be white marks at the base. The Crown Squirrelfish (below) is very similar. To separate these two with certainty the two spines on the gill covers must be examined: the Hawaiian Squirrelfish has an upper spine much longer than the lower. Species name from *xanthos* ("yellow") and *erythrum* ("red"). To 6.5 in. Endemic. Photo: "Black Rock," leeward O'ahu. 20 ft.

CROWN SQUIRRELFISH • 'ala'ihi
Sargocentron diadema (Lacepède, 1802).

By day looking very much like the Hawaiian Squirrelfish (above), this less common species is most easily identified at night when it may develop several white marks on the upper sides. White marks on the dorsal fin (when raised) look like a crown or diadem, hence the common and scientific names. The silvery stripes are more evenly spaced than those of the Hawaiian Squirrelfish. The spines on the gill covers are of almost equal size, the upper slightly longer. To 6.5 in. Indo-Pacific. Photo: Kailua Pier, Hawai'i. 20 ft. (night)

PEPPERED SQUIRRELFISH • 'ala'ihi
Sargocentron punctatissimum (Cuvier, 1829).

Although almost never seen by day, this small, abundant species is often encountered at night. It is pinkish red, peppered with small black spots. After dark a pale stripe develops down the center of the body. The dorsal fin, when raised, displays white marks in a perfect arc. To 5 in. Indo-Pacific. Photo: Kailua Pier, Hawai'i. 15 ft. (night).

YELLOWSTRIPE SQUIRRELFISH • 'ala'ihi
Sargocentron ensiferum (Jordan & Evermann, 1903)

Bright yellow stripes contrast with red on this strikingly pretty squirrelfish, which is usually seen alone under an isolated coral head. Preferring depths greater than 60 feet it is not uncommon off the south shore of Maui or off the Kona coast of the Big Island. The species name means "sword bearer," referring to a long, backward-pointing spine on the gill cover just behind the eye. To about 1 ft. Known from Japan, New Caledonia, Hawai'i, and Pitcairn. The very similar Goldline Squirrelfish *(Neoniphon aurolineatus)* is illustrated and described on page 183. Photo: Bob Owens. Molokini Island. 60 ft.

BLUESTRIPE SQUIRRELFISH • 'ala'ihi
Sargocentron tiere (Cuvier, 1829).
(TAHITIAN SQUIRRELFISH)

In bright light, iridescent blue stripes gleam lengthwise along the lower sides of this relatively large, uncommon squirrelfish. Viewed from the front, the snout has whitish markings that almost encircle the eye. At night a bright white bar develops down the center of the body and another at the base of the tail. By day this fish remains deep within the reef and is infrequently seen. It prefers depths of 40 feet or less. The species name was taken from a Tahitian word for squirrelfish. To about 12 in. Indo-Pacific. Photo: Hanauma Bay, O'ahu. 20 ft.

LONGJAW SQUIRRELFISH • 'ala'ihi
Sargocentron spiniferum (Forsskål, 1775).
(SABER SQUIRRELFISH)

The largest of its family, this species is easy to recognize: the body is uniform orange red, the fins (except for the bright red dorsal) are yellowish, and it has a long sad-looking face. A long venomous spine projects back from the lower gill cover. This might have been the species called in old Hawai'i **'ala'ihi kalaloa** ("long-spike **'ala'ihi**"). Easy to approach, it is encountered most often along the Kona Coast at about 50 feet. Species name means "spiny." To 18 in. Indo-Pacific. Photo: Hanauma Bay, O'ahu. 30 ft.

BRICK SOLDIERFISH • 'ū'ū
Myripristis amaena (Castelnau, 1873).

Of the three similar soldierfishes pictured here, this is the easiest to identify; its soft dorsal, anal and tail fins are plain red without white edges. Preferring depths less than 25 feet, it is most likely to be seen by snorkelers and shallow divers. To about 10 in. Restricted to the Pacific islands. Photo: Palea Point, O'ahu 15 ft.

BIG-SCALE SOLDIERFISH • 'ū'ū
Myripristis berndti Jordan & Evermann, 1903.

Large scales and a strongly projecting lower jaw separate this common species from the Pearly Soldierfish (below). Both have white on the leading edges of the fins. The dorsal fin, when raised, shows orange yellow. The largest Hawaiian soldierfish, it was named for Mr. E. Louis Berndt, inspector of the Honolulu Fish Market in the early years of this century. To 11 in. East Africa to the Americas. Photo: Hanauma Bay, O'ahu. 20 ft.

PEARLY SOLDIERFISH • 'ū'ū
Myripristis kuntee Cuvier, 1831.
(EPAULETTE SOLDIERFISH)

This fish varies from red to pinkish with a satiny or pearly sheen. The leading edges of the fins are white. The shoulder bar is darker and more distinct than that of the preceding species, the scales are slightly smaller, and the lower jaw less projecting. The dorsal fin, when raised, shows yellow. This species is generally seen at depths of 15 to 50 feet. To about 7.5 in. Indo-Pacific. Photo: Hanauma Bay, Oahu. 40 ft.

123

Feeding school of Yellow Tangs *(Zebrasoma flavescens)*. Hanauma Bay, O'ahu. 20 ft.

Surgeonfishes, or tangs, are probably the most numerous and prominent of all Hawaiian reef fishes. Each surgeonfish carries at the base of its tail fin two knifelike spines or scalpels — one on each side. Ordinarily these scalpels lie flat in a groove. A simple swipe of the tail automatically flips one out, ready for action against enemy or intruder. In unicornfishes (subfamily Nasinae) the scalpels are replaced by extremely sharp bony projections. In either case, these fishes are quite capable of causing serious injury to predators or rivals. The common name "surgeonfish" was inspired by the deep, painful cuts they occasionally inflict on careless humans, typically while being removed from a net or spear. But don't blame the fish; its scalpels, or the areas around them, are often brightly colored as a warning. In some species the scalpels and fin spines are mildly venomous, causing wounds that are slow to heal. Well-behaved divers and snorkelers, however, have little to fear from surgeonfishes.

Surgeonfishes are typically oval in shape with thin (compressed) bodies and scales so small as to seem nonexistent. They propel themselves with winglike beats of their pectoral fins, as do wrasses and parrotfishes. Although a few species feed on plankton, the majority are algae eaters with mouths adapted for either scraping the surface of rocks and dead coral or nibbling leafy seaweeds.

Because algae grows best in bright light, most surgeonfishes are shallow-water creatures. Some, such as the mid-size Achilles Tang and Whitespotted Surgeonfish, inhabit the turbulent surge zone. Smaller species, such as Convict Tangs and Brown Surgeonfish, prefer calmer waters, often browsing the reef in large mixed schools. Moving together in a group affords protection from predators and, more importantly, enables them to overcome the territorial defenses of other algae-eating fishes. One of these is the Pacific Gregory, an aggressive and common little damselfish that vigorously defends its own patch of algae against individual intruders. It can only dart about in helpless frustration when several hundred peacefully grazing surgeonfishes sweep through its territory.

Some larger species, such as the Yellowfin Surgeonfish, feed on the almost microscopic algae growing on sandy bottoms. This must be slow going indeed, and it is not surprising that the taste of concentrated fishfood drives these large surgeons wild. Before fish feeding was banned in Hanauma Bay, O'ahu, they would mill and swarm around humans in shallow water, providing excitement for both children adults.

Included in the surgeonfish family are the unicornfishes, many species of which grow a long horn on the forehead. Some are plankton eaters that school well above the bottom, often in deeper water than other surgeonfishes. Although there appears to be no Hawaiian name for surgeonfishes in general, the unicornfishes are all known as **kala**, which also means "thorn." In old Hawai'i a person who could well defend himself was praised as "a **kala** fish with a sharp tail." The family name originates in the Greek word *akanthos* ("thorn").

Twenty-three species of surgeonfishes occur in Hawaiian waters; 19 are described here. Included also is the closely related Moorish Idol, the only member of the family Zanclidae. Moorish Idols lack a scalpel and resemble butterflyfishes in appearance and behavior. However, a careful observer will notice that, like surgeonfishes (and unlike butterflyfishes), they swim largely with their pectoral fins. Their family name is from the Greek *zanclon* ("sickle").

The smaller, more colorful surgeonfishes make good aquarium specimens. Most are territorial in the wild and are best kept as single specimens or in small schools where their aggressive tendencies are dampened. Although herbivorous by nature, tangs are quick to accept high-protein animal food in captivity. To avoid malnutrition the aquarist should provide a diet of at least 50 percent vegetable matter. Algae-covered stones or fresh seaweed from the ocean are best. Commercially prepared frozen fishfoods made from these ingredients are available. Finely chopped spinach or other greens are an alternative. (It is helpful to either freeze these greens or dip them in boiling water for a few seconds to break down the indigestible cellulose contained in all terrestrial plants.) Yet another possibility is dried Japanese seaweed. Pet surgeonfishes quickly consume and control any green algae growing in the aquarium.

ACHILLES TANG · **pāku'iku'i**
Acanthurus achilles Shaw, 1803.
A bright red teardrop-shape patch over the scalpel identifies this species; the body is black. Common along rocky shores with moderate wave action, these active fishes seem to spend most of their time driving intruders away. A short charge and a sudden turn, to expose a scalpel, does the job nicely. When agitated, their bodies and flared fins take on a reddish glow. Smaller specimens are excellent aquarium fishes. Aggressive to their own kind, they are best kept singly. Named for the Greek warrior Achilles, who symbolizes youthful grace, beauty and valor. To 10 inches. Restricted to the islands of the Pacific (but rare in Micronesia). Photo: Hālona Blowhole, O'ahu. 20 ft.

GOLDRIM SURGEONFISH *Acanthurus nigricans* (Linnaeus, 1758).
(Whitecheek Surgeonfish)
Similar to the Achilles Tang in habits and appearance, these have yellow around the scalpel and white on the tail fin. When agitated they extend their dorsal and anal fins, appearing rimmed in gold and surrounded by a thin margin of electric blue. Although uncommon in Hawai'i, they are abundant at Puakō Reef on the Kona Coast of the Big Island. Occasional pairs can usually be seen at many other locations. This species occasionally hybridizes with the more common Achilles Tang. Species name means "blackish." To 8 in. Indonesia to the Americas. Photo: Palea Point, O'ahu. 20 ft.

125

RINGTAIL SURGEONFISH • pualu
Acanthurus blochii Valenciennes, 1835.

Less abundant than the common **pualo**, (or Yellowfin Surgeonfish) below, these are dark, usually with a white ring around the tail. Several other surgeonfishes, however, can adopt this color pattern. Its dark pectoral fins will separate it from both the Yellowfin Surgeonfish and the **palani**. A yellow band to the rear of the eye differentiates it from the much smaller Bluelined Surgeon. It is common at Hanauma Bay, O'ahu, where it often swims with the Yellowfin Surgeonfish. Named after German ichthyologist M.E. Bloch (1723-1799) who first scientifically described many fishes in this book. To 17 in. Indo-Pacific. Photo: Hanauma Bay, O'ahu. 10 ft.

EYESTRIPE SURGEONFISH • palani
Acanthurus dussumieri Valenciennes, 1835.

A white scalpel immediately separates the **palani** from similar species such as the Yellowfin and Ringtail Surgeonfishes. It can alter its color from light blue to almost black, often with a white ring around the tail. The dorsal fin is a beautiful ochre color. Any large surgeonfish resting under a ledge is likely to be this species. It prefers depths of 20 feet or more. Large specimens have an unusually large, rounded snout. The **palani** has a strong odor when cooked; a Hawaiian riddle based on this name means "odor reaching to heaven." To 18 in. Indo-Pacific. Photo: "Golden Arches," Kona Coast, Hawai'i. 25 ft.

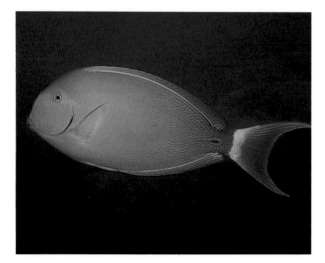

YELLOWFIN SURGEONFISH • pualu
Acanthurus xanthopterus Valenciennes, 1835.

Large **pualu** are familiar to beachgoers and snorkelers at fish-feeding sites where they eagerly surround anyone offering food. They are purplish gray with yellow and blue banded dorsal and anal fins, and deep blue lyre-shape tails. The yellow pectoral fins are especially important for identification because the species can alter its body color to almost black with a white ring around the tail (thus appearing much like the Ringtail Surgeonfish which has black pectorals). The caudal spine is black, distinguishing it from the Eyestripe Surgeonfish or **palani**. Species name means "yellow-fin." To 22 in. East Africa to the Americas. Photo: Hanauma Bay, O'ahu. 10 ft.

WHITEBAR SURGEONFISH • mäikoiko
Acanthurus leucopareius (Jenkins, 1903).

Easy to identify, this species has a prominent white bar behind the eye; the body is grayish brown. It often schools, either alone or with the Convict Tang, and is common close to shore. Species name means "white cheek." To 10 in. Restricted to the subtropical Pacific islands. Photo: "Makaha Caves," leeward O'ahu. 30 ft.

WHITESPOTTED SURGEONFISH • 'api
Acanthurus guttatus Bloch & Schneider, 1801.
(MUSTARD TANG)

Whitespotted Surgeons have an almost circular brown body with white bars in front and many white spots in back. The pectoral fins are intense lemon yellow. A long sloping snout terminates in a thick upper lip. Inhabiting turbulent, rocky shores, they are adept at riding the foamy surge into the shallows to nibble for a few seconds at algae before being swept back into deeper water. It has been suggested that their many white spots help hide them in the bubbles. These fish usually occur in small groups but sometimes browse the reef in large schools. The species name means "spotted." To 11 in. Indo-Pacific. Photo: Hanauma Bay, O'ahu. 2 ft.

BROWN SURGEONFISH • mä'i'i'i
Acanthurus nigrofuscus (Forsskål, 1775).
(LAVENDER TANG)

These shallow-water surgeonfish are grayish brown but with a definite lavender tinge, especially on the fins. Dull orange spots dot the head. There are small dark spots above and below the base of the tail. Common and drab, few snorkelers and divers pay them much attention, but they are interesting nonetheless. In some locations, such as inside the reef at Hanauma Bay, O'ahu, they are territorial, defending small areas primarily against other herbivores, especially the Convict Tang. In other places, such as the "Haleiwa Trench," O'ahu, they behave quite differently, browsing the reef in large schools, often *with* Convict Tangs. From February to October at certain select spots, such as over the hot water outfall at Kahe Point, O'ahu, they spawn daily in sometimes huge aggregations. Finally, the largest bacteria known to science live in their gut, apparently aiding digestion. The species name means "dark," the Hawaiian name, "tiny." To 8 in. Indo-Pacific. Photo: Kahe Point Beach Park, O'ahu, 15 ft.

BLUELINE SURGEONFISH • **maiko**
Acanthurus nigroris Valenciennes, 1835.
   Common reef fishes, these are dark brownish gray with fine, somewhat wavy blue lines running lengthwise along the body and two small dark spots, above and below the base of the tail. Like many surgeonfishes, they can change color to almost black with a white ring around the tail, but the blue lines always remain faintly visible. Species name means "blackness." To 10 in. Pacific Islands. Photo: Hōnaunau, Hawai'i. 20 ft.

Orangeband Surgeonfish - adult ∧   juvenile ∨

ORANGEBAND SURGEONFISH • **na'ena'e**
Acanthurus olivaceus Bloch & Schneider, 1801.
   This large surgeonfish always has a short orange band ringed in blue on its shoulder. It can change color rapidly from light olive to cleanly divided light and dark to completely dark. Often browsing in groups, usually over sandy patches, it occasionally joins other surgeonfishes in large, mixed schools. Juveniles, which are bright yellow without an orange band, might be confused with the Yellow Tang. Species name means "olive color." To 12 in. Pacific Ocean. Photos: Hanauma Bay, O'ahu. 25 ft. juvenile. Pūpūkea, O'ahu. 30 ft.

THOMPSON'S SURGEONFISH
Acanthurus thompsoni (Fowler, 1923).
This small plankton-eating surgeonfish occurs in midwater either singly, in small groups, or in aggregations of hundreds. It is uniformly bluegray to dark brown, almost black. There is a single black spot above the base of the crescent-shape tail. (Outside Hawaiian waters the tail is bright white.) These fish are perhaps most common along the Big Island's Kona Coast. Juveniles occur in beds of Finger Coral *(Porites compressa)*. The name honors John W. Thompson, a technician and artist at the Bishop Museum from 1901 to 1928. (Four Hawaiian fishes are named for Thompson, two of them endemic. He must have been quite a guy!) To 10 in. but usually smaller. Indo-Pacific. Photo: *Mahi* wreck, O'ahu. 60 ft.

CONVICT TANG • **manini**
Acanthurus triostegus (Linnaeus, 1758).
Abundant and well-known, **manini** are light greenish or yellowish white with six black bars (the convict's stripes). Common everywhere except in areas of heavy coral growth, they often browse the reef in large, dense schools. Juveniles are found in tidepools and inlets, even where the water is brackish. Although illegal to sell commercially, young **manini** are good beginning aquarium fishes; they can be captured by children and are attractive and hardy. Only in Hawai'i does this widespread species have the narrow, oblique bar under the pectoral fin, and the Hawaiian population is sometimes given the subspecies name *sandvicensis*. Although **manini** were a favored food fish in old Hawai'i, the popular name has come to mean undersized or stingy. To 10 in. East Africa to the Americas. Photos: Pūpūkea, O'ahu. 50ft.

GOLD-RING SURGEONFISH • **kole** ●
Ctenochaetus strigosus (Bennett, 1828).
(GOLD-RING BRISTLETOOTH)

The **kole** has a bright gold ring around the eye. The dark body is marked with many fine horizontal lines, and the mouth is surrounded by blue. Juveniles are sometimes dull yellow. In old Hawai'i these fish were placed under the posts of a new home to ensure good luck. The species name means "thin" or "meager." The Hawaiian name means "raw" (which was how it was eaten). The Gold-Ring Surgeonfish has recently been re-classified as a Hawaiian endemic. Several similar species occur elsewhere in the Indo-Pacific. To 7 in. Photo: Hanauma Bay, O'ahu. 30 ft.

BLACK SURGEONFISH
Ctenochaetus hawaiiensis Randall, 1955.
(CHEVRON TANG)

The mouth of this surgeonfish resembles that of a rabbit. It is black, almost entirely covered with close-set fine light longitudinal lines. The dorsal and anal fins are deep and sail-like when extended. The species is uncommon in Hawai'i except on the Big Island. On O'ahu it may be seen regularly near the mouth of Hanauma Bay. Juveniles, cinnamon orange with blue markings, are highly prized aquarium fishes sold under the name Chevron Tang. They are usually found at depths between 60 and 100 feet in areas of heavy coral cover, whereas adults prefer shallower locations. To 11 in. Pacific Islands. Photo: juvenile. Hōnaunau, Hawai'i. 60 ft. adult. Hanauma Bay, O'ahu. 20 ft.

Black Surgeonfish - juvenile ∧   adult ∨

YELLOW TANG · **lau-ī-pala**
Zebrasoma flavescens (Bennett, 1828).

Except for a white tail spine, these beauties are entirely bright yellow. Along the calm Kona Coast they can frequently be identified from shore as they graze in the shallows. Underwater, schools of these golden fishes flowing over the reef are a sight unique to Hawai'i; although ranging as far as Japan and Guam, the species is abundant only here. Juveniles, thin and delicate as wafers, have greatly elevated dorsal and anal fins. They do not school like adults, and are especially common in stands of finger coral. Hawaii's most popular export, Yellow Tangs do well in captivity, although they cannot easily be kept with their own kind. Their mouths are adapted for browsing soft filamentous algae, and they may have difficulty with large chunks of solid food. The species name means "yellow," the Hawaiian name, "yellowed ti-leaf." To almost 8 in. Hawai'i, Marshall Islands, Mariana Islands, Southern Japan. Photo: Hanauma Bay, O'ahu. 30 ft.

SAILFIN TANG · **māne'one'o**
Zebrasoma veliferum (Bloch, 1797).

Named for their remarkable, sail-like dorsal and anal fins, these tangs are banded brown and white. If alarmed, they extend their fins, greatly enlarging their apparent size. The attractive juveniles, banded yellow and black, have permanently extended "sails." Juveniles are solitary but adults often swim in pairs, occasionally in schools. The species name means "carrying a sail." Some fishes, when eaten raw, cause an unpleasant sensation in the throat. This may be one; the Hawaiian name means "itchy" or "irritating." To 15 in. Indo-Pacific. Photo: Kahalu'u, Hawai'i. 2 ft.

PALETAIL UNICORNFISH · kala lōlō
Naso brevirostris (Valenciennes, 1835).
(SPOTTED UNICORNFISH)

These unicornfishes are plankton eaters. They have a prominent horn and a white tail fin containing a darkish spot. Large adults have small spots or lines on their sides. Schooling well off the bottom, often in the company of the Sleek Unicornfish (below), these fish can be hard to approach. Occasionally they enter shallow water where they can be seen by snorkelers. Divers can inspect them at night, when they sleep on the bottom. Although an adult's horn may be almost the length of its head, the species name means "short-horned." Perhaps the original specimen was not fully grown. Subadults have only a nub and juveniles lack the horn entirely. The Hawaiian word lōlō mean "lazy" or "crazy." To 24 in. Indo-Pacific. Hanauma Bay, O'ahu. 5 ft.

SLEEK UNICORNFISH · kala holo; 'ōpelu kala
Naso hexacanthus (Bleeker, 1855).

This hornless unicornfish has a sleek, symmetrical shape. It can change almost instantly from a metallic blue gray to entirely dark, but usually only its silhouette is seen against the blue. A plankton eater, it schools in midwater, often with the Paletail Unicornfish (above) and is difficult to approach unless it descends to the bottom to be serviced by cleaner wrasses. Schools often rest in caves, fleeing when a diver comes near. The species name means "six spines." The Hawaiian word holo means "swift." Fishermen also call it 'ōpelu kala because 'ōpelu (Mackerel Scad) are often nearby. To 30 in. Indo-Pacific. Photo: Pai'olu'olu Point, O'ahu. 60 ft.

BLUESPINE UNICORNFISH · kala
Naso unicornis (Forsskål, 1775)

These plain, light color unicornfishes sport a medium-size horn and almost fluorescent blue tail spines. When browsing on algae in shallow water they often darken except for a light shoulder patch. Males have tail streamers. Small specimens lack the horn. This is the horned unicornfish most commonly seen by snorkelers. It usually occurs singly but schools are sometimes encountered. The Hawaiian name means "thorn." In old Hawai'i its tough skin was used for making drumheads. To 27 in. Indo-Pacific. Photo: Kahalu'u, Hawai'i. 3 ft.

ORANGESPINE UNICORNFISH
• umauma-lei
Naso lituratus (Bloch & Schneider, 1801).
(NASO TANG)

Bright orange lips, a graceful curve of yellow from eye to mouth (somewhat like a **lei**), and brilliant orange caudal spines identify this attractive hornless unicornfish. It is common in shallow water where it feeds on seaweeds. Large males have tail streamers. When chasing other fishes the dull yellow mark on the forehead becomes intensely yellow, looking almost like a headlight. Viewed from above, the orange, forward curving tail spines look convincingly sharp. Species name means "blotted out" or "blurred." Hawaiian name from **umauma** ("chest") and **lei** ("garland"). In a large enough aquarium, one of these makes a winning display. Two will almost certainly fight. The species may take several weeks to begin feeding. Unfortunately, juveniles are dull in color compared to adults. To 18 in. Indo-Pacific. Photo: Magic Island, O'ahu. 30 ft.

MOORISH IDOL • **kihikihi**
Zanclus cornutus, (Linnaeus, 1758).

Moorish Idols, with their perfect blend of form and color, are the classic coral reef fish. Living symbols of the exotic undersea world, they have light gold bodies marked with jet-black bands, long orange and white striped snouts, and graceful trailing filaments. Moorish Idols often swim in pairs, occasionally in small schools, and to view them underwater is always a delight. Although unrelated, they are remarkably similar to the Pennant Butterflyfish. Immature (post-larval) Moorish Idols develop hornlike spines which later fall off, thus the species name, meaning "horned." The Hawaiian name ("curves," "corners," "angular," "zigzag") was applied to a number of fishes, including hammerhead sharks. Moorish Idols are difficult to maintain in captivity. Active, surprisingly aggressive, and often hard to feed, they do best in a large tank in groups of three or more. To about 8 in. East Africa to the Americas. Photo: Hanauma Bay, O'ahu. 10 ft.

TILEFISHES
(MALACANTHIDAE)

Tilefishes, often called sand tilefishes or blanquillos, are a small family of slender elongated fishes that dwell in burrows or mounds in sandy or rubbly areas. They hover several feet over the bottom, retreating to their holes if too closely approached. Some species are quite colorful and of interest to aquarists. Although considerably larger than most aquarium fishes they are peaceful and do not bother their tankmates. Only one species is known from Hawai'i.

FLAGTAIL TILEFISH • **maka-'ā**
Malacanthus brevirostris Guichenot, 1848.
(Quakerfish; Striped Blanquillo)
    A lovely fish, very fluid in its movements, the Flagtail Tilefish is named for the two black stripes on its tail fin. It is bluish white overall and not often seen, although fairly common at Mākua, O'ahu. Do not confuse it with the much smaller Indigo Dartfish which shares the same habitat. The species name means "short snout." To about 1 ft. East Africa to the Americas. Photo: Pūpūkea, O'ahu. 20 ft.

TRIGGERFISHES
(BALISTIDAE)

Hawai'i's unofficial state fish, the Reef or Picasso Triggerfish *(Rhinecanthus rectangulus)*.

Triggerfishes are named for the unusual arrangement of their two dorsal spines. The first spine, thick and strong, can be erected and locked into place internally with the second, which is shorter. At the slightest danger, most triggerfishes dive into a hole or crevice and erect their spine, becoming very difficult to remove. In theory, if the second spine (the "trigger") is depressed, the locking mechanism will release, and the surprised triggerfish can be pulled from its refuge. This procedure is not recommended, however, as surprised triggerfishes can deliver a nasty bite. In Hawaiian, triggerfishes are called **humuhumu** ("to stitch pieces together") perhaps referring to the geometric patterns of some species.

Triggerfishes have tough skins and small but strong jaws and mouths with which they feed on crustaceans, echinoderms, coral or almost anything. Because their eyes are placed far back on the body, several species seem to be at least half head. Many triggerfishes are plankton eaters. All swim by rippling their soft dorsal and anal fins. This enables them to move backward as well as forward, an advantage while maneuvering in and out of small spaces. They lay their eggs in nests on the bottom where they are guarded, usually by the male. Some species (not in Hawai'i) will charge and even bite divers who approach their nests.

Triggerfishes belong to the order Tetraodontiformes, which includes other curious fishes such as the filefishes, pufferfishes and boxfishes. Of perhaps 20 Indo-Pacific species, ten are known from Hawai'i and eight described here.

In the aquarium **humuhumu** are "personality fishes," hardy and easy to feed. They can also be real troublemakers. Large ones are pugnacious and are best kept alone. With their sharp, chisel-like teeth they make short work of any invertebrates in the tank; they have even been known to sever plastic air hoses and destroy glass heaters. They will also rearrange the rocks in your aquarium to suit themselves. Baby **humuhumu** can often be collected in late summer in shallow, rocky areas. If you are lucky, they will hole up in a loose piece of coral which can simply be picked up and put in a bucket. A new triggerfish may stay in its refuge for many days before emerging.

BLACK TRIGGERFISH • humuhumu-'ele'ele
Melichthys niger (Bloch, 1786).
(BLACK DURGON)
   These are very dark with two conspicuous light blue lines along the bases of the soft dorsal and anal fins. When agitated they display a radiating pattern of iridescent blue lines between the eyes. Black Triggerfishes often aggregate above the reef, feeding on plankton and drifting algae. Both the species and Hawaiian names mean "black." To about 1 ft. Found in tropical seas worldwide. Triggerfishes of the genus *Melichthys* are also known as durgons. Photo: Hōnaunau, Hawai'i. 20 ft.

PINKTAIL TRIGGERFISH • humuhumu-hi'u-kole
Melichthys vidua (Solander, 1844).
(PINKTAIL DURGON)
   These are dark brown with clear to whitish anal and soft dorsal fins and a white and pink tail. Although they do not school, their habits are similar to those of the Black Triggerfish. The species name means "widow," the Hawaiian name, "raw tail" or "red tail." It is reported to be less aggressive in captivity than many other triggerfishes. To about 13 in. Indo-Pacific. Photo: *Mahi* wreck, O'ahu. 60 ft.

REEF TRIGGERFISH • **humuhumu-nukunuku-ā-puaʻa**
Rhinecanthus rectangulus (Bloch & Schneider, 1801).
(PICASSO TRIGGERFISH)

Colored lines, geometrically arranged, give this curiously patterned fish one of its common names, Picasso Triggerfish. The position of its eyes, high and about one third of the way down the tan body, enables it to attack long-spined sea urchins. Although common on shallow reef flats, it is one of the most difficult fishes to approach or photograph. The descriptive words **humuhumu-nukunuku-ā-puaʻa** mean "nose like a pig" and the fish grunts like a pig when pulled from the water. The famous song "My Little Grass Shack" features this fish. According to legend, the pig demigod **Kama-puaʻa** once escaped the wrath of the volcano goddess **Pele** by turning into a triggerfish. Lefend also relates that in the guise of a triggerfish he once saved some children from a shark. Schoolchildren and others across the state returned the favor in 1984 by electing the **humuhumu** Hawaiʻi's State Fish. Fish experts argued in favor of other species, but children's' **hula** groups dancing to the tune of the famous song captured the hearts of the voters. Out some 60,000 votes cast—some from as far away as Maine, Massachusetts, and Arizona—the triggerfish won with 16,577, followed by the **manini** (8,742), the **lauwiliwili nukunuku ʻoiʻoi** (8,543), and the **hinalea lauwili** (6,206). The story, however, does not end there: Displeased with the election, certain fish experts persuaded the Legislature to limit the **humu**'s term to five years! Its term has now elapsed, but so far no one has suggested a successor to this popular fish. To 10 in. Indo-Pacific. Photo: Hanauma Bay, Oʻahu. 10 ft

LAGOON TRIGGERFISH • **humuhumu-nukunuku-a-puaʻa**
Rhinecanthus aculeatus (Linneaus, 1758).

This beautiful but uncommon triggerfish sports a blue hat, yellow lips bordered with blue, and a yellow bridle. It has much black on the upper body, and diagonal white bands on the lower rear side. Viewed from above, a bullseye mark is conspicuous on its back. Rows of rough file-like spines at the base of the tail give protection when the fish retreats into a hole (true of all *Rhinecanthus*). It prefers a sandier, weedier habitat than the similar Reef Triggerfish (above) and is not seen at most dive sites. Good places to look for it are Makapuʻu Beach Park, Oʻahu, the south end of Mākaha Beach, Oʻahu, and Kahaluʻu Beach Park, Kailua-Kona, Hawaiʻi. It shares its Hawaiian name with the Reef Triggerfish. Pugnacious in captivity, it is best kept alone. The species name means "sharp-pointed." To 1 ft. Indo-Pacific. Photo: Hanauma Bay, Oʻahu. 5 ft.

LEI TRIGGERFISH · **humuhumu-lei**
Sufflamen bursa (Bloch & Schneider, 1801).
(Whiteline Triggerfish)

Two curved bands, like strands of a lei running up from the base of the pectoral fin, give this fish its name. The bands may be brown, gray or yellow. The body is grayish-brown and white. A thin white line runs diagonally from mouth to anal fin. This species is easier to maintain in captivity than most other triggerfishes. To 8.5 in. Indo-Pacific. Photo: Hanauma Bay, O'ahu. 30 ft.

BRIDLED TRIGGERFISH · **humuhumu-mimi**
Sufflamen fraenatus (Latreille, 1804).

Drab in appearance, this triggerfish is uniformly brown to blackish brown, often with a white ring around the base of the tail. Males have a white or yellow stripe running down from the corner of the mouth, somewhat like the traces of a bridle. Both sexes have a band under the chin. The young are light in color with a dark back. To the Hawaiians this was a smelly fish, hence the name **mimi** ("urine"). The species name means "bridle." To 15 in. Indo-Pacific. Photos: male. *Mahi* wreck, O'ahu. 50 ft. female. Kawaihoa (Portlock) Point, O'ahu. 30 ft. juvenile. Mākua, O'ahu. 30 ft.

Bridled Triggerfish - male ∧   female ∨   juvenile ∨

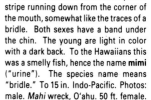

Gilded Triggerfish - male ∧

female ∨

GILDED TRIGGERFISH • **humuhumu**
Xanthichthys auromarginatus (Bennett, 1831).

These small triggerfishes are gray with a white mark on each scale. The beautiful males have a blue patch on the throat and blue fins edged in gold; females are plainer. Plankton eaters, they swim in midwater at depths of 30 feet or more, most commonly off the Kona Coast of the Big Island. They are less aggressive in captivity than many other triggerfishes. To almost 8 in. Found in scattered Indo-Pacific localities. Photos: Kaiwi Point, Hawai'i. 30 ft.

CROSSHATCH TRIGGERFISH
Xanthichthys mento (Jordan & Gilbert, 1882)

Preferring deep water, these impressive triggerfishes are rare at sport diving depths off the main islands (but fairly common in the northwestern chain). Males have blue lines on the chin and a tail rimmed in red; the sides are light yellow, crosshatched in black. Females are grayish blue (crosshatched in black) and lack the red tail. The species is similar to the Gilded Triggerfish (above), but larger. To about 12 in. Sub-tropical Pacific. Photo: Midway Island. 90 ft.

139

Trumpetfish • **nūnū** *(Aulostomus chinensis)*, Makapuʻu, Oʻahu. 30 ft.

Familiar to all snorkelers and divers, these remarkably long predators can be seen hovering over the reef almost any time. In the early morning or late afternoon they become especially active, carefully stalking small fishes and literally sucking them into their tubelike mouths with an often-audible "whomp." Their mouths are capable of enormous expansion, permitting them to swallow fishes as large in diameter as themselves.

The sticklike trumpetfishes are solitary but the sinuous cornetfishes occasionally hunt in groups. Trumpetfishes have vertically narrow (compressed) bodies; cornetfishes are horizontally flattened with a long filament extending from the tail fin. Both belong to the order Syngnathiformes, tube-mouth fishes that includes the pipefishes and seahorses. One species of each is known from Hawaiʻi. Neither should be confused with the surface-dwelling needlefishes.

Very small trumpet or cornetfishes make interesting pets. They must initially be fed with live guppies or other small fishes, but can be weaned to frozen whole fishes (thawed, of course, before feeding). A trumpetfish will occasionally yawn, expanding its narrow snout to amazing proportions. Needless to say, it should not be kept with other small fishes of value.

Both these fishes received their common names from a fancied resemblance to musical instruments and are sometimes called flutemouths. Their family names derive from *aulos* ("flute") and *fistula* ("pipe"). In Hawaiian they were known as **nūnū** or **nuhu**.

TRUMPETFISH • **nūnū**
Aulostomus chinensis (Linnaeus, 1766).

Inflexible and sticklike, these fishes are usually gray or brown, sometimes with pale vertical bars or longitudinal stripes; in Hawai'i a bright yellow color phase is common. They have a barbel on the chin that may serve as a lure. Propulsion is achieved by fluttering dorsal and anal fins set far back on the body. Trumpetfishes are a common sight on Hawaiian reefs. They ambush or stalk their prey, maneuvering slowly and carefully within striking range, often from a vertical position. They sometimes approach by swimming closely alongside another fish, such as a puffer or parrotfish, or by accompanying schools of surgeonfishes. When swarms of Milletseed Butterflyfishes attack a patch of Hawaiian Sergeant eggs a yellow trumpetfish will often turn up, taking advantage of its color and the general confusion to nab a small fish. While quite conspicuous from the side, Trumpetfishes are almost impossible to see from the perspective of their prey — head on. The species name means "Chinese." To 27 in. Indo-Pacific. Photo: Hanauma Bay, O'ahu. 70 ft.

CORNETFISH • **nūnū**
Fistularia commersonii Rüppell, 1838.

Cornetfishes have a long, whiplike filament extending from the center of the tail. Their flattened bodies are greenish, with light blue lines and dots on the back. To blend with their surroundings they can rapidly assume a pattern of dark bars. Unlike Trumpetfishes, Cornetfishes flex from side to side as they swim. Slightly less common than Trumpetfishes, they grow much larger. The species name honors the famous French biologist, Philibert Commerson (1727-1773). To 4.5 ft. (including the tail filament). Indo-Pacific. Photo: Hanauma Bay, O'ahu. 3 ft.

Elegant Coris *(Coris venusta)* - male. Magic Island, O'ahu. 25 ft.

No account of coral reef fishes could be complete without the wrasses. Wherever fishes have been hand-fed, these greedy, colorful characters are almost unavoidable. Slender and fast moving, they seem to fly through the water with winglike beats of their pectoral fins. Although a diverse group, most wrasses are elongated, cigar-shape fishes with one continuous dorsal fin. Some, such as the Saddle and Old Woman wrasses, are bold and will readily approach humans for food. Others, such as the jewel-like Fourline Wrasse, are shy and seldom seen. Wrasses are among the most common and fascinating of reef fishes. The Hawaiian Islands, with over 40 species, are an excellent location for observing them.

Characteristic of the family are bright, gaudy color patterns which vary dramatically with age and sex. Because of this wrasses are one of the most complex families to classify. Until recently, for example, males and females of some fishes were thought to represent completely separate species. The same was true for adults and juveniles. To add to the confusion, dominant males ("terminal males" or "supermales") are more vividly colored than ordinary males. For this reason, rather than separating wrasses by sex it is more accurate to divide them into "initial" and "terminal" growth phases.

The initial phase can consist solely of females or of both sexes, depending on species. Most adult wrasses are initial phase fishes. They look alike and are reproductively mature. If both sexes are present, they are capable of spawning together in a group. Comparatively few of them enter the terminal phase.

Terminal phase wrasses are always male. Though less numerous, they are more noticeable due to their brighter colors. Terminal phase males are dominant; they typically hold a territory and spawn individually with the females within it.

These social arrangements may be complex, but they are flexible; many wrasse species are able to change from female to male to suit the needs of the group. If the dominant male is removed, the largest or most aggressive of the initial phase females reverses sex and assumes his role. In fact, all dominant males begin adult life as females. Wrasses "born" male never become dominant and are doomed to a life of mediocrity.

Wrasses have thick lips and sharp teeth that often project slightly forward and are easily seen. They are carnivorous, typically preying upon small invertebrates. One Hawaiian wrasse feeds primarily on fishes, several others on plankton. Possibly the most unusual with respect to feeding habits are the small cleaners, which pick parasites and mucus from the skin and gills of other fishes. Cleaner wrasses inhabit a specific territory, such as a coral head, and attract attention by swimming up and down with a curious dancing motion. Any fish pausing at the cleaning station will get serviced by them. They enter the mouths of large fishes with impunity.

Most Hawaiian wrasses are small to mid-size, the biggest growing to about 20 inches. In 1967, however, a "giant **hīnālea**" weighing 64 pounds and measuring 3.5 feet in length was found in a Honolulu fish market. Experts from the Waikīkī Aquarium identified it as a stray Humphead or Napoleon Wrasse *(Cheilinus undulatus)*, an enormous, chunky Indo-Pacific fish which grows to over six feet in length and attains a weight of at least 400 pounds. Although they are not normally found in Hawai'i, another of these huge wrasses was seen in 2001 off the Kona Coast of the Big Island at a depth of 120 feet.

During the day wrasses depend on speed and agility to escape predation; at night they seek refuge in holes and cracks, or bury themselves in the sand. A few species spend the night in tidepools. As aquarium animals they receive mixed reviews. Although hardy and colorful, many species are "pacers," too active for the small aquarium; others hide much of the time. A few are relentless diggers. If juveniles are kept, some thought needs to be given to their future growth; wrasses are voracious eaters and mature quickly. The tendency of almost all species to bury themselves at night may keep them from being seen during the "peak" evening aquarium-viewing hours. They also bury themselves when frightened. A newly-introduced wrasse can remain out of sight for so long that the aquarist might conclude it has died or jumped out of the tank. Many species, including some of the smaller ones, are aggressive toward members of their own species.

The general Hawaiian name **hīnālea** is applied to most (but not all) wrasses; many of the smaller varieties have no known Hawaiian names. In old Hawai'i a pungent condiment was made using partially decomposed wrasses, crushed **kukui** nuts and chili pepper; a person with bad breath was sometimes referred to unkindly as "a dish of **hīnālea** sauce."

The family name comes from the Greek name *labros*, also meaning "greedy." The word "wrasse" derives from either the Celtic *urach* or the Cornish *gwragh,* take your pick. With over 600 species, the wrasses form a very large family, second only to the gobies. Hawai'i has 43 species, 13 of them endemic. Twenty-seven are described below.

Flame Wrasse *(Cirrhilabrus jordani)*. Molokini Island, Maui. 80 ft.

terminal ∧

PSYCHEDELIC WRASSE ●
Anampses chrysocephalus Randall, 1958.
(Redtail Wrasse; Psych Head)

Terminal phase males are brown with a splendid orange-and-blue head. Initial phase fishes (females), dark brown with fine white spots, sport a bright red tail. Females often move in groups and can sometimes be seen by snorkelers in shallow water. The solitary males are encountered less frequently, preferring depths of 50 feet or more. In the aquarium trade females are known as Redtail Wrasses and males as Psych Heads. The species name means "golden-head." These active fishes do poorly in captivity. Unless kept in a small group, females pace frantically up and down the glass. Males often waste away for no apparent reason. To 7 in. Endemic. Photos: terminal ph. *Mahi* wreck, O'ahu, 70 ft. initial ph. Hanauma Bay, O'ahu. 40 ft.

initial ∨

PEARL WRASSE • 'ōpule ●

Anampses cuvier Quoy & Gaimard, 1824.

Initial phase fishes (females) are dark, decorated with lines of white dots like strings of pearls. Terminal males are dull blue green with brighter blue markings on the head and tail, sometimes with a light vertical bar on the side. Seen most often in rocky areas close to shore, they also enter deeper water. Females are skittish but the colorful males can sometimes be closely approached. Named after French biologist Baron Georges Cuvier (1769-1832), who originally described many of the fishes in this book. Hawaiian name means "variegated in color." To 14 in. Endemic. Photos: initial ph. Kahe Point, O'ahu. 15 ft. terminal ph.. Lana'i Lookout, O'ahu. 40 ft.

initial ∧

terminal ∨

juvenile ∧

HAWAIIAN HOGFISH • **a'awa**
Bodianus bilunulatus (Lacepède, 1801).
  Juveniles are mostly black becoming bright yellow on top of the head and back. As they grow the yellow loses its intensity and the black recedes into a spot under the soft dorsal fin, leaving a light-color body with dark streaks on the head and many fine longitudinal lines. Terminal males, rarely seen in less than 50 feet, become blotchy purplish gray. Despite the popular name the species is not endemic, but Hawaiian specimens differ slightly and are recognized as the subspecies *albotaeniatus*. The species name means "two crescents," the subspecies, "white line." To 20 in. Indo-Pacific. Photos: Juvenile. Makua, Oahu. 20 ft. initial ph. Hanauma Bay, O'ahu. 20 ft. terminal ph. "Sheraton Caverns," south shore Kaua'i. 50 ft.

initial ∧   terminal ∨

146

TWOSPOT WRASSE
Oxycheilinus bimaculatus
(Valenciennes, 1840)

Males and females of this species are much the same: males light greenish brown, females reddish and darker. Both have delicately colored spots and lines which intensify in males during courtship. Males have a distinct wedge-shape tail fin with a backward pointing spikelike projection at the top. In both sexes the tail fin is often held closed, appearing pointed. These wrasses occur on rubble and sand bottoms, often near seaweed. They are seldom seen over coral. The species name, meaning "two spots," refers to a pair of dark spots, one in the center of the side, the other (seldom conspicuous) just behind the eye. To 6 in. Indo-Pacific. Photo: male. Magic Island, O'ahu. 30 ft.

RINGTAIL WRASSE · pō'ou
Oxycheilinus unifasciatus (Streets, 1877)

Unusual for their family, these wrasses are predators of other fishes. They typically hover several feet off the bottom, head angled down and ready to strike. They also eat crustaceans and echinoderms. Generally they are dark on the back and light on the underside, but their overall color—reddish, greenish or gray—can change rapidly, may be mottled or uniform, and has little to do with sex. A white ring around the base of the tail, usually present, can disappear in seconds. The species name means "one bar," most likely referring to the tail ring. To 18 in. Central and Western Pacific. Photos: Hanauma Bay, O'ahu. 25-30 ft.

CIGAR WRASSE • kūpou
Cheilio inermis (Forsskål, 1775).

The long, slender body shape is unique among Hawaiian wrasses. The color is light greenish brown, brown, or occasionally yellow. Terminal males have an irregular yellow orange and black patch on the upper side. The species prefers sandy, weedy or rubbly areas. The head lacks scales, thus the species name: "bare." To 19 in. Indo-Pacific. Photos: Hanauma Bay, O'ahu. 25 ft.

Cigar Wrasse - initial ∧   terminal ∨

FLAME WRASSE ●
Cirrhilabrus jordani Snyder, 1904.

These wrasses live in harems — numerous females dominated by a single male — usually at depths over 100 feet on rubble bottoms. They feed on plankton and unlike most wrasses swim by rippling their soft dorsal fin. Initial phase fishes (females) are scarlet on the back, pinkish red on the sides (appearing grayish at depth). Terminal males are scarlet on the back and tail, yellow on the sides. Males engage in frequent territorial and sexual displays, standing on their tails, flaring their fins and flashing bright lines along the body. Flame Wrasses are common on some dives off O'ahu's west shore and also at Molokini Island. They make excellent aquarium fishes (one male only to a tank) but may be inactive for several days when first introduced. They secrete a mucus cocoon at night. Keep them with peaceful fishes such as pygmy angelfishes. Named for American ichthyologist David Starr Jordan (1851-1932). To 4 in. Endemic. Photos: initial ph. Marjorie L. Awai, Waikiki. 40ft., terminal ph. Molokini Island, 80 ft.

Flame Wrasse - initial ∧   terminal ∨

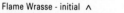

initial ∧

LINED CORIS • mālamalama ●
Coris ballieui Vaillant & Sauvage, 1875.

Muted rather than gaudy colors characterize these seldom seen wrasses, which prefer sandy or rubbly bottoms at 60 feet or more. Initial adults, faded yellow and rose marked with fine horizontal white lines, often have a series of brown markings on the upper side. Terminal males are grayish blue, becoming yellowish or pinkish on the upper front, often with a darker band on the side. Like many wrasses of the genus *Coris,* they have a prolonged first dorsal spine. Perhaps Monsieur Ballieu, an early French consul in Honolulu, provided hospitality to the two visiting French scientists who then named this fish in his honor. Two other Hawaiian fishes bear his name as well, a scorpionfish and another wrasse. To 12 in. Endemic. Photos: Marjorie L. Awai, Maunalua Bay, Oʻahu. 65 ft.

terminal ∨

juvenile ∧

initial ∧   terminal ∨

YELLOWSTRIPE CORIS • hilu ●
Coris flavovittata (Bennett, 1829).

Juveniles are dark with four or five yellowish white longitudinal stripes. Initial adults are white below eye-level, dark above, with two white stripes running lengthwise along the back. Terminal males are mottled light blue green overall. These wrasses are solitary by nature and relatively uncommon at most dive sites, although they are abundant in the Northwestern Hawaiian Islands. An old legend relates that two gods, brothers, each took the form of a **hilu**. One of them was caught by fishermen and put on the fire. The other brother, taking human form, rescued it and released it into the sea, but not before the fire had seared it with the lengthwise stripes which persist to this day. Species name: "yellow striped." Hawaiian name: "well behaved." Women who ate **hilu** while pregnant were said to bear quiet, refined children. To 20 in. Endemic. Photos: juvenile. Pūpūkea, O'ahu. 35 ft. initial ph. Makapu'u, O'ahu. 20 ft. terminal ph. Midway Island. 45 ft.

YELLOWTAIL CORIS • **hīnālea 'aki-lolo**
Coris gaimard (Quoy & Gaimard, 1824).
(RAINBOW WRASSE)

Like living rainbows, initial adults
have a green blue body speckled with
brilliant blue spots, a bright yellow tail,
and orange red dorsal and anal fins
edged with electric blue. Terminal males
are darker, often with a lighter vertical
bar down the center of the body. Juveniles are bright red with a series of white
saddles along the top of head and back.
This species is probably the most popular aquarium wrasse, juveniles being
especially interesting to observe as their
color gradually changes to the adult pattern. The Hawaiian name means "brain-
biting" (the fish was used in the treatment of head diseases). Named after an
officer on the French ship *Uranie*, which
visited Hawai'i in 1819. Gaimard helped
collect and describe the first biological
specimens of many fishes in this book.
Males to about 15 in., initial adults
smaller. Indo-Pacific. Photos: juvenile.
Kahe Point, O'ahu. 20 ft. initial ph. Puakō,
Hawai'i. 40 ft. terminal ph. Kaiwi Point,
Hawai'i. 40 ft.

juvenile ∧

initial ∧   terminal ∨

151

ELEGANT CORIS ●
Coris venusta Vaillant & Sauvage, 1875.

Although abundant in many areas such as the popular snorkeling beaches of O'ahu's north shore, the nondescript juveniles and subadults of this species are apt to be overlooked. Adults in deeper water, however, can be quite colorful when they spread their fins in bright light. Males have two color forms, one predominantly dull green with orange stripes on the head and body (illustrated above) and the other with a yellow head and fore-body and bluish or pink stripes (see page 142). Juveniles are light overall with a dark stripe on the head. The species is appropriately named after Venus, Roman goddess of beauty. It is hardy in captivity. To about 7 in. Endemic. Photos: Magic Island, O'ahu. 20 ft.

BIRD WRASSE • **hīnālea 'i'iwi** (terminal ph.); **hīnālea 'aki-lolo** (initial ph.)
Gomphosus varius Lacepède, 1801.

Bird Wrasses are easily identified by their long curved snout. Terminal males are dark green; initial adults are white in front, darkening to black. Active fishes, they are always on the go. The species name means "different." The Hawaiian name for the terminal phase refers to the 'i'iwi, or Scarlet Hawaiian Honeycreeper, an endemic bird with a long curved bill. The initial phase name means "brain biting," possibly because these fishes were used in the treatment of brain diseases. To 12 inches. Pacific Ocean (with a similar species in the Indian Ocean). Photos: Hanauma Bay, O'ahu. 20 ft.

Bird Wrasse - initial ∧   terminal ∨

ORNATE WRASSE · Iā'ō
Halichoeres ornatissimus (Garrett, 1863).

A colorful and common shallow-water wrasse, this fish is reddish with complex iridescent green markings. Juveniles are predominantly green with one or two black spots on the dorsal fin. The species name means "ornate," the Hawaiian name, "sugar-cane leaf." To 6 in. Western Pacific. Photo: Magic Island, O'ahu. 30 ft.

HAWAIIAN CLEANER WRASSE ●
Labroides phthirophagus Randall, 1958.

These small, beautiful wrasses make their living by picking parasites, and perhaps dead tissue, from the bodies of larger fishes. Adults are yellow and magenta with a black stripe from head to tail; juveniles are black with an intense blue line along the back. At night they often encase themselves in thick mucus, as do some parrotfishes. Unlike the less colorful Indo-Pacific Cleaner Wrasse (*L. dimidiatus*), the Hawaiian Cleaner Wrasse will not eat fishfood in captivity and eventually wastes away. Removing it from the reef is detrimental to other fishes. Aquarists, please do not buy this fish; trade in such species should be discouraged. The species name means "louse eater." To 4 in. Endemic. Photos: juvenile. Hōnaunau, Hawai'i. 15 ft. adult. Kealakekua Bay, Hawai'i. 20 ft.

Hawaiian Cleaner Wrasse - juvenile ∧   adult ∨

SHORTNOSE WRASSE ●
Macropharyngodon geoffroy (Quoy &
Gaimard, 1824).
(POTTER'S WRASSE)
These handsome orange wrasses
are covered with iridescent blue spots.
They swim with their dorsal and anal
fins extended and, because of their
shape and color, are easily mistaken at
first glance for a Potter's Angelfish. The
initial and terminal phases are similar;
terminal males are larger and have a
red spot at the front of their dorsal fin.
Although colorful and peaceful in captivity, they often waste away (possibly
because of an insufficient diet). To 6 in.
Endemic. Photo: Magic Island, O'ahu.
25 ft.

ROCKMOVER
Novaculichthys taeniourus (Lacepède,
1801).
(DRAGON WRASSE)
Juveniles, popularly called Dragon
Wrasses, are among the most bizarre
fishes on the reef. They have filamentous
extensions on their fins and swim with a
swaying motion, like drifting seaweed.
Adults lose the filaments, becoming dark
with white marks on each scale (appearing grayish at a distance) with a white bar
through the tail. They are usually seen
nosing about the bottom, sometimes actually moving or overturning rocks in
search of prey. The young make interesting aquarium fishes, but beware when
they grow up—adults are not called
Rockmovers for nothing. The species
name means "ribbonlike." To 12 in. East
Africa to the Americas. Photo: juvenile.
Magic Island, O'ahu. 25 ft. adult, Molokini
Island, Maui. 15ft.

Rockmover - juvenile ∧   adult ∨

DISAPPEARING WRASSE
Pseudocheilinus evanidus Jordan &
Evermann, 1903.
(SCARLET WRASSE)

These are red (appearing grayish
red underwater) with many fine white
lines along the length of the body and a
white streak under the eye. They are
found in coral-rich areas and seldom
stray far from cover. The species name
of this shy fish means "disappearing."
Hardy in captivity. To about 3 in. Indo-
Pacific. Photo: Hōnaunau, Hawai'i. 40 ft.

EIGHTLINE WRASSE
Pseudocheilinus octotaenia Jenkins,
1900.

Yellowish tan to pinkish, this wrasse
has eight dark lines along its body. Although the boldest member of its genus
in Hawai'i, it seldom ventures far into
the open. Aggressive in captivity, it is
best kept with larger fishes. The species
name means "eight lines." To 5 in.
Indo-Pacific. Photo: Hōnaunau, Hawai'i.
70 ft.

FOURLINE WRASSE
Pseudocheilinus tetrataenia Schultz,
1960.
(NEON WRASSE)

These shy beauties are orange red
with four blue lines on the upper side
from head to tail and a blue white diagonal streak from the snout to the pelvic
fin. Remaining within the coral, they are
glimpsed only while darting from one
crevice to another. They become more
outgoing in captivity, however, and are
a good choice for "mini-reef" aquariums. The species name means "four
lines." To 2.7 in. Central and Western
Pacific. Photo: Kahe Point, O'ahu. 15 ft.

PENCIL WRASSE
Pseudojuloides cerasinus (Snyder, 1904).
(SMALLTAIL WRASSE)

   Terminal males are blue and green, striped lengthwise with even brighter blue and yellow. They are known in the aquarium trade as Blue Pencil Wrasses. The rosy red initial phase fishes (females) are called Pink Pencil Wrasses. Both prefer depths of 40 feet or more. Males keep harems and display to their females by flicking the first few rays of their dorsal fin up and down. They are active fishes. Hardy in captivity. The species name means "cherry color." To almost 5 in. Indo-Pacific. Photos: Magic Island, O'ahu. 25 ft.

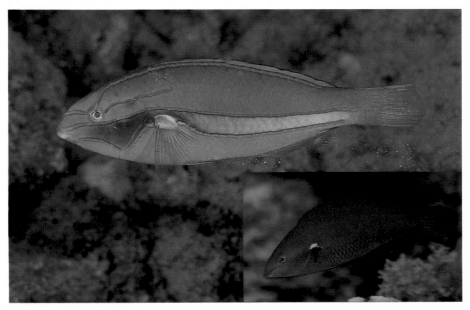

BELTED WRASSE • 'ōmaka   ●
Stethojulis balteata (Quoy & Gaimard), 1824.
(ORANGE-BAR WRASSE)

   Terminal males are mostly green with several vivid blue lines on head and body and a broad orange stripe from pectoral fin to tail. Initial adults (both sexes) are grayish with a bright yellow spot at the base of the pectoral fin. Fast-moving, always on the go, these pretty wrasses do poorly in captivity. The species name means "girdled." To almost 6 in. Endemic. Photos: initial ph. Kahe Point, O'ahu. 15 ft. terminal ph. Hanauma Bay, O'ahu. 30 ft.

156

OLD WOMAN WRASSE • **hīnālea luahine** ●
Thalassoma ballieui (Vaillant & Sauvage, 1875).
(BLACKTAIL WRASSE)

These large, rather plain wrasses have little fear of humans. Initial-phase adults (both sexes) are grayish with a thin vertical reddish line on each scale; terminal males are similar with a darker head, dull blue under the chin, and a black tail. Juveniles are bright green. The name honors Théo Ballieu, a French diplomat in Honolulu at the time of King Kalākaua. The Hawaiian name means "old woman." To about 15 in. Endemic. Photos: initial phase. Hanauma Bay, O'ahu. 10 ft. juvenile. Magic Island, O`ahu. 20 ft.

SADDLE WRASSE • **hīnālea lau-wili**
Thalassoma duperrey (Quoy & Gaimard, 1824).

These endemics are the most abundant wrasses in Hawai'i. They are blue-green with a dull orange band behind the head. Terminal males have a crescent-shape (lunate) tail fin and a whitish area behind the orange band, which they can turn on and off. Juveniles are lighter, lack the orange band, and have a dark stripe running through the eye from snout to the tail. Juveniles sometimes clean other fish, somewhat like the Hawaiian Cleaner Wrasse. The species name honors physicist Louis Isodore Duperrey (1786-1865), 2nd lieutenant of the French ship *Uranie* which visited Hawai'i in 1819. The Hawaiian name means "turning" or "twisting." To 10 in. Endemic. Photos: terminal male. Hanauma Bay, O'ahu. 3ft.; juvenile. Kahe Point, O'ahu. 15ft.

Sunset Wrasse - initial ∨   terminal ∧

SUNSET WRASSE
Thalassoma lutescens (Lay & Bennett, 1839).
(LIME GREEN WRASSE)

Uncommon in Hawai'i, the Sunset Wrasse is widespread elsewhere in the Indo-Pacific. It is closely related to the Saddle Wrasse, with which it occasionally hybridizes. Initial adults are golden; the gaudy terminal males are bright green with complex markings on the head. The species name means "yellow" (after the initial phase). To 7.5 in. Sri Lanka to the Americas. Photos: initial ph. "Golden Arches," Kona Coast, Hawai'i. 20 ft. terminal ph. Kealakekua Bay, Hawai'i. 10 ft.

SURGE WRASSE • **hou**
Thalassoma purpureum (Forsskål, 1775).

These large, fast-moving wrasses inhabit shallow water where wave action is strong. Terminal males are blue green with pink stripes and marks on the head and body. Initial adults (both sexes) are almost identical to initial phase Christmas Wrasses (below), but grow considerably larger. Prized as food in ancient Hawai'i, they were caught at night in the tidepools where they sleep. Not common. The species name means "purple." To 16 in. Indo-Pacific. Photo: terminal ph. Kahalu'u, Hawai'i. 5 ft.

FIVESTRIPE WRASSE
Thalassoma quinquevittatum (Lay & Bennett, 1839).

The complex purple, green and yellow colors of this wrasse almost defy description. First recorded from Hawai'i in 1980, it is an uncommon (but not rare) inhabitant of shallow reef flats near the surge zone, an area not much frequented by divers. Initial and terminal phases are similar. It sometimes hybridizes with the Saddle Wrasse. The species name means "five stripes." To about 5 in. Indo-Pacific. Photo: Kahe Point, O'ahu. 10 ft.

CHRISTMAS WRASSE • 'āwela
Thalassoma trilobatum (Lacepède, 1801).

Terminal males have ladderlike, blue green markings on a reddish body. Drab by comparison, initial adults (both sexes) are brown and green. These fast-moving wrasses inhabit shallow reef flats in the surge zone and are more easily seen by snorkelers than by divers. At night they sometimes sleep in tidepools just above the water line where they can be discovered by flash-light. Species name means "three lobes." Also called **hou** in Hawaiian. A hardy but active aquarium fish. To about 11 in. Indo-Pacific. Photos: Hanauma Bay, O'ahu. 15 ft.

Christmas Wrasse - initial ∧   terminal ∨

adult ∧

juvenile ∧

BLACKSIDE RAZORFISH · **lae nihi** ●
Iniistius umbrilatus (Jenkins, 1901)

   Razorfishes (or razor wrasses) have high, compressed bodies and live over sand, into which they dive when threatened. The endemic Blackside Razorfish is the most common razorfish in the islands. Juveniles, with three dark bars, remain close to the reef and are probably seen more often than adults, which roam widely over the sand in slightly deeper water. Initial phase adults are pale gray with a large black patch on the side and an area of bluish iridescence under it. Terminal males in courtship display appear half dark and half light (dark half in front). The species name means "shadowed," the Hawaiian name "sharp forehead." Until recently placed in the genus *Xyrichtys*. To about 9 in. Endemic. Photos: Kahe Point, O'ahu. 20-30 ft. (The Celebese Razorfish, *I. celebicus,* is similar but with a brownish patch; it is generally less common.)

adult ∧

PEACOCK RAZORFISH · **lae nihi**
Iniistius pavo (Valenciennes, 1840)

   This razorfish is easily identified by the long dorsal filament which can be flicked up and down. It is lightly barred in gray (often with a whitish patch on the side) and has a small black spot high on the side above the pectoral fin. Juveniles, darker and variable in color, are best recognized by the long stem-like dorsal filament projecting forward above the head. Very small juveniles twist and bend as they swim, almost exactly mimicking a drifting bit of leaf or weed. Juveniles do well in captivity but should be released when they grow too large. (Somewhat similar and sharing the same habitat, the Whiteside Razorfish, *I. aneitensis,* has a snow white patch on the side while the rarely seen *I. baldwini,* has a white patch bordered by yellow with a small black patch above and prefers depths of 70 feet or more.) Species name means "peacock;" Hawaiian name, "sharp forehead." To 12 in. East Africa to the Americas. Photos: Kahe Point, O'ahu. 30 ft.

juvenile ∧

160

CATCHING YOUR OWN AQUARIUM FISHES

If you are an aquarist living in Hawai'i sooner or later you will want to catch your own aquarium fishes. Once you discover how much fun this is you may never buy again.

Before collecting specimens you must obtain at no charge an aquarium fish collecting permit from the State of Hawai'i Department of Land and Natural Resources, Division of Aquatic Resources. The address is 1151 Punchbowl Street, Room 330, Honolulu, HI 96813. Obtain from the same office a current copy of the Hawaii Fishing Regulations. Restricted areas and species are listed both on the permit and in the pamphlet.

No book can teach you to how to catch coral reef fishes. It is a skill best learned by practice. Each collector has his or her favorite techniques. Below, however, are a few hints for beginners.

Most amateur collectors use hand nets. Try to find one made from fine monofilament; the ordinary cotton type are too easy for fishes to see and avoid. You may have to mount the net yourself.

You will also want something to help chase fishes into the net. Some use a long thin rod or stick, others prefer using another handnet. A stick can be poked into hiding places while a conspicuous cotton net can be used to maneuver fishes into a less visible monofilament net. Unfortunately, struggling fishes easily damage themselves in monofilament nets. Either restrain the fish by holding it or use a softer cotton net for transporting it to the collecting bucket.

Although "slurp guns," sometimes available in dive shops, seem an easy shortcut to success, they require practice to use effectively. You can't just go out and start slurping up fishes. On the other hand, some small fishes which hole up in the coral can most easily be caught with these devices.

Do not place fishes you have caught in a collapsible mesh "goody bag." Abrasion will quickly kill them. Use a container with solid sides that is weighted to rest on the bottom. Bait buckets with spring-loaded lids are convenient. You may need to drill additional holes to ensure good water circulation.

Some aquarists construct small traps using window screening or fine mesh wire netting. The traps have a funnel entrance, wide on the outside and narrow on the inside which are easy to swim into but difficult to get out of. Traps can be left in a likely spot for several hours or overnight. Luring fishes inside with a piece of a broken white plate is often as effective as using edible bait. Be sure to check traps often; fishes will damage themselves if left for too long.

Scuba divers should catch fishes in shallow water only. Those caught deeper than about 25 feet will probably require hours of decompression before they can be brought safely to the surface. As pressure decreases, air in their swim bladders will expand causing them to float uncontrollably. They are unlikely to survive.

If you are visiting Hawai'i you might be able to get your fishes professionally bagged in oxygen for the trip back home at one of the Honolulu pet stores that sell marine fishes. One place to try is Modern Pet Center at 818 Sheridan Street (949-4916).

Please note that it is illegal in Hawai'i to take coral or rocks with marine life attached.

PHOTOGRAPHING FISHES

Far more challenging than catching fishes is capturing good portraits of them. "A combination of hunting and art," underwater photographer David Doubilet calls this skill. Increasing numbers of divers and snorkelers are discovering that underwater photography is one of the main reasons they dive.

Most use waterproof rangefinder cameras with wide-angle lenses (such as the popular Nikonos) to capture reef scenes, divers, and large marine creatures. Macro lenses and wire framers attach easily to these cameras for shooting closeups. But, as many discover, these popular systems are poor for fish photography. Focusing must be estimated — difficult on small moving targets. Although wide-angle lenses can overcome this (everything is in focus), most fish subjects appear too small and distant.

The solution is the single lens reflex (SLR) camera, which allows the photographer to actively compose and focus through the camera lens itself. Although a highly sophisticated (and costly) professional underwater SLR is offered by Nikon, most divers interested in fish photography continue to use ordinary SLRs in underwater housings. Most of the photographs in this book were taken with such a system: a Minolta X-700 SLR camera mounted in a relatively inexpensive plexiglass housing made in the U.S.A. by Ikelite.

A weakness of many housed camera systems is a viewfinder too small to be used through face mask and housing. Several discontinued manual SLR cameras (as well some recent high-end models) can be fitted with special large viewfinders originally designed for sports photography. These solve the problem and are a pleasure to use underwater. The popular Ikelite housings come with a viewfinder extender (the "Supereye") that delivers a small but workable image with most other SLRs. It takes time to get used to focusing with a Supereye.

Autofocus underwater works well in general but introduces problems of its own. In macro work, for example, where depth of field is minimal, any motion between camera and subject makes it difficult for the camera to focus. Another problem is the near necessity for subjects to be centered in the frame: if the fish moves, the camera re-focuses on the background. Whichever system you use, seeing and focusing are often easier when wearing a black mask rather than one of the clear silicone type.

The lens of choice for most fish portrait work is a 90 or 100 mm macro lens. In clear water it can capture anything from a small goby to a large surgeonfish. For bigger fishes, or where fishes are unafraid of divers, 50 mm or even 35 mm lenses give excellent results.

Because of the filtering effect of seawater, colors underwater are usually disappointing unless a strobe is used. Powerful strobes permit smaller apertures and greater depth of field, but are heavy and awkward to carry. The author finds twin low-power Ikelite MV substrobes quite adequate for most fish portraits. Mounted close to the lens, they point straight forward, eliminating the need for constant adjustment. If possible, use a sync speed faster than the standard 1/60th of a second; this helps minimize blurring of a moving subject due to ambient light exposure. Automatic TTL metering yields excellent results in most cases as long as the subject occupies 65% or more of the frame.

Film choice is not critical for fish closeups. With a strobe, ordinary 100 ISO film is satisfactory; with ambient light alone, faster film is preferable. (Snorkelers near the surface can obtain surprisingly good pictures with fast film and ambient light. The photograph of two Moorish Idols in this book was taken on Ekatachrome 400 using an SLR housed in an inexpensive plastic bag housing made by the German firm Ewa Marine.) Print film, because of its wide exposure latitude, is easiest to use, yielding acceptable results with closeup subjects. Its low contrast, however, makes it less suitable for wider angle work. Serious photographers almost always use slide film for superior color, contrast and reproducibility. Most of the photographs in this book were taken on Fuji Velvia exposed at ASA 80 and pushed one stop.

Some final tips: You rarely get good fish portraits by chasing your subjects. By remaining in an area for a long time, however, you can often take a series of excellent photos — the fishes get used to you. Subjects that are feeding, resting, or being cleaned are easiest. Approach them slowly, with a minimum of bubbles. (If you are a diver, be careful about holding your breath. On ascent, this dangerous habit can lead to ruptured lungs and air embolism.)

Fishes in open water can be photographed with a dramatic black background simply by using a small enough f-stop to eliminate most ambient light. Natural-looking deep blue backgrounds are more difficult to achieve: your f-stop must be set to balance both ambient and artificial light.

For further discussion of equipment and techniques consult the comprehensive **Manual of Underwater Photography** by de Couet and Green (listed under Photography in the chapter Further Reading). In Honolulu, you can meet other underwater photographers through the Underwater Photographic Society of Hawai'i. It sponsors club dives and meets about once a month. Inquire at dive shops or camera stores for locations and times.

Finally, as many have pointed out, the number of good pictures obtained will be in direct proportion to the amount of film exposed — so keep on diving and keep on taking pictures.

SOURCE MATERIALS

Most of the technical and cultural information presented in this book was drawn from the following publications (listed in approximate order of usefulness). Other sources are listed under "Further Reading".

IDENTIFICATION, CLASSIFICATION, GEOGRAPHIC RANGE, MAXIMUM LENGTH
Randall, John E. 1985. **Guide to Hawaiian reef fishes.** Newtown Square, Pennsylvania: Harrowood Books.

Myers, Robert F., 1989. **Micronesian reef fishes.** Barrigada, Guam: Coral Graphics.

Tinker, Spencer W., 1978. **Fishes of Hawaii.** Honolulu: Hawaiian Service.

Randall, John E., G.R. Allen & R.C. Steene. 1990. **Fishes of the Great Barrier Reef and Coral Sea.** Honolulu: University of Hawaii Press.

Eschmeyer, William N. 1990. **Catalog of the genera of recent fishes.** San Francisco : California Academy of Sciences. 697 p.

HAWAIIAN NAMES AND CULTURAL INFORMATION
Titcomb, Margaret, 1972. **Native use of fish in Hawaii** (2nd ed.). Honolulu: University Press of Hawaii.

Pukui, Mary Kawena & S.H. Elbert, 1971. **Hawaiian dictionary.** Honolulu: University Press of Hawaii.

Hobson, Edmund & E.H. Chave, 1990. **Hawaiian reef animals** (revised ed.). Honolulu: University of Hawaii Press.

Jordan, David Starr & B.W. Evermann, 1973. **The shore fishes of Hawaii.** Rutland, Vermont: Charles E. Tuttle Co. (first printed in 1905 under different title)

THE ENVIRONMENT
Gosline, William & Vernon E. Brock, 1960. **Handbook of Hawaiian Fishes.** Honolulu: University of Hawaii Press.

Fielding, Ann, & Ed Robinson, 1987. **An Underwater Guide to Hawai'i.** Honolulu: University of Hawaii Press.

SCIENTIFIC NAMES
Brown, Roland Wilbur, 1956. **Composition of scientific words.** Washington, D.C.: Smithsonian Institution Press.

FURTHER READING

The previous section lists the most important books on Hawaiian fishes. The following supplemental material includes magazine, journal and newspaper articles as well as a few books. It is organized into five sections: A) Diving, snorkeling and beach guides; B) Fishes by family; C) Fishes, general; D) Aquarium guides; E) Underwater photography.

A) DIVING, SNORKELING AND BEACH GUIDES

Balder, A.P. 1992. **Marine atlas of the Hawaiian Islands**. Honolulu: University of Hawai'i Press. 120 p. (A complete set of nautical charts for serious marine navigators. Author is a dedicated diver.)

Canham, Rod. 1991. **Hawaii below: favorites, tips and secrets of the diving pros**. San Diego: Watersport Publishing. 235 p. (Comprehensive rundown on Hawaii's dive sites, concentrating on boat dives. Includes good information for the fish watcher but no detailed maps. Supplementary material for tourists is included).

Clark, John R.K. 1977-1990. **Beaches of the Big Island; Beaches of Kaua'i and Ni'ihau; Beaches of Maui County; Beaches of O'ahu**. Honolulu: University of Hawai'i Press. 4 vols. (Detailed descriptions of every beach in the state. Rich in historical information. Good maps. Skimpy on diving and snorkeling information.).

Dresie, Dick. [no date] **Let's go shore dive'n' on the Kona Coast**. [Kailua-Kona]: DPD Associates. [44 p.] (Chatty and informative descriptions of 27 favorite shore dives on the Big Island. Detailed descriptions of entry points, but no maps.)

Scott, Susan & David R. Schrichte. 1993. **Exploring Hanauma Bay**. Honolulu: University of Hawaii Press. 90 p.

Thorne, Chuck & Lou Zitnik. 1984. **The divers' guide to Hawaii**. Hawaii Divers Guide: P.O. Box 1461, Kahalui, Maui 96732. 248 p. (The most comprehensive guide to shore dives and snorkeling sites. Includes detailed maps plus information on weather patterns, currents, tides and more.)

Thorne, Chuck. 1988. **The divers' guide to Maui**. Maui Dive Guide, P.O. Box 1461, Kahalui, HI 96732. 80 p. (An updated Maui version of the above.)

B) FISHES BY FAMILY

ANGELFISHES and BUTTERFLYFISHES

Allen, Gerald R. & Roger Steene. 1979. **Butterfly and angelfishes of the world, vols. 1-2.** Mentor, Ohio: Aquarium Systems. (The most complete reference available. Well illustrated. Includes aquarium information.)

Carlson, Bruce A. 1982. **The Masked angelfish, *Genicanthus personatus* Randall, 1974.** *Freshwater and Marine Aquarium* 5(5):31-32; May 1982

Lobel, Phil S. 1975. **Hawaiian angelfishes**. *Marine Aquarist* 6(4):30

Miklosz, John C. 1976. **Hawaiian butterflies**. *Marine Aquarist* 7(2):19

Pyle, Richard L. 1990. **The Masked angelfish, *Genicanthus personatus* Randall**. *Freshwater and Marine Aquarium* 13(10):112; Oct. 1990.

Pyle, Richard L. 1992. **Centropyge loriculus x potteri, another hybrid angelfish**. *Freshwater and Marine Aquarium* 15(8):40; Aug. 1992.

Taylor, Edward C. **Marine angelfishes — thinking small**. 1983. *Tropical Fish Hobbyist* 31(9) May 1983.

Turk, Christopher T., & Devin Bartley. 1989. **Marine fish and invertebrate nutrition, part 3: angelfish and butterflyfishes**. *Freshwater and Marine Aquarium* 12(9):20 Sept. 1989.

Verbin, Mark S. 1991. **Marine angelfish**. *Marine Fish Monthly* 6(8) Sept. 1991.

BARRACUDAS

Markerich, Mike. 1983. **Opelu mama — a barracuda friend and fishing companion**. *Honolulu Star-Bulletin & Advertiser*, April 3, 1983, A-15.

Markerich, Mike. 1984. **The "opelu mama" — a barracuda with a job to do.** *Honolulu Star-Bulletin & Advertiser*, Dec. 16, 1984, F-1.

BLENNIES

Carlson, Bruce A. 1992. **Life history and reproductive success of *Exallias brevis*.** Ph.D. thesis, University of Hawai'i.

BOXFISHES

Pyle, Richard L. 1989. **Whitley's Boxfish, *Ostracion whitleyi* Fowler.** *Freshwater and Marine Aquarium* 12(7):58; July 1989.

Randall, John E. 1972. **The Hawaiian trunkfishes of the genus *Ostracion*.** *Copeia* 1972(4):757-767.

DAMSELFISHES

Allen, Gerald R. 1991. **Damselfishes of the world.** Melle, Germany: Mergus. (The most complete book available on these fishes. Well illustrated. Includes aquarium information.)

Fenner, Bob and Cindi Camp. 1991. **Damselfishes, saltwater bread and butter.** *Freshwater and Marine Aquarium* 14(10) Oct. 1991.

Randall, John E. & S.N. Swerdloff. 1973. **A review of the damselfish genus Chromis from the Hawaiian Islands, with descriptions of three new species.** *Pacific Science* 27(4):327-349.

EELS

Dick, Danny & Jennifer Piltz. 1985. **The distribution and abundance of the garden eel, *Gorgasia hawaiiensis*, at Puako, Hawaii.** *Proceedings of the 10th annual student symposium on marine affairs.*

Randall, John E. & J.R. Chess. 1979. **A new species of garden eel (Congrinae: Heterocongrinae) of the genus *Gorgasia* from Hawaii.** *Pacific Science*, 33(1):17-23.

Randall, John E. 1969. **How dangerous is the moray eel?** *Australian Natural History*, June 1969.

FROGFISHES

Michael, Scott W. 1991. **Commerson's Frogfish *Antennarius commersoni* (Latreille).** *Freshwater and Marine Aquarium* 14(11) Nov. 1991.

Pietsch, T.W. and D.B. Grobecker. 1987. **Frogfishes of the world: systematics, zoogeography, and behavioral ecology.** Stanford, Calif.: Stanford University Press, 1987. 420 p. (mainly for specialists.)

GOBIES and DARTFISHES

Baldwin, Wayne J. 1972. **A new genus and new species of Hawaiian gobiid fish.** *Pacific Science* 26: 125-128. (A description of Mainland's Goby, *Psilogobius mainlandi*.)

Carlson, Bruce A. 1982. ***Nemateleotris magnifica* Fowler 1938.** *Freshwater and Marine Aquarium* 5(1):8; Jan. 1982.

Davis, William P. & John E. Randall. 1977. **The systematics, biology and zoogeography of *Ptereleotris heteropterus* (Pisces: Gobiidae).** *Proceedings of the 3rd Coral Reef Symposium (Miami)*: 261-266.

Hunziker, Ray. 1990. **Gobies in the marine aquarium.** *Tropical Fish Hobbyist* 38(11):40; July 1990

Spies, Gunter. 1991. **Little known and seldom seen: the tiny coral gobies of the genus Bryaninops.** *Tropical Fish Hobbyist* 40(1):78; Sept. 1991.

GROUPERS and ANTHIAS

Anon. 1956. **354-pound sea bass speared.** *Honolulu Advertiser*, December 31, 1956, A-1.

——. 1958. **Skin divers conquer giant sea bass.** *Honolulu Advertiser*, March 3, 1958, A-8.

——. 1989. 1989. **Catch of the day: 554-pound sea bass.** *Honolulu Advertiser*, June 30, 1989, A-18.

Carlson, Bruce A. 1983. **The longfin bass, *Anthias ventralis*, Randall, 1979.** *Freshwater and Marine Aquarium* 7(8):45-46; Aug. 1984.

Privitera, Lisa A. 1991. **The sunset basslet, *Liopropoma aurora* (Jordan and Evermann).** *Freshwater and Marine Aquarium* 14(3) March 1991.

Pyle, Richard L. 1991. **The Hawaiian deep anthias *Holanthias fuscipinnis* (Jenkins).** *Freshwater* *and Marine Aquarium* 14(12) Dec. 1991.

Randall, John E. 1979. **A review of the serranid fish genus *Anthias* of the Hawaiian Islands, with descriptions of two new species.** *Contrib. Sci. Natur. Hist. Mus. Los Angeles County,* 1979. 302:1-13.

Randall, John E. & S. Ralston. 1984. **A new species of serranid fish of the genus *Anthias* from the Hawaiian Islands and Johnston Island.** *Pacific Science* 38(3):220-227.

HAWKFISHES

Takeshita, Glenn Y. 1975. **Long-snouted hawkfish.** *Marine Aquarist* 6(6):27.

LIZARDFISHES

Waples, R.S. and J.E. Randall. 1988. **A revision of the Hawaiian lizardfishes of the genus *Synodus*, with descriptions of four new species.** Pacific Science 42(3-4): 178-213.

NEEDLEFISHES

McCabe, M.J., et al. 1978. **A fatal brain injury caused by a needlefish.** Neuroradiology 15: 137-139. (Injury of a 10-year old boy on Kauai)

PIPEFISHES and SEAHORSES

Dawson, C.E. 1985. **Indo-Pacific pipefishes: (Red Sea to the Americas).** Ocean Springs, Miss.: Gulf Coast Research Laboratory. 230 p. (Mainly for specialists).

Sprung, Julian. 1989. **Hand fed horses.** *Freshwater and Marine Aquarium* 12(3):74-75; March 1989

Volkart, Bill. 1992. **Seahorses, treasures of the sea.** *Freshwater and Marine Aquarium* 15(5): 44-45; May 1992.

PUFFERS

Allen, Gerald R. & John E. Randall. 1977. **Review of the sharpnose pufferfishes (subfamily *Canthigasterinae*) of the Indo-Pacific.** *Records of the Western Australian Museum* 30(17): 475-517. (Color plates of each species).

Michael, Scott W. 1991. **An aquarist's guide to the tobies (genus *Canthigaster*), parts 1-2.** *Freshwater and Marine Aquarium* 14(1) Jan. 1991; 14(2) Feb. 1991.

RAYS

Addison, Clark. 1993. **Man meets manta.** *Discover Diving* 11(1):74-76; Jan/Feb. 1993.

SCORPIONFISHES

Donovan, Paul. 1992. **The Family Scorpaenidae, a tank of lions and stones.** *Freshwater and Marine Aquarium* 15(3):8-11. March 1992.

Eschmeyer, William N. & J.E. Randall. 1975. **The scorpaenid fishes of the Hawaiian Islands, including new species and new records.** *Proceedings of the California Academy of Sciences,* 4th series 40(11):265-333.

Fox, Gregory A. 1989. **Venomous and potentially dangerous marine animals, pt. 1. The scorpionfish family.** *Freshwater and Marine Aquarium* 12(12):8-9; Dec. 1989.

SHARKS

Balazs, George H. **Shark attacks in the Hawaiian Islands involving fatality.** (register updated regularly and available from National Marine Fisheries Service, Honolulu).

Glodek, Garrett S. 1992. **Shark biology.** *Freshwater and Marine Aquarium* 15(3):171-181. March 1992.

Lineaweaver, Thomas H. & R.H. Backus, 1984. **The Natural history of sharks.** New York: Nick Lyons Books/Schocken Books. 234 p. (Beautifully written. Still an excellent book on the subject although no longer completely up-to-date.)

Suzumoto, Arnold, R.L. Pyle & R.B. Reeve. 1991. **Sharks Hawai'i.** Honolulu: Bishop Museum Press. 44 p.

Taylor, Leighton. 1993. **Sharks of Hawai'i: their biology and cultural significance.** University of Hawai'i Press. 126 p. (The best book on Hawaiian sharks, illustrated with paintings and drawings. Includes Balazs' shark attack listing up to December 1992.)

Tinker, Spencer Wilkie & Charles J. DeLuca. 1973. **Sharks & rays: a handbook of the sharks and rays of Hawaii and the Central Pacific Ocean**. Rutland, Vermont : Charles E. Tuttle Company. 80 p. (Material drawn from the first author's **Fishes of Hawaii**).

SNAPPERS

Tabata, Raymond S., ed. **Transcripts of "Taape: what needs to be done?" workshop, November 7, 1979.** University of Hawaii College Sea Grant Program. Working paper no. 46.

SURGEONFISHES and MOORISH IDOLS

DeBernardo, James P. 1982. **Keeping the moorish idol.** *Freshwater and Marine Aquarium* 5(11) Nov. 1982.

Jones, Lawrence L.C. 1983. **Care and maintenance of tangs in captivity, part 1 & 2.** *Freshwater and Marine Aquarium* 6(11) Nov. 1983; 7(3) March 1984.

Lobel, Philip S. 1984. **The Hawaiian chevron tang, *Ctenochaetus hawaiiensis*.** *Freshwater and Marine Aquarium* 7(3) March 1984.

Turk, Christopher T. & Devin M. Bartley. 1990. **Marine fish and invertebrate nutrition, part 4: surgeonfish (Acanthuridae) and damselfish (Pomacentridae).** *Freshwater and Marine Aquarium* 13(1):96; Jan. 1990.

TRIGGERFISHES

Emmens, Cliff W., 1984. **Triggerfishes.** *Tropical Fish Hobbyist* 32(9):55-59. May 1984.

Parker, Nancy J. 1977. **Picasso trigger.** *Marine Aquarist* 8(1) 1977.

Ryan, Tim. 1984. **Humuhumu winner of popular vote for Hawaii's state fish.** *Honolulu-Star Bulletin*, December 15, 1984. Page A-1.

WRASSES

Anon. 1967. **Giant hinalea.** *Honolulu Star-Bulletin*, July 12, 1967. Page E-1.

Gonzalez, Deane. 1979. **The exquisite Hawaiian flame wrasse.** *Freshwater and Marine Aquarium* 12(6):26; June. 1979.

Michael, Scott W. **An aquarist's guide to the wrasses of the genus Pseudocheilinus.** *Freshwater and Marine Aquarium* 13(9):9-10; Sept. 1990.

Privitera, Lisa A. 1992. **The Hawaiian flame wrasse *Cirrhilabrus jordani* Snyder** *Freshwater and Marine Aquarium* 15(9):152; Sept. 1992.

Pyle, Richard L. 1992. **The neon wrasse: *Bodianus sanguineus* (Jordan and Evermann).** *Freshwater and Marine Aquarium* 14(12):144; Dec. 1992.

Randall, John E. 1976. **A review of the Hawaiian labrid fishes of the genus Coris.** *UO. Japan Society of Ichthyology. Tokyo* 26:1-10

Takeshita, Glenn Y. 1977. **Hawaiian flame wrasse.** *Marine Aquarist* 7(8):44

C) FISHES, GENERAL

Bartley, Devin M. & Christopher T. Turk. 1991. **Nutrition and feeding in the marine environment, part 5: the carnivores.** *Freshwater and Marine Aquarium* 14(2) Feb. 1991.

Carpenter, Russell & Blyth Carpenter. 1981. **Fish watching in Hawaii**. San Mateo, Calif.: Natural World Press. 120 p. (Excellent discussion of fish behavior, biology, ecology).

Clark, Athline M. 1978. **Dangerous marine organisms of Hawaii.** Sea Grant Advisory Report UNIHI-SEAGRANT-AR-78-01. 27 p.

Conde, B. 1982. **Longevity of marine tropicals at the Nancy Aquarium.** *Revue Francaise d'Aquariologie* 9(4) March 1, 1983.

Debelius, Helmut. 1986. **Fishes for the invertebrate aquarium**. Essen, Germany: Edition Kernen. 160 p. (Informative discussion of fishes for the "mini-reef" aquarium. Well illustrated.)

Goodson, Gar. 1977. **The many-splendored fishes of Hawaii**. Palos Verdes Estates, Calif.: Marquest Colorguide Books. 91 p.

Hanauer, Eric. 1993. **Let the critters be critters.** *Discover Diving* 11(1):97-98; Jan/Feb. 1993. (on fish feeding by divers)

Hoover, John. 1994. **Expedition to Midway.** Freshwater and Marine Aquarium 17(5): 200-210; May, 1994.

Hourigan, T.F & E.S. Reese. 1987. **Mid-ocean isolation and the evolution of Hawaiian reef fishes.** *Trends in ecology and evolution* 2(7): 187-191.

Kosaki, Randall K., et al. 1991. **New records of fishes from Johnston Atoll, with notes on biogeography.** *Pacific Science* 45(2):186-203.

Parker, Nancy J. 1974. **Hawaiian collecting.** *Marine Aquarist* 5(1):28-38.

Perrine, Doug. 1989. **Reef fish feedings: amusement or nuisance?** *Sea Frontiers* 35(5):272; Sept -Oct. 1989.

Randall, John E., et al. 1993. **Annotated checklist of the fishes of Midway Atoll, Northwestern Hawaiian Islands.** *Pacific Science* 47(4):356-400

Randall, John E. 1980. **Conserving marine fishes.** *ORYX, Journal of the Fauna Preservation Society* 15(3):287-291; April 1980.

Randall, John E. 1980. **New records of fishes from the Hawaiian Islands.** *Pacific Science* 34(3):211-232.

Randall, John E. 1973. **The endemic shore fishes of the Hawaiian Islands, Lord Howe Island and Easter Island.** *Colloque Commerson 1973 O.R.S.T.O.M. Travaux et documents* no. 47.

Randall, John E., et al. 1993. **Eleven new records and validations of shore fishes from the Hawaiian Islands.** *Pacific Science* 47(3):222-239.

Randall, John E., Phillip S. Lobel & E.H. Chave. 1985. **Annotated checklist of the fishes of Johnston Island.** *Pacific Science* 39(1):24-80.

Randall, John E. & Richard K. Kanayama. 1972. **Hawaiian fish immigrants.** *Sea Frontiers* 18(3):144-153.

Severns, Mike & Pauline Fiene-Severns. 1993. **Molokini Island: Hawaii's premier marine reserve.** Wailuku, Hawaii: Pacific Islands Publishing. (Features stunning underwater photographs of unusual and rare fishes as well as other marine life.)

Wilson, Roberta & James Q. Wilson. 1985. **Watching fishes: life and behavior on coral reefs.** New York: Harper & Row. 275 p. (An informative discussion of fish behavior and biology).

D) AQUARIUM GUIDES

Emmens, C. W. 1988. **Marine fishes and invertebrates in your own home.** Neptune City, N.J.: T.F.H. 189 p.

Moe, Martin A. 1982. **The marine aquarium handbook: beginner to breeder.** Marathon, Fla.: Norns Publishing Co. 169 p. (The best short guide for beginners as well as a reference for advanced aquarists. Covers only traditional undergravel or canister filtration.)

Moe, Martin A. 1989. **The marine aquarium reference: systems and invertebrates.** Plantation, Fla.: Green Turtle Publications. 510 p. (The most complete reference available. Highly recommended.)

Spotte, Stephen. 1973. **Marine aquarium keeping: the science, animals and art.** New York: Wiley. 171 p. (A good introductory guide, although somewhat dated.)

E) UNDERWATER PHOTOGRAPHY

de Couet, Heinz-Gert & Andrew Green. 1989. **The manual of underwater photography.** Wiesbaden: Verlag Christa Hemmen. 394 p. (A thorough introduction and reference. Highly recommended. A 2nd ed. in German is available.)

TABLE OF INVALID OR INCORRECT SCIENTIFIC NAMES

Although generally stable, scientific names are not free from change. Earlier books still in print may use any of the names below in reference to the fishes in this book. The majority are "synonyms," invalid names resulting from a species being described and named more than once. See the chapter Classification and Names for more information.

Some invalid names result from revisions in classification. For example, the Moorish Idol, originally thought to be a butterflyfish, was first named *Chaetodon cornutus*. Later, scientists placed it in its own family, Zanclidae, and the valid name became *Zanclus cornutus*.

A few species names below are perfectly valid, but incorrect when applied to Hawaiian fishes. For example, an earlier book may list the surgeonfish *Acanthurus mata* as occuring in Hawai'i. *Acanthurus mata* (*A. mata*, for short) is a valid species not found in Hawai'i. The Hawaiian fish long thought to be *A. mata* is actually *A. blochii*.

INVALID NAME - VALID NAME

Acanthurus aliala = *A. nigricans* (Goldrim Surgeonfish)
Acanthurus glaucopareius = *A. nigricans* (Goldrim Surgeonfish)
Acanthurus elongatus = a common misidentification of *A. nigrofuscus* (Lavender Tang)
Acanthurus mata = a common misidentification of *A. blochii* (Ringtail Surgeon)
Acanthurus sandvicensis = *A. triostegus sandvicensis* (Convict Tang)

Adioryx = *Sargocentron* (a squirrelfish genus)

Anampses godeffroyi = *A. cuvier* (Pearl Wrasse)

Anampses rubrocaudatus = *A. chrysocephalus* (Psychedelic Wrasse)

Anthias = *Pseudanthias* (a genus in the family Serranidae)

Aphareus furcata = *Aphareus furca* (Forktail Snapper)

Apogon snyderi = *A. kallopterus* (Iridescent Cardinalfish)
Apogon erythrinus = probably *A. coccineus* (Ruby Cardinalfish)

Apolemichthys arcuatus = *Holacanthus arcuatus* (Bandit Angelfish)

Belone platyura = *Platybelone argalus* (Flat-Tailed Needlefish)

Bodianus albotaeniatus = *B. bilunulatus* (Hawaiian Hogfish)

Brachirus barberi = *Dendrochirus barberi* (Green Lionfish)

Caesioperca thompsoni = *Pseudanthias thompsoni* (Hawaiian Anthias)

Calotomus sandwicensis = *C. carolinus* (Star-Eye Parrotfish)

Cantherhines albopunctatus = *C. dumerilii* (Barred Filefish)
Cantherhines carolae = *C. dumerilii* (Barred Filefish)

Canthigaster cinctus = *C. coronata* (Crown Toby)
Canthigaster bitaeniata = *C. rivulata* (Maze Toby)

INVALID NAME - VALID NAME

Carangoides ferdau = a common misidentification of *C. orthogrammus* (Yellowspotted Jack)

Caranx stellatus = *C. melampygus* (Bluefin Trevally)
Caranx elacate = *C. sexfasciatus* (Bigeye Jack)

Carcharhinus milberti = *C. plumbeus* (Sandbar Shark)
Carcharhinus menisorrah = a common misidentification of *C. amblyrhyncos* (Gray Reef Shark)

Centropyge flammeus = *C. loriculus* (Flame Angelfish)

Chaenomugil leuciscus = *Neomyxus leuciscus* (Acute-Jawed Mullet)

Chaetodon corallicola = *C. kleinii* (Bluehead Butterflyfish)

Cheilinus rodochrous = *C. unifasciatus* (Ringtail Wrasse)

Cirrhitus alternus = *C. pinnulatus* (Stocky Hawkfish)

Coris eydouxi = *C. flavovittata* (Yellowstripe Coris)
Coris greenovii = *C. gaimard* (Yellowtail Coris)
Coris lepomis = *C. flavovittata* (Yellowstripe Coris)
Coris rosea = *C. ballieui* (Lined Coris)

Decapterus pinnulatus = *D. macarellus* (Mackerel Scad)

Dendrochirus chloreus = *D. barberi* (Green Lionfish)
Dendrochirus hudsoni = *D. barberi* (Green Lionfish)

Doryhamphus melanopleura = *D. excisus* (Bluestripe Pipefish)

Dunckerocampus baldwini = *Doryrhamphus baldwini* (Redstripe Pipefish)

Echidna zebra = *Gymnomuraena zebra* (Zebra Moray)

Epinephelus tauvina = a common misidentification of *E. lanceolatus* (Giant Grouper)

Flammeo = *Neoniphon* (a squirrelfish genus)

Forcipiger cyrano = *F. longirostris* (Rare Longnose Butterflyfish)
Forcipiger inornatus = *F. longirostris*

INVALID NAME - VALID NAME

Gomphosus tricolor = G. varius (Bird Wrasse)

Gymnothorax hepaticus = G. albimarginatus
(Whitemargin Moray)
Gymnothorax petelli = G. rueppelliae (Yellowhead Moray)

Hemipteronotus = Xyrichtys (a wrasse genus)

Hemitaurichthys zoster = a common misidentification of
H. polylepis (Pyramid Butterfly)

Histiopterus typus = a common misidentification of
Evistias acutirostris (Whiskered Boarfish)

Holocentrus = Sargocentron (a Squirrelfish genus)

Malacanthus hoedti = M. brevirostris (Sand Tilefish)

Megaprotodon trifascialis = Chaetodon trifascialis
(Chevron Butterflyfish)

Melichthys piceus = M. niger (Black Triggerfish)
Melichthys niger = M. niger (Black Triggerfish)

Mugiloididae = Pinguipedidae (Sandperches)

Mulloides = Mulloidichthys (a Goatfish genus)
Mulloides auriflamma = Mulloidichthys vanicolensis
(Yellowfin Goatfish)
Mulloidichthys samoensis = M. flavolineatus
(White Goatfish)

Muraena kailuae = Enchelycore pardalis (Dragon Moray)
Muraena pardalis = Enchelycore pardalis (Dragon Moray)

Myripristis argyromus = M. amaena (Brick Soldierfish)
Myripristis borbonicus = M. kuntee (Shoulderbar Soldierfish)
Myripristis murdjan = a common misidentification of *M. berndti*
(Bigscale Soldierfish)
Myripristis multiradiatus = M. kuntee (Shoulderbar Soldierfish)

Novaculichthys bifer = N. taeniourus (Rockmover, or
Dragon Wrasse)

Odontanthias fuscipinnis = Holanthias fuscipinnis
(Hawaiian Deep Anthias)

Ostracion camurum = Ostracion meleagris (Spotted Boxfish)
Ostracion lentiginosus = Ostracion meleagris (Spotted Boxfish)

INVALID NAME - VALID NAME

Ostracion sebae = Ostracion meleagris (Spotted Boxfish)

Parapercidae = Pinguipedidae (Sandperches)

Parupeneus chyserydros = P. cyclostomus (Blue Goatfish)

Pikea aurora = Liopropoma aurora (Sunset Basslet)

Pomacentrus jenkinsi = Stegastes fasciolatus
(Pacific Gregory)

Runula = Plagiotremus (a blenny genus)

Quisquilius = Priolepis (a goby genus)

Sargocentron lacteoguttatum = S. punctatissimum
(Peppered Squirrelfish)

Scarus ahula = Scarus perspicillatus (Spectacled Parrotfish)
Scarus forsteri = S. psittacus (Palenose Parrotfish)
Scarus lauia = S. dubius (Regal Parrotfish)
Scarus paluca = S. rubroviolaceus (Redlip Parrotfish)

Scomberoides sanctipetri = S. lysan (Leatherback)

Scorpaena coniorta = Sebastapistes coniorta
(Speckled Scorpionfish)

Sphyraena acutipinnis = possible synonym of *S. helleri*
(Heller's Barracuda)

Strongylura gigantea = Tylosurus crocodilis
(Crocodile Needlefish)

Synodus variegatus = prior to 1989 confused with
S. dermatogenys.

Thalassoma fuscum = T. trilobatum (Christmas Wrasse)
Thalassoma stuckiae = Gomphosus varius (Bird Wrasse)
Trachurops crumenophthalmus = Selar crumenophthalmus
(Bigeye Scad)

Upeneus arge = U. taeniopterus (Bandtail Goatfish)
Uropterygius tigrinus = Scuticaria tigrinus (Tiger Moray)

Zanclus canescens = Z. cornutus (Moorish Idol)

A

Achilles Tang, 125
Acute-Jawed Mullet, 90, 180
Agile Chromis, 43
Amberjack, 85
Ambon Toby, 101
Angelfish, Bandit, 13,16
 Emperor, 13
 Fisher's, 14
 Flame, 15
 Japanese Pygmy, 13
 Masked, 16
 Potter's, 15
Anthias, Bicolor, 76
 Hawaiian Longfin, 77
 Hawaiian Yellow, 75, 179
 Thompson's, 77
Arc-Eye Hawkfish, 80

B

Banded Cardinalfish, 38
Bandit Angelfish, 13,16
Bandtail Goatfish, 69
Bannerfish, 36
Barracuda, Great, 18
 Heller's, 18
Barred Filefish, 58
Basslet, Sunset, 75,179
Bearded Brotula, 56
Belted Wrasse, 156
Bicolor Anthias, 76
Big-Scale Soldierfish, 123
Bigeye, 19
Bigeye Emperor, 118
Bigeye Jack, 84
Bigeye Scad, 86 .
Bigeye, Hawaiian, 19
Bird Wrasse, 152
Black Durgon, 136
Black Surgeonfish, 130
Black Triggerfish, 136
Blackfin Chromis, 45
Blacklip Butterflyfish, 29
Blackside Hawkfish, 81
Blackspot Sergeant, 43
Blacktail Snapper, 117
Blenny, Ewa, 22
 Gargantuan, 21, 179
 Marbled, 22
 Scale-Eating, 22
 Scarface, 20,21
 Shortbodied, 21
 Spotted Coral, 21
 Zebra, 22
Blue Goatfish, 67
Blue Ulua, 83
Blue-Eye Damselfish, 47
Bluefin Trevally, 83
Bluehead Butterflyfish, 29
Blueline Surgeonfish, 128
Bluespine Unicornfish, 132
Bluestripe Butterflyfish, 29
Bluestripe Pipefish, 98
Bluestripe Snapper, 116,118

Bluestripe Soldierfish, 122
Boarfish, Whiskered, 23
Bonefish, 87
Boxfish, Spotted, 24,25
 Whitley's, 25
Brassy Chub, 39,180
Brick Soldierfish, 122
Bridled Triggerfish, 138
Bright-Eye Damselfish, 46
Brotula, Bearded, 56
Brown Stingray, 105
Brown Surgeonfish, 127
Bullethead Parrotfish, 96
Businessman Butterflyfish, 36
Butterflyfish, Blacklip, 29
 Bluehead, 29
 Bluestripe, 29
 Businessman, 36
 Chevron, 27
 Fourspot, 31
 Klein's, 29
 Lined, 29
 Longnose, 34
 Melon, 33
 Milletseed, 26,30
 Multiband, 31
 Ornate, 31
 Oval, 33
 Pebbled, 31
 Pennant, 36
 Pyramid, 35
 Raccoon, 30
 Rare Longnose, 34
 Redfin, 33
 Reticulated, 32
 Saddleback, 28
 Speckled, 28
 Teardrop, 33
 Thompson's, 36
 Threadfin, 28
 Tinker's, 32

C

Cardinalfish, Banded, 38
 Iridescent, 37,38
 Ruby, 38
 Spotted, 38
Chevron Butterflyfish, 27
Chevron Tang, 130
Chocolate Dip Chromis, 43
Christmas Wrasse, 159
Chromis, Agile, 43
 Blackfin, 45
 Chocolate Dip, 43
 Oval, 44
 Threespot, 45
Chubs, Gray, 39,40
Chub, Lowfin, 180
Cigar Wrasse, 148
Cocos Frill Goby, 71
Commerson's Frogfish, 63,64
Conger, Mustache, 49
Convict Tang, 129
Coris, Elegant, 142,152
Coris, Lined, 149

Coris Yellowstripe, 150
 Yellowtail, 151
Cornetfish, 141
Cowfish, Thornback, 25
Crocodile Needlefish, 91
Crosshatch Triggerfish, 139
Crown Squirrelfish, 121
Crown Toby, 101
Curious Wormfish, 73

D

Damselfish, Blue-Eye, 47
 Bright-Eye, 46
 Hawaiian Domino, 46
 Hawaiian Rock, 47
 Onespot, 46
Dartfish, Fire, 73
 Indigo, 73
Dascyllus, Hawaiian, 46
Decoy Scorpionfish, 108,182
Devil Scorpionfish, 110
Disappearing Wrasse, 155
Doublebar Goatfish, 67
Dragon Moray, 52
Dragon Wrasse, 154
Durgon, Black, 136
 Pinktail, 136
Dwarf Moray, 54

E

Eel, Conger, 48
 Crocodile Snake, 56,181
 Freckled Snaked, 181
 Hawaiian Garden, 49
 Magnificent Snake, 56
 Moray, see Moray
 Spotted Snake, 56
 White, 49
Eightline Wrasse, 155
Elegant Coris, 142,152
Emperor Angelfish, 13
Emperor, Bigeye, 118
Epaulette Soldierfish, 123
Ewa Fang Blenny, 22
Eyestripe Surgeonfish, 126

F

Fantail Filefish, 57,59
Filefish, Barred, 59
 Fantail, 57,58
 Hawaiian, 59
 Lacefin, 59
 Scrawled, 58
 Scribbled, 58
 Shy, 59
 Squaretail, 59
 Yellowtail, 58
Fire Dartfish, 73
Fisher's Angelfish, 14
Fisher's Seahorse, 98
Fivestripe Wrasse, 159
Flagtail Tilefish, 134
Flagtail, Hawaiian, 60
Flame Angelfish, 15
Flame Wrasse, 148

Flametail Snapper, 117
Flat-Tail Needlefish, 91
Flatfish, Manyray, 61,62
Flounder, Panther, 62
  Peacock, 61,62
Flying Gurnard, 111
Forcepsfish, 34
Forktail Snapper, 117
Fourline Wrasse, 155
Fourspot Butterflyfish, 31
Freckled Hawkfish, 81
Frogfish, Commerson's, 63,64
  Giant, 63,64

G
Galapagos Shark, 113
Gargantuan Blenny, 21
Gaping Needlefish, 91
Giant Frogfish, 63,64
Giant Grouper, 74
Giant Moray, 51
Giant Trevally, 83
Gilded Triggerfish, 139
Goatfish, Bandtail, 69
  Blue, 67
  Doublebar, 67
  Manybar, 68
  Orange, 66
  Sidespot, 69
  Whitesaddle, 65,69
  Yellow-Saddle, 67
  Yellowbanded, 65,69
  Yellowfin, 66
  White, 66
Goby, Cocos Frill, 71
  Golden Green, 72
  Halfspotted, 71
  Mainland's, 71
  Noble, 71
  Shoulder-Spot, 70,71
  Taylor's, 71
  Wire Coral, 72
Gold-Ring Surgeonfish, 130
Golden Green Goby, 72
Golden Trevally, 84
Goldline Squirrelfish, 121,183
Goldrim Surgeonfish, 125
Gray Reef Shark, 112
Gray Snapper, 117
Great Barracuda, 18
Great White Shark, 114
Green Jobfish, 117
Green Lionfish, 108
Gregory, Pacific, 47
Grouper, Giant, 74
  Hawaiian Black, 74,75
  Peacock, 75
Guineafowl Puffer, 100
Gurnard, Flying, 111

H
Halfspotted Goby, 70
Hawaiian Bigeye, 19
Hawaiian Black Grouper, 74,75
Hawaiian Cleaner Wrasse, 153
Hawaiian Crocodile Eel, 56,181
Hawaiian Dascyllus, 46

Hawaiian Domino Damselfish, 46
Hawaiian Filefish, 58
Hawaiian Flagtail, 60
Hawaiian Garden Eel, 49
Hawaiian Hogfish, 146
Hawaiian Ladyfish, 87
Hawaiian Lionfish, VII, 109
Hawaiian Longfin Anthias, 77
Hawaiian Morwong, 79,81
Hawaiian Rock Damselfish, 47
Hawaiian Sergeant, 41,42
Hawaiian Squirrelfish, 120
Hawaiian Stingray, 105
Hawaiian Tarpon, 87
Hawaiian Turkeyfish, 109
Hawaiian Whitespotted Toby, 102
Hawaiian Yellow Anthias, 75, 179
Hawkfish, Arc-Eye, 80
  Blackside, 81
  Freckled, 81
  Longnose, 80
  Redbarred, 79
  Stocky, 78,79
  Twospot, 79
Heller's Barracuda, 18
Henshaw's Eel, 56, 181
Highfin Chub, 39, 180
Hogfish, Hawaiian, 146
Humphead Wrasse, 143

I
Indigo Dartfish, 73
Indo-Pacific Sergeant, 9, 41
Iridescent Cardinalfish, 37,38

J
Jack, Bigeye, 84
  Jumping, 22
  Thicklipped, 85
  Yellowspotted, 83
Japanese Pygmy Angelfish, 13
Jobfish, Green, 117
  Smalltooth, 117
Jumping Jack, 22

K
Klein's Butterflyfish, 29
Knifejaw, Spotted, 182

L
Lacefin Filefish, 59
Ladyfish, Hawaiian, 87
Lagoon Triggerfish, 137
Lantern Toby, 101
Lavender Tang, 127
Leaf Scorpionfish, 111
Leatherback, 85
Lei Triggerfish, 135,138
Lime Green Wrasse, 158
Lined Butterflyfish, 29
Lined Coris, 149
Lionfish, Green, 108
  Hawaiian, 109
Lizardfish, Clearfin, 88
  Hawaiian, 88
  Orangemouth, 89
  Reef, 88,89
  Twospot, 89

Longfin Anthias, 77
Longjaw Squirrelfish, 122
Longnose Butterflyfish, 34
Longnose Hawkfish, 80

M
Mackerel Scad, 86
Mainland's Goby, 70
Manta Ray, 105
Manybar Goatfish, 68
Manyray Flatfish, 61,62
Marbled Blenny, 22
Masked Angelfish, 16
Maze Toby, 102
Melon Butterflyfish, 33
Milkfish, 87
Milletseed Butterflyfish, 26,30
Moorish Idol, 125,133
Moray, Dragon, 52
  Dwarf, 54
  Giant, 51
  Snowflake, 51
  Stout, 53
  Tiger, 55
  Undulated, 55
  Viper, 50,52
  Whitemargin, 50,51
  Whitemouth, 54
  Yellowhead, 55
  Yellowmargin, 53
  Yellowmouth, 54
  Zebra, 52
Morwong, Hawaiian, 79,81
Mullet, Acute-Jawed, 180
Mullet, Sharpnose, 90
Mullet, Striped, 90
Multiband Butterflyfish, 31
Mustache Conger, 49
Mustard Tang, 127

N
Napoleon Wrasse, 143
Needlefish, Crocodile, 91
  Flat-Tail, 91
  Gaping, 91
Neon Wrasse, 155
Noble Goby, 70

O
Old Woman Wrasse, 157
Onespot Damselfish, 46
Orange Goatfish, 66
Orangeband Surgeonfish, 128
Orangemouth Lizardfish, 88,89
Orangespine Unicornfish, 133
Ornate Butterflyfish, 31
Ornate Wrasse, 153
Oval Butterflyfish, 33
Oval Chromis, 41, 44

P
Pacific Gregory, 47
Palenose Parrotfish, 95
Panther Flounder, 62
Parrotfish, Bullethead, 95
  Palenose, 96
  Redlip, 96
  Regal, 94

Spectacled, 92,95
Star-Eye, 93
Parrotfish, Yellowbar, 94
Peacock Flounder, 61,62
Peacock Grouper, 75
Pearl Wrasse, 145
Pearly Soldierfish, 123
Pebbled Butterflyfish, 31
Pencil Wrasse, 156
Pennant Butterflyfish, 36
Pennantfish, 36
Peppered Squirrelfish, 121
Picasso Triggerfish, 137
Pig Ulua, 85
Pinktail Durgon, 136
Pinktail Triggerfish, 136
Pipefish, Bluestripe, 98
 Redstripe, 97,98
Porcupinefish, 99
 Giant, 103
 Longspine, 103
Potter's Angelfish, 15
Potter's Wrasse, 154
Psychedelic Wrasse, 144
Puffer, Guineafowl, 100
 Spotted, 100
 Stars and Stripes, 100
 Stripebelly, 100
 Velcro, 100
Pyramid Butterflyfish, 35

R
Raccoon Butterflyfish, 30
Rainbow Runner, 84
Rainbow Wrasse, 151
Rare Longnose Butterflyfish, 34
Ray, Manta, 105
 Spotted Eagle, 104, 106
Razorfish, 160
Redbarred Hawkfish, 79
Redfin Butterflyfish, 33
Redlip Parrotfish, 96
Redspotted Sandperch, 106
Redstripe Pipefish, 97,98
Redtail Wrasse, 144
Reef Lizardfish, 88,89
Reef Triggerfish, 137
Regal Parrotfish, 94
Remora, 104
Reticulated Butterflyfish, 32
Ringtail Surgeonfish, 126
Ringtail Wrasse, 147
Rockmover Wrasse, 154
Rough-Scale Soldierfish, 119,183
Ruby Cardinalfish, 38
Runner, Rainbow, 84

S
Saddle Wrasse, 157
Saddleback Butterflyfish, 28
Sailfin Tang, 131
Sandbar Shark, 115
Sandperch, Redspotted, 106
Sargassumfish, 63
Scad, Bigeye, 86
 Mackerel, 86
Scale-Eating Fang Blenny, 22

Scalloped Hammerhead Shark, 114
Scarface Blenny, 20,21
Scarlet Wrasse, 155
Scorpionfish, Decoy, 108,182
 Devil, 110
 Leaf, 111
 Speckled, 111
 Titan, 107,110
Scribbled Filefish, 58
Seahorse, Spotted, 98
 Fisher's, 98
Sergeant, Blackspot, 43
 Hawaiian, 41,42
Sergeant Major, 42
Shark, Galapagos, 113
 Gray Reef, 112
 Great White, 114
 Sandbar, 115
 Scalloped Hammerhead, 114
 Tiger, 114
 Whale, 115
 Whitetip Reef, 115
Sharpnose Mullet, 180
Shortbodied Blenny, 21
Shortnose Wrasse, 154
Shy Filefish, 59
Sidespot Goatfish, 69
Sleek Unicornfish, 132
Slender Sand Wrasse, 182
Smallscale Snapper, 116
Smalltail Wrasse, 156
Smalltooth Jobfish, 117
Snake eels, 56,181
Snapper, Blacktail, 117
 Bluestripe, 116,118
 Flametail, 117
 Forktail, 117
 Gray, 117
 Smallscale, 116
Snowflake Eel, 51
Soldierfish, Big-Scale, 123
 Brick, 122
 Epaulette, 123
 Pearly, 123
 Rough-Scale, 119,183
 Tahitian, 122
 Yellowfin, 119,183
Speckled Butterflyfish, 28
Speckled Scorpionfish, 111
Spectacled Parrotfish, 92,95
Spiny Porcupinefish, 103
Spiny Seahorse, 98
Spotfin Squirrelfish, 120
Spotted Boxfish, 24,25
Spotted Cardinalfish, 38
Spotted Coral Blenny, 21
Spotted Eagle Ray, 104, 106
Spotted Knifejaw, 182
Spotted Puffer, 100
Spotted Seahorse, 98
Spotted Snake Eel, 56
Spotted Unicornfish, 132
Squaretail Filefish, 58
Squirrelfish, Bluestripe, 122
 Crown, 121
 Goldline, 121,183
 Hawaiian, 120
 Longjaw, 122

Peppered, 121
Spotfin, 120
Squirrelfish, Yellowstripe, 121
Star-Eye Parrotfish, 93
Stars and Stripes Puffer, 100
Stingray, Brown, 105
 Hawaiian, 105
Stocky Hawkfish, 78,79
Stonefish, 107,108
Stout Moray, 53
Stripebelly Puffer, 100
Stripey, 39, 40
Suckerfish, 104
Sunset Basslet, 75,179
Sunset Wrasse, 158
Surge Wrasse, 158
Surgeonfish, Black, 130
 Blueline, 128
 Brown, 127
 Eyestripe, 126
 Gold-Ring, 130
 Goldrim, 125
 Orangeband, 128
 Ringtail, 126
 Thompson's, 129
 Whitebar, 127
 Whitecheek, 125
 Whitespotted, 127
 Yellowfin, 126

T
Tahitian Squirrelfish, 122
Tang, Achilles, 125
 Chevron, 130
 Convict, 129
 Lavender, 127
 Mustard, 127
 Sailfin, 131
 Yellow, 124, 131
Tarpon, Hawaiian, 87
Taylor's Goby, 70
Teardrop Butterflyfish, 33
Tenpounder, 87
Thicklipped Jack, 85
Thompson's Anthias, 77
Thompson's Butterflyfish, 36
Thompson's Surgeonfish, 129
Thornback Cowfish, 25
Threadfin, 90
Threadfin Butterflyfish, 28
Threespot Chromis, 45
Tiger Moray, 55
Tiger Shark, 114
Tilefish, Flagtail, 134
Tinker's Butterflyfish, 32
Titan Scorpionfish, 107,110
Toby, Ambon, 101
 Crown, 101
 Hawaiian Whitespotted, 102
 Lantern, 101
 Maze, 102
Trevally, Bluefin, 83
 Giant, 83
 Golden, 84
Triggerfish, Black, 136
 Bridled, 138
 Crosshatch, 139
 Gilded, 139

Lagoon, 137
Triggerfish, Lei, 138
  Picasso, 135, 137
  Pinktail, 136
  Reef, 135, 137
  Whiteline, 135,138
Trumpetfish, 140,141
Turkeyfish, Hawaiian, 109
Twospot Hawkfish, 79
Twospot Lizardfish, 89
Twospot Wrasse, 147

U
Ulua, Blue, 83
  Pig, 85
  White, 83
  Yellow, 84
Undulated Moray, 55
Unicornfish, Bluespine, 132
  Orangespine, 133
  Sleek, 132
  Spotted, 132

V
Velcro Puffer, 100
Viper Moray, 50

W
Whale Shark, 115
Whip Coral Goby, 72
Whiskered Boarfish, 23
White Eel, 49
White Goatfish, 66
White Ulua, 83

Whitebar Surgeonfish, 127
Whitecheek Surgeonfish, 125
Whiteline Triggerfish, 135,138
Whitemargin Moray, 50,51
Whitemouth Moray, 54
Whitesaddle Goatfish, 65,69
Whitespotted Surgeonfish, 127
Whitetip Reef Shark, 115
Whitley's Boxfish, 25
Wormfish, Curious, 73
Wrasse, Belted, 156
  Bird, 152
  Christmas, 159
  Cigar, 148
  Disappearing, 155
  Dragon, 154
  Eightline, 155
  Fivestripe, 159
  Flame, 148
  Fourline, 155
  Hawaiian Cleaner, 153
  Humphead, 143
  Lime Green, 158
  Napoleon, 143
  Neon, 155
  Old Woman, 157
  Ornate, 153
  Pearl, 145
  Pencil, 156
  Potter's, 154
  Psychedelic, 144
  Rainbow, 151
  Redtail, 144
  Ringtail, 147

Rockmover, 154
Wrasse, Saddle, 157
  Scarlet, 155
  Shortnose, 154
  Slender Sand, 182
  Smalltail, 156
  Sunset, 158
  Surge, 158
  Twospot, 147

Y
Yellow Seahorse, 98
Yellow Tang, 131
Yellow Ulua, 84
Yellow-Saddle Goatfish, 67
Yellowbanded Goatfish, 65,69
Yellowbar Parrotfish, 94
Yellowfin Goatfish, 66
Yellowfin Soldierfish, 119,183
Yellowfin Surgeonfish, 126
Yellowhead Moray, 55
Yellowmargin Moray, 53
Yellowmouth Moray, 54
Yellowspotted Jack, 83
Yellowstripe Coris, 150
Yellowstripe Squirrelfish, 121
Yellowtail Coris, 151
Yellowtail Filefish, 59

Z
Zebra Blenny, 22
Zebra Moray, 52

INDEX OF HAWAIIAN NAMES

A

a'awa, 146
'aha, 91
āholehole, 60
akule, 86
'ala'ihi, 119-122,183
'ala'ihi kalaloa, 122
'ālo'ilo'i, 46
'ama'ama, 90
'api, 127
awa, 87
awa'aua, 87
'āwela, 159
'āweoweo, 19

E

enenue, 39,40,180

H

hāhālua, 105
hailepo, 104,106
halalu, 86
hāpu'u, 74,75
hihimanu, 105
hilu, 150
hīnālea 'aki-lolo, 151,152
hīnālea 'i'iwi, 152
hīnālea lau-wili, 157
hīnālea luahine, 157
hou, 158
humuhumu-ele'ele, 136
humuhumu-hi'u-kole, 136
humuhumu-lei, 138
humuhumu-mimi, 138
humuhumu-nukunuku-a'pua'a, 137

K

kāhala, 85
kākū, 18
kala, 132
kala holo, 132
kala lolo, 132
kamanu, 84
kawele'ā, 18
kihikihi, 125,133
kīkākapu, 29-31,33,79,81
kōkala, 99, 103
kole, 130
kūmū, 65,69
kupipi, 43
kūpou, 148

L

lae-nihi, 160
lai, 85
lā'o, 153
lau-hau, 31
lau-ī-pala, 131
lau-wiliwili, 26,30
lau-wiliwili-nukunuku-oi'oi, 34
lauia, 94
loloa'u, 111
loulu, 58

M

mā'i'i'i, 127
maiko, 128
māikoiko, 127
maka-'ā, 134
makukana, 25
mālamalama, 149
mamo, 41,42
māne'one'o, 131
manini, 129
manō, 113
manō-lālā-kea, 115
manō-kihikihi, 114
moa, 24,25
moano, 68,69
moano ukali-ulua, 67
moi, 90
mū, 118
munu, 67

N

na'ena'e, 128
nenue, 39,40,180
niuhi, 114
nohu, 107,108,110
nohu 'omakaha, 110
nohu pinao, 109
nuhu, 140,141
nū, 140,141

O

'ō'ili, 58,59
'ō'ili lepa, 59
'ō'ili-'uwī'uwī, 57,58
ō'io, 87
'ōmaka, 156
'omilu, 83
onaga, 116
o'opu-alamo'o, 70
o'opu-hue, 100
o'opu-'ohune, 71
'opakapaka, 116
'ōpelu, 86
'ōpule, 145

P

pāki'i, 61,62
pāku-iku'i, 125
palani, 126
pāo'o, 20,21,22
pili-ko'a, 79,80,81
pinao, 111
po'o-pa'a, 78,79
pō'ou, 147
pualu, 126
puhi, 52-55,181
puhi-kāpā, 51
puhi-kauila, 50, 52
puhi-lā'au, 56
puhi-lau-milo, 55
puhi-'oni'o, 54
puhi-paka, 53
puhi-palahoana, 56
puhi-ūhā, 49
pu'u olai, 101

R

roi, 75

T

ta'ape, 116,118
to-au, 117

U

uhu, 93-96
uhu 'ahu'ula, 92,95
uhu 'ele'ele, 96
uhu pālukaluka, 96
uhu uliuli, 92,95
uku, 117
'ulae, 88,89
'ula 'ula, 116
ulua, 84,85
ulua pa'opa'o, 84
ulua-aukea, 83
umauma-lei, 133
uouoa, 90,180
'upāpalu, 37,38
'ū'ū, 122,123,183

W

wahanui, 117
weke'ā, 66
weke pueo, 69
weke-'ula, 66

INDEX OF SCIENTIFIC NAMES

A
abdominalis, Abudefduf, 41,42
Ablennes hians, 91
Abudefduf abdominalis, 41,42
sordidus, 43
Acanthurus achilles, 125
blochii, 126
dussumieri, 126
guttatus, 127
leucopareius, 127
nigricans, 125
nigrofuscus, 127
nigroris, 128
olivaceus, 128
thompsoni, 129
triostegus, 129
xanthopterus, 126
achilles, Acanthurus, 125
aculeatus, Rhinecanthus, 137
acutirostris, Evistias, 23
Aetobatus narinari, 104, 106
agilis, Chromis, 43
albimarginatus, Gymnothorax, 50,51
albisella, Dascyllus, 46
Albula sp., 87
alfredi, Manta, 105
Aluterus monoceros, 58
scriptus, 58
amaena, Myripristis, 122
Amblycirrhitus bimacula, 79
amblyrhynchos, Carcharhinus, 112
amboinensis, Canthigaster, 101
Anampses chrysocephalus, 144
cuvier, 145
aneitensis, Xyrichtys, 160
anjerensis, Gnatholepis, 70,71
Antennarius commerson, 63,64
Aphareus furca, 117
Apogon erythrinus, 38
kallopterus, 37,38
maculiferus, 38
menesemus, 38
taeniopterus, 38
Aprion virescens, 117
arcatus, Paracirrhites, 80
arcuatus, Desmoholacanthus, 13,16
argalus, Platybelone, 91
argus, Cephalopholis, 75
Ariosoma marginatum, 48
Arothron hispidus, 100
meleagris, 100
aspricaudus, Pervagor, 58
Asterropteryx semipunctatus, 70
Aulostomus chinensis, 140,141
aureoviridis, Priolepis, 72
auriga, Chaetodon, 28
aurolineatus, Neoniphon, 121,183
auromarginatus, Xanthichthys, 139
aurora, Liopropoma, 75,179

B
baldwini, Doryrhamphus, 97,98
baldwini, Xyrichtys, 160
ballieui, Coris, 149
ballieui, Thalassoma, 157
balteata, Stethojulis, 156
barberi, Dendrochirus, 108
barracuda, Sphyraena, 18
Bathygobius cocosensis, 71
berndti, Myripristis, 123

bicolor, Pseudanthias, 76
bifasciatus, Parupeneus, 67
bigibbus, Kyphosus, 39,40
bilunulatus, Bodianus, 146
bimacula, Amblycirrhitus, 79
bimaculatus, Oxycheilinus, 147
binotatus, Synodus, 89
bipinnulatus, Elagatis, 84
birostris, Manta, 104
blochii, Acanthurus, 126
Bodianus bilunulatus, 146
Bothus mancus, 61,62
pantherinus, 62
Brachysomophis crocodilinus, 56,181
brevirostis, Malacanthus, 134
brevirostris, Naso, 132
brevis, Dasyatis, 105
brevis, Exallias, 21
Brotula multibarbata, 56
townsendi, 56
Bryaninops yongei, 72
bursa, Sufflamen, 138

C
cacopsis, Scorpaenopsis, 107,110
Callechelys lutea, 181
Calotomus carolinus, 93
zonarchus, 94
canina, Enchelynassa, 50
Cantherhines dumerilii, 58
sandwichiensis, 58
verecundus, 59
Canthigaster amboinensis, 101
coronata, 101
epilampra, 101
jactator, 102
rivulata, 102
Carangoides ferdau, 83
orthogrammus, 83
Caranx ignobilis, 83
melampygus, 83
sexfasciatus, 84
Carcharhinus amblyrhynchos, 112
galapagensis, 113
plumbeus, 113
Carcharodon carcharias, 114
carolinus, Calotomus, 93
Centropyge fisheri, 14
interrupta, 13
loricula, 15
potteri, 15
Cephalopholis argus, 75
cephalus, Mugil, 90
cerasinus, Pseudojuloides, 156
Chaetodon auriga, 28
citrinellus, 28
ephippium, 28
fremblii, 29
kleinii, 29
lineolatus, 29
lunula, 30
lunulatus, 33
miliaris, 26,30
modestus, 27
multicinctus, 31
ornatissimus, 31
quadrimaculatus, 31
reticulatus, 32
tinkeri, 32
trifascialis, 27

Chaetodon, ulietensis, 27
unimaculatus, 33
Chanos chanos, 87
Cheilinus undulatus, 143
Cheilio inermis, 148
Cheilodactylus vittatus, 79,81
chinensis, Aulostomus, 140,141
Chlorurus sordidus, 92,96
perspicillatus, 92,95
Chromis agilis, 43
hanui, 43
ovalis, 44
vanderbilti, 45
verater, 45
chryseres, Myripristis, 119,183
chrysocephalus, Anampses, 144
cinerascens, Kyphosus, 39,180
cinereus, Conger, 49
Cirrhilabrus jordani, 148
Cirrhitops fasciatus, 79
Cirrhitus pinnulatus, 78,79
Cirripectes obscurus, 21
vanderbilti, 20,21
citrinellus, Chaetodon, 28
cocosensis, Bathygobius, 71
commerson, Antennarius, 63,64
commersonii, Fistularia, 141
concolor, Lentipes, 70
Conger cinereus, 49
oligoporus, 48
coniorta, Sebastapistes, 111
Coris ballieui, 149
flavovittata, 150
gaimard, 151
venusta, 142,152
cornutus, Zanclus, 125,133
coronata, Canthigaster, 101
crocodilis, Tylosurus, 91
crocodilinus, Brachysomophis, 56, 181
cruentatus, Heteropriacanthus, 19
crumenophthalmus, Selar, 86
Ctenochaetus hawaiiensis, 130
strigosus, 130
curiosus, Gunnelichthys, 73
cuvier, Anampses, 145
cuvier, Galeocerdo, 114
cyclostomus, Parupeneus, 67
Cymolutes lecluse, 182

D
Dactyloptena orientalis, 111
Dascyllus albisella, 46
Dasyatis dipterura, 105
lata, 105
Decapterus macarellus, 86
Dendrochirus barberi, 108
dentex, Pseudocaranx, 85
dermatogenys, Synodus, 88
Desmoholacanthus arcuatus, 13, 16
diabolus, Scorpaenopsis, 110
diadema, Sargocentron, 121
Diodon holocanthus, 103
hystrix, 99,103
diphreutes, Heniochus, 36
Doryrhamphus baldwini, 97,98
excisus, 98
dubius, Scarus, 94
dumerili, Seriola, 85
dumerilii, Cantherhines, 59
duperrey, Thalassoma, 157

dussumieri, Acanthurus, 126

E
Echeneis naucrates, 104
Echidna nebulosa, 51
Elagatis bipinnulata, 84
Elops hawaiiensis, 87
Enchelycore pardalis, 52
Enchelynassa canina, 50
engeli, Moolgarda, 90
ensiferum, Sargocentron, 121
Entomacrodus marmoratus, 22
ephippium, Chaetodon, 28
epilampra, Canthigaster, 101
Epinephelus lanceolatus, 74,75
   quernus, 74,75
eugenius, Priolepis, 71
eurostus, Gymnothorax, 53
evanidus, Pseudocheilinus, 155
Evistias acutirostris, 23
ewaensis, Plagiotremus, 22
Exallias brevis, 21
excisus, Doryrhamphus, 98

F
fasciatus, Cirrhitops, 79
fasciatus, Oplegnathus, 182
fasciolatus, Stegastes, 47
fisheri, Centropyge, 14
fisheri, Hippocampus, 98
Fistularia commersonii, 141
flamma, Saurida, 89, 124
flavescens, Zebrasoma, 131
flavimarginatus, Gymnothorax, 53
flavissimus, Forcipiger, 34
flavolineatus, Mulloidichthys, 66
flavovittata, Coris, 150
Forcipiger flavissimus, 34
   longirostris, 34
fornasini, Lactoria, 25
forsteri, Paracirrhites, 81
fraenatus, Sufflamen, 138
fremblii, Chaetodon, 29
fulvus, Lutjanus, 117
furca, Aphareus, 117
fuscipinnis, Holanthias, 75, 179

G
gaimard, Coris, 151
galapagensis, Carcharhinus, 113
Galeocerdo cuvier, 114
Genicanthus personatus, 16
geoffroy, Macropharyngodon, 154
Gnathanodon speciosus, 84
Gnatholepis anjerensis, 70,71
Gomphosus varius, 152
Gorgasia hawaiiensis, 49
goslinei, Plagiotremus, 22
grandoculis, Monotaxis, 118
Gunnellichthys curiosus, 73
guttatus, Acanthurus, 127
Gymnomuraena zebra, 52
Gymnothorax albimarginatus, 50,51
   eurostus, 53
   flavimarginatus, 53
   javanicus, 51
   melatremus, 54
   meleagris, 54
   nudivomer, 54
   rueppelliae, 55
   undulatus, 55

H
Halichoeres ornatissimus, 153
hanui, Chromis, 43

hawaiiensis, Ctenochaetus, 130
hawaiiensis, Elops, 87
hawaiiensis, Gorgasia, 49
hawaiiensis, Pseudanthias, 77
helleri, Sphyraena, 18
Hemitaurichthys polylepis, 35
   thompsoni, 36
Heniochus acuminatus, 36
   diphreutes, 36
henshawi, Brachysomophis, 56,181
Heteropriacanthus cruentatus, 19
heteroptera, Ptereleotris, 73
hexacanthus, Naso, 132
hians, Ablennes, 91
Hippocampus fisheri, 98
   kuda, 98
hispidus, Arothron, 100
Histrio histrio, 63
Holacanthus arcuatus, 13,16
Holanthias fuscipinnis, 75, 179
holocanthus, Diodon, 103
hystrix, Diodon, 99,103

I
ignobilis, Caranx, 83
imparipennis, Plectroglyphidodon, 46
imperator, Pomacanthus, 13
inermis, Cheilio, 148
interrupta, Centropyge, 13
Iracundus signifer, 182
Istiblennius zebra, 22

J
jactator, Canthigaster, 102
javanicus, Gymnothorax, 51
johnstonianus, Plectroglyphidodon, 47
jordani, Cirrhilabrus, 148

K
kallopterus, Apogon, 37,38
kasmira, Lutjanus, 116,118
kleinii, Chaetodon, 29
kuda, Hippocampus, 98
Kuhlia sandvicensis, 60
kuntee, Myripristis, 123
Kyphosus bigibbus, 39,40
   cinerascens, 39,180
   vaigiensis, 39,180

L
Labroides phthirophagus, 153
Lactoria fornasini, 25
lanceolatus, Epinephelus, 74
latus, Dasyatis, 105
lecluse, Cymolutes, 182
Lentipes concolor, 70
leuciscus, Neomyxus, 90,180
leucopareius, Acanthurus, 127
lewini, Sphyrna, 114
lima, Plectrypops, 119,183
lineolatus, Chaetodon, 29
Liopropoma aurora, 75,179
lituratus, Naso, 133
longirostris, Forcipiger, 34
loricula, Centropyge, 15
lunula, Chaetodon, 30
lunulatus, Chaetodon, 33
lutescens, Thalassoma, 158
lutea, Callechelys, 181
Lutjanus fulvus, 117
   kasmira, 116,118
lysan, Scomberoides, 85

M
macarellus, Decapterus, 86

Macropharyngodon geoffroy, 154
maculiferus, Apogon, 38
maculosus, Myrichthys, 56
magnifica, Nemateleotris, 73
magnificus, Myrichthys, 56
mainlandi, Psilogobius, 71
Malacanthus brevirostris, 134
mancus, Bothus, 61,62
Manta alfredi, 105
   birostris, 104
marginatum, Ariosoma, 48
marmoratus, Entomacrodus, 22
meeki, Priacanthus, 19
megalodon, Carcharodon, 114
melampygus, Caranx, 83
melatremus, Gymnothorax, 54
meleagris, Arothron, 100
meleagris, Gymnothorax, 54
meleagris, Ostracion, 24,25
Melichthys niger, 136
   vidua, 136
menesemus, Apogon, 38
mento, Xanthichthys, 139
Microcanthus strigatus, 40
miliaris, Chaetodon, 26,30
monocerus, Aluterus, 58
Monotaxis grandoculis, 118
Moolgarda engeli, 90
Mugil cephalus, 90
Mulloidichthys flavolineatus, 66
   pflugeri, 66
   vanicolensis, 66
multibarbatus, Brotula, 56
multicinctus, Chaetodon, 31
multifasciatus, Parupeneus, 68
Myrichthys maculosus, 56
   magnificus, 56
Myripristis amaena, 122
   berndti, 123
   chyseres, 119,183
   kuntee, 123

N
narinari, Aetobatus, 104, 106
Naso brevirostris, 132
   hexacanthus, 132
   lituratus, 133
   unicornis, 132
naucrates, Echeneis, 104
nebulosa, Echidna, 51
Nemateleotris magnifica, 73
Neomyxus leuciscus, 90,180
Neoniphon aurolineatus, 121,183
   sammara, 120
niger, Melichthys, 136
nigricans, Acanthurus, 125
nigrofuscus, Acanthurus, 127
nigroris, Acanthurus, 128
Novaculichthys taeniourus, 154
nudivomer, Gymnothorax, 54

O
obesus, Triaenodon, 115
obscurus, Cirripectes, 21
octotaenia, Pseudocheilinus, 155
oligoporus, Conger, 48
olivaceus, Acanthurus, 128
Oplegnathus fasciatus, 182
   punctatus, 182
orientalis, Dactyloptena, 111
ornatissimus, Chaetodon, 31
ornatissimus, Halichoeres, 153
orthogrammus, Carangoides, 83
Ostracion meleagris, 24,25
   whitleyi, 25

ovalis, Chromis, 44
Oxycheilinus bimaculatus, 147
    unifasciatus, 147
Oxycirrhites typus, 80

P
pantherinus, Bothus, 62
Paracirrhites arcatus, 80
    forsteri, 81
Parapercis schauinslandi, 106
pardalis, Enchelycore, 52
Parupeneus bifasciatus, 67
    cyclostomus, 67
    multifasciatus, 68
    pleurostigma, 69
    porphyreus, 65,69
pavo, Xyrichtys, 160
personatus, Genicanthus, 16
perspicillatus, Chlorurus, 92,95
Pervagor aspricaudus, 59
    spilosoma, 57,59
pflugeri, Mulloidichthys, 66
phthirophagus, Labroides, 153
pinnulatus, Cirrhitus, 78,79
Plagiotremus ewaensis, 22
    goslinei, 22
Platybelone argalus, 91
Plectroglyphidodon imparipennis, 46
    johnstonianus, 47
    sindonis, 47
Plectrypops lima, 119,183
pleurostigma, Parupeneus, 69
plumbeus, Carcharhinus, 115
Polydactylus sexfilis, 90
polylepis, Hemitaurichthys, 35
Pomacanthus imperator, 13
porphyreus, Parupeneus, 65,69
potteri, Centropyge, 15
Priacanthus meeki, 19
Priolepis aureoviridis, 72
    eugenius, 71
Pseudanthias bicolor, 76
    hawaiiensis, 77
    thompsoni, 77
    ventralis, 77
Pseudocaranx dentex, 85
Pseudocheilinus evanidus, 155
    octotaenia, 155
    tetrataenia, 155
Pseudojuloides cerasinus, 156
Psilogobius mainlandi, 70
psittacus, Scarus, 96
Ptereleotris heteroptera, 73
Pterois sphex, 109
punctatissimum, Sargocentron, 121
punctatus, Oplegnathus, 182
purpureum, Thalassoma, 158

Q
quadrimaculatus, Chaetodon, 31
quernus, Epinephelus, 74,75
quinquevittatum, Thalassoma, 159

R
rectangulus, Rhinecanthus, 135, 137
reticulatus, Chaetodon, 32
Rhincodon typus, 115
Rhinecanthus aculeatus, 137

Rhinecanthus rectangulus, 137
rivulata, Canthigaster, 102
rubroviolaceus, Scarus, 96
ruppelliae, Gymnothorax, 55

S
sammara, Neoniphon, 120
sandvicensis, Kuhlia, 60
sandwichiensis, Cantherhines, 59
Sargocentron diadema, 121
    ensiferum, 121
    punctatissimum, 121
    spiniferum, 122
    tiere, 122
    xantherythrum, 120
Saurida flamma, 88,89
Scarus dubius, 94
    psittacus, 95
    rubroviolaceus, 96
    schauinslandi, Parapercis, 106
Scomberoides lysan, 85
Scorpaenopsis cacopsis, 107,110
    diabolus, 110
scriptus, Aluterus, 58
Scuticaria tigrina, 55
Sebastapistes coniorta, 111
Selar crumenophthalmus, 86
semipunctatus, Asterropteryx, 70
Seriola dumerili, 85
sexfasciatus, Caranx, 84
sexfilis, polydactylus, 90
signifer, Iracundus, 182
sindonis, Plectroglyphidodon, 47
sordidus, Abudefduf, 43
sordidus, Chlorurus, 92,95
speciosus, Gnathanodon, 84
sphex, Pterois, VII, 109
Sphyraena barracuda, 18
    helleri, 18
Sphyrna lewini, 114
spilosoma, Pervagor, 57,58
spiniferum, Sargocentron, 122
Stegastes fasciolatus, 47
Stethojulis balteata, 156
strigatus, Microcanthus, 39, 40
strigosus, Ctenochaetus, 130
Sufflamen bursa, 135,138
    fraenatus, 138
Synodus binotatus, 89
    dermatogenys, 88
    ulae, 88
    variegatus, 88,89

T
Taenianotus triacanthus, 111
taeniopterus, Apogon, 38
taeniopterus, Upeneus, 69
taeniourus, Novaculichthys, 154
taylori, Trimma, 70
tetrataenia, Pseudocheilinus, 155
Thalassoma ballieui, 157
    duperrey, 157
    lutescens, 158
    purpureum, 158
    quinquevittatum, 159
    trilobatum, 159
    thompsoni, Acanthurus, 129
    thompsoni, Hemitaurichthys, 36

thompsoni, Pseudanthias, 77
tiere, Sargocentron, 122
tigrinus, Uropterygius, 55
tinkeri, Chaetodon, 32
townsendi, Brotula, 56
triacanthus, Taenianotus, 111
Triaenodon obesus, 115
trifascialis, Chaetodon, 27
trifasciatus, Chaetodon, 33
Trimma taylori, 70
triostegus, Acanthurus, 129
Tylosurus crocodilus, 91
typus, Oxycirrhites, 80
typus, Rhincodon, 115

U
ulae, Synodus, 88
umbrilatus, Xyrichtys, 160
undulatus, Cheilinus, 143
undulatus, Gymnothorax, 55
unicornis, Naso, 132
unifasciatus, Oxycheilinus, 147
unimaculatus, Chaetodon, 33
Upeneus taeniopterus, 69
    vittatus, 65,69

V
vaigiensis, Abudefduf, 9, 42
    Kyphosus, 39,180
vanderbilti, Chromis, 45
vanderbilti, Cirripectes, 20,21
vanicolensis, Mulloidichthys, 66
variegatus, Synodus,89
varius, Gomphosus, 152
veliferum, Zebrasoma, 131
ventralis, Pseudanthias, 77
venusta, Coris, 142,152
verater, Chromis, 45
verecundus, Cantherhines, 59
vidua, Melichthys, 136
virescens, Aprion, 117
vittatus, Cheilodactylus, 79,81
vittatus, Upeneus, 65,69

W
whitleyi, Ostracion, 25

X
xantherythrum, Sargocentron, 120
Xanthichthys auromarginatus, 139
    mento, 139
xanthopterus, Acanthurus, 126
Xyrichtys aneitensis, 160
    baldwini, 160
    pavo, 160
    umbrilatus, 160

Y
yongei, Bryaninops, 72

Z
Zanclus cornutus, 125,133
zebra, Gymnomuraena, 52
zebra, Istiblennius, 22
Zebrasoma flavescens, 131
    veliferum, 131
zonarchus, Calotomus, 94

This appendix, added with the 2nd printing, contains photographs and descriptions of 15 additional Hawaiian reef fishes.

SUNSET BASSLET ●
Liopropoma aurora (Jordan & Evermann, 1903).

Rosy red, with yellow markings, this is one of Hawaii's prettiest but least known endemic fishes. In the same family as groupers and anthias, it is a secretive species usually associated with depths greater than 150 feet (although it has been seen as shallow as 70 feet). It is most likely to be found in the open in the late afternoon or evening. Otherwise, look for it in caves and under overhangs. Its stocky red body and flaring yellow-edged fins should make identification easy, but without artificial light to bring out the red it could go unnoticed. The few aquarium specimens collected to date have done well. The species name means "dawn." To about 6 in. Endemic. Photo: Lisa Privitera, aquarium specimen collected off Waianae, O'ahu at 190 ft.

HAWAIIAN YELLOW ANTHIAS ●
Holanthias fuscipinnis (Jenkins, 1901)

This rare and spectacular Hawaiian endemic was first photographed alive in 1989 at Molokini Island, to the surprise of scientists who had always assumed it to live beyond the depth range of scuba divers. It has since been found as shallow as 140 feet, usually in small groups around ledges and in caves. Orange yellow trimmed with crimson and violet, it is closely related to the colorful anthias of the grouper family (pictured on pages 76-77). The few specimens ever to have been collected have proved hardy and peaceful in captivity. To about 9 in. Endemic. Photo: Mike Severns, Molokini Island. 180 ft.

GARGANTUAN BLENNY • pāo'o ●
Cirripectes obscurus (Borodin, 1927)

These are the largest blennies in Hawai'i. Bright spots, like pinpoints of light, speckle the head and front of their dark bodies. During the spawning season (January-March) males develop splendid red heads and yellow pectoral fins. Although infrequently seen, these fish are not uncommon in the shallow surge zone along steep rocky shores down to about 20 ft. To find them, pick a super-calm day and look under overhangs and in crevices, especially in surge channels that you wouldn't normally enter. The endemic Hawaiian Rock Damselfish often lives nearby. The species name means "dark." To about 7 in. Endemic. Photo: Makapu'u, O'ahu. 15 ft. (male and female with eggs)

HIGHFIN CHUB • **nenue**
Kyphosus cinarescens (Forsskål, 1775).
(SNUBNOSE CHUB)

Flaring soft dorsal and anal fins distinguish this species from the common Brown Chub (page 40). The snub nose is another identifying feature. Body color varies from light gray to blackish with light flecks. Highfin Chubs are territorial, occurring alone or in small groups. They are often actively engaged in driving away intruders and do not roam the reef in large schools. Species name means "ash color." To about 14 in. Indo-Pacific. Photo: Hanauma Bay, O`ahu. 3 ft.

LOWFIN CHUB • **nenue**
Kyphosus vaigiensis (Quoy & Gaimard, 1825).
(BRASSY CHUB)

These chubs usually have brassy yellow marks faintly visible about the mouth, eyes and at the edges of the gill covers (brighter in small individuals). The prominent scale rows give a slightly striped appearance. Evenly spaced pale spots appear on their backs and sides when they are grazing; if threatened they darken their body, dramatically intensifying these spots. When snorkeling look for these chubs near the turbulent surge zone where small specimens occur individually or in groups. Lowfin Chubs also occur offshore in large schools. The species name is from the Indonesian island of Waigeo. To about 20 in. Indo-Pacific. Photo: Hanauma Bay, O'ahu. 3 ft.

ACUTE-JAWED MULLET • **uouoa**
Neomyxus leuciscus (Gunther, 1871).

Known locally as False Mullet, or False **'ama'ama**, these have a distinctive yellow spot above the base of the pectoral fin and a sharper snout than the common Striped Mullet (page 90). They typically swim in small fast-moving schools, often grazing directly off the rocky reef rather foraging along the sandy bottom. Viewed from the front, their lower jaws meet at a very sharp angle, hence the common name. The head, if eaten, is said to cause nightmares unless an offering is first made to Pahulu, King of the Ghosts. To about

HENSHAW'S SNAKE EEL • **puhi** ●
Brachysomophis henshawi Jordan &
Snyder, 1904.
(CROCODILE SNAKE EEL)

   This ugly customer lives in sand,
often near the edge of the reef. With
only the top of its reddish head showing, it lies in wait for fish or crustaceans
to pass within striking range. Powerful
jaws, a muscular body and fast reflexes
make it a formidable predator. At least
one diver in Hawai'i has been seriously
bitten by one of these eels while lying
on the sand taking a picture. The name
honors naturalist Henry W. Henshaw
(1850-1930), who lived in Hilo in the
early 1900s. To about 3.5 ft. Although
once considered endemic to Hawai'i,
this eel has an Indo-Pacific distribution.
Photo: Mike Severns, Molokini Island,
Maui. 85 ft.

FRECKLED SNAKE EEL • **puhi** ●
Callechelys luteus Snyder, 1904.

   These endemic snake eels are not
uncommon in some sandy areas, their
heads protruding perpendicularly several inches from the bottom. Light colored with small black and yellow spots,
they blend in with the sand and are
easily overlooked. Their long slender
bodies (attaining at least 3 feet with a
diameter of about 1 inch) remain buried
during the day. Species name means
"yellow." To 41 in. Endemic. Photo:
Kahe Point, O'ahu. 30 ft.

STEINDACHNER'S MORAY • **puhi** ●
Gymnothorax steindachneri Jordan &
Evermann, 1903.

   This Hawaiian endemic is more
abundant in the cooler seas of the Northwestern Hawaiian Islands than around
the main islands, where it occurs mainly
at depths of 100 feet or more. It is easily
recognized by the dark lines under the
mouth (looking like creases or folds in
the loose skin), a dark mark at the corner of the mouth, and a prominent dark
spot over the gill opening. The body is
light brown covered with irregular dark
spots. The species name honors the
19th century German ichthyologist,
Franz Steindachner, who originally described and named several fishes in
this book. To at least 2 ft. Endemic.

SPOTTED KNIFEJAW
Oplegnathus punctatus (Temminck &
Schlegel, 1844)

Knifejaws (or false parrotfishes)
have beaks much like true parrotfishes.
They belong, however, to the unrelated
family Oplegnathidae, associated more
often with temperate than with tropical
waters. Spotted Knifejaws have a bright
white face. Their dark gray bodies are
densely covered with black spots (most
evident on the head and fins). Younger
fishes are lighter, with highly contrasting spots. Usually occurring deeper
than 100 feet, they shelter in caves and
under ledges. This species and the
striking Barred Knifejaw, *O. fasciatus*,
(very rare in the main islands), are most
common in the northwestern Hawaiian
chain, their larvae probably brought
here from Japan by the Kuroshio Current. Japan and Hawai'i. Photo: Midway Island. 40 ft.

DECOY SCORPIONFISH • nohu
Iracundus signifer (Jordan & Evermann,
1903)

This unusual species uses its dorsal fin as a lure to attract prey. The
black spot resembles the eye of a small
fish, the gap between the 1st and 2nd
spines looks like an upturned mouth,
and an elongated dorsal spine mimics a
dorsal fin. When "fishing" the Decoy
Scorpionfish snaps and waves its lure
in a surprisingly realistic fashion. However, it is often active at night when,
presumably, the deception would go
unnoticed. It inhabits the rubble zone
at the bases of ledges, usually on the
leeward sides of the islands. Species
name means "bearing marks." To 5 in.
Indo-Pacific. Photo: "Manta Ray Bay,"
Kona Coast, Hawai'i. 30 ft.

HAWAIIAN KNIFE FISH ●
Cymolutes lecluse (Quoy & Gaimard,
1824)
(SLENDER SAND WRASSE)

These pearly white sand-diving
wrasses are more slender (less deep-
bodied) than the razorfishes that share
their habitat. Males have a tiny dark
spot high on the upper side, about mid-
body; females have a dark spot high on
the base of the tail. The slightly barred
juveniles show both dark spots. The
species prefers sandy areas with some
current, not too far from the edge of the
reef, and is frequently found in small
groups consisting of a male and 3-5
females. To about 6 in. Endemic. Photo:
Kahe Point, O'ahu. 25ft. Photo: Kahe
Point, O'ahu. 25 ft.

YELLOWFIN SOLDIERFISH • 'ū'ū
Myripristis chryseres Jordan & Evermann, 1903.

With their golden yellow fins, these are perhaps the loveliest of Hawaii's soldierfishes. They are deep dwellers occasionally encountered by divers, usually at depths exceeding 100 feet. In the Northwestern Hawaiian Islands, however, these fishes can be seen in as little as 40 feet (probably because the water is cooler). The species name means "golden." To about 10 in. Indo-Pacific. Photo: Mike Severns. Molokini Island, Maui. 120 ft.

GOLDLINE SQUIRRELFISH • 'ala'ihi
Neoniphon aurolineatus (Lienard, 1839).

One of two Hawaiian squirrelfishes with bright yellow body stripes, the Goldline Squirrelfish can be most easily distinguished from its look-alike, the more solitary Yellowstripe Squirrelfish (page 121), by its tendency to aggregate in groups. It has a more strongly projecting lower jaw and lacks a long spine on the gill cover. These attractive fishes are usually seen under ledges and in caves at depths of about 100 feet. Species name means "gold lined." To about 10 in. Indo-Pacific. Photo: Mākua, O'ahu. 100 ft.

ROUGH-SCALE SOLDIERFISH • 'ū'ū
Plectrypops lima (Valenciennes, 1831)

This chunky soldierfish is a uniform orange red, lacking markings. Unlike other soldierfishes, its tail has very rounded lobes. Dwelling in the far recesses of caves and crevices, it is almost never seen by day. Even after dark it seldom leaves its cave. It is rough to the touch and the species name means "file." To about 6 in. Indo-Pacific. Photo: Lāna'i Lookout, O'ahu. 30 ft.